THE EDITING OF THE HEBREW PSALTER

SOCIETY OF BIBLICAL LITERATURE

DISSERTATION SERIES

Number 76

The Editing of the Hebrew Psalter
by
Gerald Henry Wilson

Gerald Henry Wilson

THE EDITING OF THE HEBREW PSALTER

Scholars Press
Chico, California

THE EDITING OF THE HEBREW PSALTER

Gerald Henry Wilson

Ph.D., 1981
Yale University

Advisor:
Robert L. Wilson

Library of Congress Cataloging in Publication Data

Wilson, Gerald Henry.
The editing of the Hebrew Psalter.

(Dissertation series / Society of Biblical Literature ; 76)
Originally presented as the author's thesis (Ph.D.)—
Yale, 1981.
Bibliography: p.
1. Bible. O.T. Psalms—Criticism, Redaction. I. Title. II.
Series: Dissertation series (Society of Biblical Literature) ;
no. 76.
BS1430.2.W55 1984 223'.2044 84-1265
ISBN 0-89130-728-1

Printed in the United States of America
on acid-free paper

To

William Sanford LaSor,
who taught me to love Hebrew;

David Allen Hubbard,
who taught me to love the Psalms;

Brevard Springs Childs,
who taught me to respect the Canon;

and
Robert Rutherford Wilson,
who guided this project through to its completion.

Contents

List of Illustrations

TABLE

FIGURE

Abbreviations

Abbreviations of commonly known periodicals not listed here conform to the style cited in *Society of Biblical Literature, Member's Handbook* (Scholars Press, 1980). Complete References are available in the Bibliography.

AJSL 26	D. D. Luckenbill, "A Neo-Babylonian Catalogue of Hymns."
"Antiquity"	William W. Hallo, "On the Antiquity of Sumerian Literature."
BAK	Hermann Hunger, *Babylonische und assyrische Kolophone.*
BASOR 88	S. N. Kramer, "The Oldest Literary Catalogue: A Sumerian List of Literary Compositions Compiled About 2000 B.C."
Bernhardt-Kramer	Inez Bernhardt and S. Kramer, "Götter-Hymnen und Kult-Gesänge der Sumerer auf zwei Keilschrift- 'Katalogen' in der Hilprecht Sammlung."
"Bezug"	Claus Wilcke, "Der aktuelle Bezug der Sammlung der sumerischen Tempelhymnen und ein Fragment eines Klageliedes."
Bibel und Qumran	*Bibel und Qumran.* Beiträge zur Erforschung der Beziehungen zwischen Bibel- und Qumranwissenschaft.
BL	S. Langdon, *Babylonian Liturgies.*
BZ	*Biblische Zeitschrift.*

"Canon and Text"	M. H. Goshen-Gottstein, "The Psalms Scroll (11QPs[a]): A Problem of Canon and Text."
Canonization	Sid Z. Leiman, *The Canonization of Hebrew Scripture* (Hamden, CT: Archon Books, 1976).
Catalogue	C. Bezold, *Catalogue of the Cuneiform Tablets in the Kounyunjik Collection of the British Museum.*
"Criticism"	Patrick W. Skehan, "Qumran and Old Testament Criticism."
CRRA	*Compte rendu de la . . . Rencontre Assyriologique Internationale.*
"Duplicates"	S. Langdon, "Unidentified Duplicates of Part of the Sumerian Liturgy 'e-lum-gud-sun.' The Titular Litany."
Einleitung	Hermann Gunkel, *Einleitung in die Psalmen.*
Exaltation	William W. Hallo and J. J. A. van Dijk, *The Exaltation of Inanna.*
"Fragments"	J. P. M. van der Ploeg, "Fragments d'un psautier de Qumran."
Gottesdienst	Anton Arens, *Die Psalmen in Gottesdienst des Alten Bundes.*
"History"	William W. Hallo, "Toward a History of Sumerian Literature."
Inscriptions	R. D. Biggs, *Inscriptions from Tell Abu Salabikh.*
IOTS	Brevard S. Childs, *Introduction to the Old Testament as Scripture.*
IVR^2	H. C. Rawlinson, *A Selection from the Miscellaneous Inscriptions of Assyria.* The Cuneiform Inscriptions of Western Asia, 2nd ed., vol. IV.
KAR	*Keilschrift aus Assur religiöse Inhalts.*
"List"	S. Langdon, "A List of Known Titles of Sumerian Penitential Psalms (ERŠAḪUNGA)."

"Liturgical Complex"	Patrick W. Skehan, "A Liturgical Complex in 11QPs[a]."
"Non-Canonical Psalms"	James A. Sanders, "Two Non-Canonical Psalms in 11QPs[a]."
OTT2	Gerhard von Rad, *Old Testament Theology,* vol. 2.
"Petit rouleau"	J. P. M. van der Ploeg, "Un petit rouleau de psaumes apocryphes (11QPsAp[a])."
"Pisqah"	Shemaryahu Talmon, "Pisqah be ʾemṣaʿ pasuq and 11QPs[a]."
PIW2	Sigmund Mowinckel, *The Psalms in Israel's Worship,* vol. 2.
Probleem	C. Th. Niemeyer, *Het Probleem van de rangschikking der Psalmen.*
PRU	*Le Palais royal d'Ugarit.*
"Psalm 1"	John T. Willis, "Psalm 1—An Entity."
Psalms Scroll	James A. Sanders, *The Dead Sea Psalms Scroll.*
"Psalms Titles"	Brevard S. Childs, "Psalms Titles and Midrashic Exegesis."
"Psaumes Apocryphes"	J. Starcky, "Psaumes apocryphes de la grotte 4 de Qumran (4QPs[f] vii-x)."
"Psaume XCI"	J. P. M. van der Ploeg, "Le Psaume XCI dans une recension de Qumran."
"Ps 151"	James A. Sanders, "Ps 151 in 11QPss."
RA 55 (1961)	S. N. Kramer, "New Literary Catalogue from Ur."
"Redaktion"	Lic. Th. W. Riedel, "Zur Redaktion des Psalters."
"Restoration"	S. Langdon, "The Assyrian Catalogue of Liturgical Texts: A Restoration of the Tablet."
"Reviewed"	James A. Sanders, "The Qumran Psalms Scroll (11QPs[a]) Reviewed."

RHR	*Revue de l'Histoire des Religions*
Scribal Character	Malachi Martin, *The Scribal Character of the Dead Sea Scrolls.*
"Scrolls and Text"	Patrick W. Skehan, "The Scrolls and the Old Testament Text."
STVC	*Sumerian Texts of Varied Contents*
"Surprises"	James A. Sanders, "Cave 11 Surprises and the Question of Canon."
TCL	Henri de Genouillac, *Textes Religieux Sumeriens, Textes Cuneiform du Louvre.*
TCS	*Texts from Cuneiform Sources.*
TCS 3	Åke Sjöberg and E. Bergmann, *The Collection of the Sumerian Temple Hymns.*
"Textform"	Otto Eissfeldt, "Eine Qumran-Textform des 91. Psalms."
Textus	*Textus. Annual of the Hebrew University Bible Project.*
TMH	*Texte und Materialien der Frau Hilprecht Sammlung im Eigentum der Friedrich-Schiller-Universität Jena.*
Tradition und Glaube	*Tradition und Glaube*; das frühe Christentum in seiner Umwelt. Festgabe für Karl Georg Kuhn zum 65. Geburtstag.
UET	*Ur Excavations, Texts.*
"Variorum"	James A. Sanders, "Variorum in the Psalms Scroll (11QPs^{a})."
VS	*Vorderasiatische Schriftdenkmaler.*
"Weisheitspsalm"	D. Lührmann, "Ein Weisheitspsalm aus Qumran."
WZJ	*Wissenschaftliche Zeitschrift der Friedrich-Schiller-Universität Jena.*

1

Methodological Considerations

In the study of the Old Testament books, it is possible to distinguish two general methodological approaches: that which concentrates on the final form of the text and is concerned to investigate the significance of the work as a whole; and, on the other hand, that which views the book as a collection of disparate elements, each of which must be separated out and considered individually as to its significance. In the case of the Hebrew Psalter, research (especially in the last century) has drawn most heavily on the latter of these two methodologies. Current Psalm scholarship emphasizes the study of individual psalms (pss), or at the most, those earlier collections of pss which can be discerned embedded within the final form of the canonical Psalter. The roots of this current trend can be traced to the influential works of the early, major figures in the field, namely Hermann Gunkel and Sigmund Mowinckel. Both men have been largely concerned to focus on individual pss, loosed from their traditional moorings in the Psalter (MT 150) and rearranged according to other criteria in groups which (in effect) ignore the canonical order.

When Gunkel does speak of the larger issue of Psalter arrangement, it is not without a degree of suspicion.[1] He is skeptical of finding any uniform principle governing the arrangement of the pss, since the final form of the Psalter is the end product of a long history of development and not the result of the plan and activity of a single editor (or group of editors).[2] Perhaps it was his skepticism of ever bringing significant order to the Psalter as a whole which led to Gunkel's break-through into *Gattungsforschung* in the pss. In this manner he was able to treat the

---

[1]Hermann Gunkel, *Einleitung in die Psalmen* (Göttingen: Vandenhoeck & Ruprecht, 1933) 436, 447. (Hereafter cited as *Einleitung*)

[2]Gunkel, *Einleitung*, 436, 447.

individual pss as independent units, divorced from their immediate or larger context, and to find unity (and therefore meaning) in the definition of ps genres and the relation of each genre to its proper cultural matrix.

Regardless of the abundance of illumination which this process has contributed to our understanding of the pss (and it has been considerable), the practical effect of *Gattungsforschung* has been to emphasize the significance of genres of similar pss (and thus isolated, individual pss) while minimizing the importance of the canonical order. As a result, the canonical arrangement comes to be viewed almost as an accidental product of an extended collection process.[3]

Mowinckel also contributes to this trend toward fragmentation in the study of the Psalter. While he does deal with the arrangement of the pss in more thorough fashion than most, he too is primarily concerned to delineate the major collections *within* MT 150. At most he speculates on how, in what order and for what purpose these were brought together.[4] Ultimately, however, Mowinckel is unable to conceive of the Psalter as a unified whole with a connected purpose.[5] This view is evident in his treatment of the "single" pss which do not conform to the expected characteristics of the collections in which they stand. These pss Mowinckel dismisses as late intrusions, and he attributes no particular purpose to their final positions.[6]

Mowinckel, then, as Gunkel before him, was more concerned to *reorganize* the individual pss within the framework of his hypothetical "Enthronement Festival" which he affirmed as the true matrix of the Psalter. Mowinckel's movement in this direction is clearly influenced by the work of Gunkel and may represent his own reaction to the previous failure of scholars to demonstrate convincing principles for the unification of the Psalter. It also explains the disproportionately small amount of time and space expended on the exposition of the larger issue of pss arrangement. Mowinckel's interests were in *reordering* the individual pss to support and to illuminate his theory and not in searching for the significance of an order which he considered superfluous and even accidental.

The widespread influence of the fragmenting approach to the pss characteristic of both Gunkel and Mowinckel is evident in the interests of

---

[3]Gunkel, *Einleitung*, 436.

[4]Sigmund Mowinckel, *The Psalms in Israel's Worship*, 2 vols. (New York: Abingdon, 1951) 193-206. (Hereafter cited as *PIW1* and *PIW2*.)

[5]Mowinckel, *PIW2*, 196-97.

[6]Mowinckel, *PIW2*, 193, 196-97.

current pss scholarship. A brief survey of recent commentaries reveals just how little time or energy is expended on the question of the arrangement of the Psalter and its significance. H.-J. Kraus includes a section of about five pages while M. Dahood disposes of all aspects of the subject in approximately two and a half.[7] Most authors are content to allude to the earlier collections underlying the canonical Psalter as evidence of the complexity of the issue and then move quickly on to the consideration of individual pss *a la* Gunkel and Mowinckel.

Current periodical literature is also dominated by the same degree of fragmentation.[8] With very rare exceptions, scholarly investigation into the pss completely ignores any question of Psalter structure of pss arrangement. The literature is almost exclusively concerned with the illumination of textual ambiguities or the further refinement of pss genres and/or cultic matrices. In short, they are concerned primarily with the development and unfolding of the theories of Gunkel and Mowinckel.

All this is not to say that the general skepticism toward the unity of MT 150 is totally unfounded. It has developed in reaction to the largely unconvincing nature of previous attempts to define a general principle of arrangement that unifies the Psalter. This has led students of the pss to conclude that (1) no general, unified principle of arrangement *can* be derived from the Psalter itself;[9] with the result that (2) all previous attempts to discover such an order have succeeded only in imposing some external, artificial order on an unwilling text.[10]

This widespread negative assessment of the search for the principles unifying the Psalter received further confirmation from the 1950 doctoral

---

[7]Mitchell Dahood, *Psalms I* (Anchor Bible; Garden City, NY: Doubleday, 1965/66) xxx-xxxii; Hans-Joachim Kraus, *Die Psalmen* (Neukirchen: Neukirchener Verlag, 1960).

[8]Brevard S. Childs, "Reflections on the Modern Study of the Psalms," *Magnalia Dei*, ed. F. M. Cross, Jr. (Garden City, NY: Doubleday, 1976) 377-88; D. J. A. Clines, "Psalm Research Since 1955," *Tyndale Bulletin* 18 (1967) 103-26; 20 (1969) 105-25; Ignatius Hunt, "Recent Psalm Study," *Worship* 41 (1967) 85-98; 47 (1973) 80-93; 49 (1975) 202-14, 283-94; 51 (1977) 127-44; R. Clements, "Interpreting the Psalms," *One Hundred Years of Old Testament Interpretation* (Philadelphia: Westminster, 1976) 76-98.

[9]Gunkel, *Einleitung*, 436; Th. C. Niemeyer, *Het Probleem van de rangschikking der Psalmen* (Leiden: Luctor et Emergo, 1950) 157. (Hereafter cited as *Probleem*.)

[10]Niemeyer, *Probleem*, 7.

dissertation of C. Th. Niemeyer, *Het Probleem van de rangschikking der Psalmen,* which must still be considered the most thorough treatment of the subject to date.[11] Niemeyer surveys the literature dealing with pss arrangement beginning with Talmud and Midrash and then proceeds to the more current materials from the first half of the nineteenth century to the date of his own work. He separates authors concerned to explore the structure and arrangement of the Psalter into two groups: (1) those who propose some unified principle governing the order of the whole Psalter and (2) those who affirm the more limited view of purposeful arrangement of *portions* of MT 150 while denying the validity of any over-arching principle guiding the arrangement of the whole.

Niemeyer's own contribution to the subject—an analysis of Talmud, Mishna, Qur'an as well as certain biblical units (Exodus 21-23; Proverbs 25-29; and the Twelve Prophets) in an attempt to derive organizational principles which might illumine the editorial process of the Psalter—leaves him ultimately unconvinced.[12] He concludes that, while principles of arrangement can be isolated within the Psalter, no single consistently applied principle can be found that binds the whole together. At most one is justified to speak of a partially intentional arrangement of portions of the Psalter (the earlier collections for example) coupled with the gradual, almost *accidental* accumulation of many subsequent pss following no discernible principle and resulting in our present MT 150 arrangement.[13]

Although general consensus has remained essentially unchanged in the thirty years since Niemeyer's work, most scholars would agree that such conclusions are always provisional and subject to the confirmation or modification of subsequent generations on the basis of new data, research and/or insights. This study contests this general skepticism on several points. First, I contend there is evidence within MT 150 itself of an editorial movement to bind the whole together. Second, I submit that the unity achieved by this process is not merely a convenient combination of disparate items into an "accidental" formal arrangement, but represents the end result of purposeful, editorial organization.

Some caution must be exercised with regard to the extent to which this final, editorial arrangement can be thought to permeate the whole of the Psalter. The recent attention given by several authors to groupings of pss within MT 150 has clearly demonstrated the complex history of the

---

[11]See above, n. 9.

[12]Niemeyer, *Probleem,* 96-121.

[13]Niemeyer, *Probleem,* 155-60.

composition of the Psalter. The Psalms of Ascents, the Qorahite and Asaphite pss, the Yahweh Malak pss and the Halleluyah pss all may indicate the prior existence of individual pss collections which were subsequently brought together in the final redaction of the Psalter.[14] Consequently, it is highly unlikely that the final form of MT 150 is the result of a completely new rearrangement of all 150 pss according to a single, editorial motive. The prior existence of these individual collections must have inhibited the editorial exercise of freedom in the final shaping of the pss. Evidence of this final, editorial unification, then, must be sought on a more limited basis. A key question which arises is: What indications are there of editorial efforts to combine and unify these originally unrelated groupings of pss? In this regard, it will be most important to look closely at the "seams" between the collections where editorial activity should be most evident.

The analysis of the Hebrew Psalter proper, which comprises the bulk of this study, falls under two major concerns. The first, in response to the initial contention above, is to isolate and describe what evidence exists of activity within the Psalter and to determine the extent of its unifying influence. Only after this data has been presented can the second concern (that of the editorial purpose which governs the organizational process) be addressed.

The first concern, then, is with the isolation and description of organizational techniques and concerns which demonstrate the existence of purposeful editorial activity in the arrangement of MT 150. In order to impart a measure of objective control to the study of the Psalter, and to avoid the pitfall of "imposing" non-existent structure on the text, I begin my analysis with several comparative texts which set parameters for the

---

[14]John D. W. Watts, "Yahweh Mālak Psalms," *TZ* 21 (1965) 341-48; Edward Lipiński, "YÂHWEH MÂLĀK," *Bib* 44 (1963) 405-60; Edward Lipiński, "Le psaumes de la royauté de Yahwé dans l'exégèse moderne," *Le Psautier* (Orientalia et Biblica Lovaniensia 4; Louvain: University Press, 1962) 133-272; Jarl H. Ulrichsen, "JHWH MĀLĀK: Einige sprachliche Beobachtungen," *VT* 27 (1977) 361-74; Cuthbert C. Keet, *A Study of the Psalms of Ascents* (London: Mitre, 1969); Gunther Wanke, *Die Zionstheologie der Korachiten*, *BZAW* 97 (1966); J. M. Miller, "The Korahites of Southern Judah," *CBQ* 32 (1970) 58-68; M. J. Buss, "The Psalms of Asaph and Korah," *JBL* 82 (1963) 382-92; K.-J. Illman, *Thema und Tradition in den Asaf Psalmen* (Åbo: Åbo Akademi, 1976); Gerhard von Rad, "Erwägungen zu den Königpsalmen," *ZAW* 17 (1940/41) 216-22; D. Michel, "Studien zu den sogenannten Thronbesteigungspsalmen," *VT* 6 (1956) 40-68.

kind of editorial techniques and concerns one might expect to find active in the organization of a group of hymnic texts such as the Psalter.

A primary consideration in the selection of this comparative literature was the *hymnic* character of the material. Niemeyer's own study suffers chiefly from his failure to limit his comparative data to hymnic texts.[15] One cannot assume that the editorial principles, techniques and concerns governing the arrangement of narrative, legal, prophetic and proverbial units are the same as or comparable to those employed in the organization of hymnic collections. For this reason the materials considered here are all concerned with the arrangement of hymnic compositions (i.e., they are all either collections of or catalogues of hymnic compositions).

A further concern in the limitation of materials is to select materials which might reasonably be expected to yield significant commentary on the editorial concerns behind the organization of the Hebrew Psalter. While American or Japanese poetry might offer some unique and fascinating comparisons, there is no reason to believe that they are sufficiently related to the Hebrew Psalter to illuminate its editorial processes. The comparative literature, therefore, is drawn from two sources: (1) texts from the larger corpus of Mesopotamian hymnic literature and (2) all the available Qumran Psalms Manuscripts (QPssMss).

THE MESOPOTAMIAN HYMNIC LITERATURE

The cuneiform hymnic literature of Mesopotamia has long been recognized as a valuable source for comparative insight into the milieu of the Old Testament in general and the Psalter in particular. Sumerian, Akkadian and Babylonian hymns have frequently been used in comparison to individual Hebrew pss and the isolation of similar features and genres has proven extremely fruitful. These hymnic texts were especially helpful in the demonstration of the functional context of the pss in the temple cult. Comparative features isolated extend so far as to include elements of terminology and phraseology.[16] The comparative value of the

---

[15]Niemeyer, *Probleem*, 96-121.

[16]C. G. Cumming, *The Assyrian and Hebrew Hymns of Praise* (New York: Columbia University Press, 1934); Geo Widengren, *The Accadian and Hebrew Psalms of Lamentation as Religious Documents* (Stockholm: Thule, 1937); Nahum Sarna, "Psalm XIX and the Near Eastern Sun-God Literature," *Papers of the Fourth World Congress of Jewish Studies* (Jerusalem, 1967).

Mesopotamian literature can be considered established and should not be underestimated. Yet, it has never, to my knowledge, been used to cast light on the organization and grouping of hymnic texts. It is not unreasonable, however, to assume that the analysis of these materials might yield data which would enhance our understanding of the organizational principles behind the arrangement of the Hebrew Psalter. The following Mesopotamian texts were chosen for comparative study discussed in chapters 2 and 3.

1. The Sumerian Temple Hymn Collection. This text consists of forty-two stereotyped hymns dedicated to an equal number of temples. It was compiled in the third millennium B.C. and is arranged according to apparent political and geographical motivations. Its chief asset is that it provides an example of an actual collection of complete, hymnic compositions preserved in their literary context. The study of its arrangement yields valuable insights into the editorial techniques employed in the organization and arrangement of individual compositions; insights which have implications for our study of the Hebrew psalter.

2. The Catalogues of Hymnic Incipits. This group of texts includes twenty-two cuneiform tablets (both whole and fragmentary) which do not contain complete hymnic compositions, but instead catalogue numerous hymns by means of their opening lines. It is possible on the basis of these incipits to infer a great deal about the types of compositions which are grouped together and other editorial considerations involved in their arrangement. Also assisting the analysis of these texts is the frequent use of summary lines and colophons which provide further understanding of the principles governing the organization of hymns.

THE QUMRAN PSALMS MANUSCRIPTS

Certainly the most fruitful texts for comparison with the Hebrew Psalter are the QPssMss. For a number of reasons they provide important new insights into the editorial arrangement of the biblical pss. First, few of these texts had been published prior to Niemeyer's study in 1950 (indeed, many remain unpublished at this date). They offer, therefore, new data previously unavailable for consideration. In addition, these are actual *Hebrew pss texts* and, as such they represent the closest parallels to MT 150 in terms of date, origin and composition. These Mss, our earliest evidence for the Hebrew text of the pss, demonstrate significant variations from MT 150 in the order of individual pss as well as the actual pss included. Canonical pss stand side-by-side with apocryphal compositions unknown to the biblical Psalter. In this regard the QPssMss allow us to view and study conflicting arrangements of the biblical pss in order to determine whether the variant organization corresponds to a variant editorial concern. Finally, these texts offer the best opportunity to study the editorial techniques which may also function in MT 150.

Two full chapters are devoted to the discussion of the QPssMss. Chapter 4 explores the preliminary questions of the nature of these texts: Are they actually alternative Psalter traditions which functioned authoritatively; or are they liturgical collections, incorporating authoritative pss, but which must be distinguished from sacred scripture? The relation of the QPssMss to MT 150 in terms of priority and dependence, as well as their significance for the transmission history of the Hebrew Psalter are also considered. The conflicting views of James A. Sanders and the late Patrick W. Skehan (among others) are analyzed and assessed.[17] This initial survey permits a clearer understanding of the significance of the Qumran data (especially the variant arrangements) for our understanding of the organization of the Hebrew Psalter.

Following the preliminary study, chapter 5 continues with a text-by-text analysis of all the available QPssMss[18] for data concerning: (1) evidence of *explicit* editorial statements in the form of superscripts (s/ss), postscripts (p/ss) or other formulae such as *halleluyahs* and doxologies; (2) evidence of *non-explicit* organizational techniques which might illuminate editorial practice in MT 150; and (3) evidence of confirmation or contradiction of the MT 150 arrangement of pss in terms of consecutive order and/or content (the addition of apocryphal compositions or the omission of canonical ones, for example). Most of the information gained from this study has important implications for the subsequent analysis of MT 150 and the remainder of chapter 5 brings together the scattered data of the individual QPssMss into groupings reflective of Qumran techniques

---

[17]See below, pp. 63-88.

[18]See below, pp. 93-115. While fragments of individual pss texts have been recovered from several caves, the preponderance of evidence for the consecutive arrangement of pss comes from caves 4 and 11. The majority of the 11QPssMss have been published either in separate articles or *DJD*, vol. 4, or Sanders's *The Dead Sea Psalm Scroll* (Ithaca, NY: Cornell University Press, 1967) (see the bibliographical references in chapter 4). For the 4QPssMss I am indebted to Patrick W. Skehan, who made available his own transcription of those Mss in his care and provided additional insights through private communications. J. P. M. van der Ploeg was also most helpful in clarifying numerous details regarding the cave 4 documents for which he is responsible.

and concerns of arrangement which can readily be related to similar practice uncovered in the biblical Psalter.

THE CANONICAL HEBREW PSALTER

Once the groundwork of comparative analysis has been laid and after parameters have been set for the editorial techniques and concerns which can be expected, the study is directed toward the main object of enquiry: the canonical Hebrew Psalter. The final chapters of this study (chapters 6 and 7) are occupied with the direct investigation of MT 150 and the detection of signs of editorial activity behind its "final form." Chapter 6 presents the exposition of the data uncovered while chapter 7 interprets the significance of that data for our understanding of the "shape" of the Psalter.

1. Evidence of Explicit Editorial Activity in MT 150. The evidence of editorial activity in the Hebrew Psalter must be considered in two categories: (1) explicit editorial statements which have been appended to the hymnic compositions, but do not form an integral part of them, and (2) tacit (non-explicit) indications of editorial method and concern. The former is represented most prominently by the s/ss or pss-headings and a single p/s at the conclusion of Ps 72. The concern here is to determine how these s/ss function to group pss within the Psalter. The comparative literature plays an important role as many authors have emphasized parallels between the biblical s/ss and the Mesopotamian hymns.

Early recourse was made to the cuneiform hymns to shed light on the obscure terminology of the pss-headings.[19] This was largely directed toward genre designations, types of instrumentation and notes concerning the manner of performance. More recently, connections have been suggested between the author designations of the biblical pss (a concern almost totally lacking in cuneiform literature) and certain Mesopotamian "Catalogues of Texts and Authors."[20] In a further development, the intriguing attempt of H. M. I. Gevaryahu to connect the biblical s/ss in

---

[19]G. R. Driver, "The Psalms in the Light of Babylonian Research," *The Psalmists*, ed. D. C. Simpson (London: Oxford University Press, 1926) 109-75; S. Langdon, "Babylonian and Hebrew Musical Terms," *JRAS* (1921) 169-91; John F. A. Sawyer, "An Analysis of the Context and Meaning of the Psalm-Headings," *Transactions of the Glasgow University Oriental Society* 22 (1967-68) 26-38.

[20]W. G. Lambert, "Authors, Ancestors, and Canonicity," *JCS* 11 (1957) 1-14; "A Catalogue of Texts and Authors," *JCS* 16 (1962) 59-77.

general and the pss-headings in particular with the colophons found at the end of many cuneiform literary tablets, has necessitated an extended discussion of the relation of these two phenomena in the light of the work on the colophons by Hermann Hunger and taking into consideration the data derived from my own study of the alphabetic cuneiform texts from Ugarit (Ras Shamra).[21]

My major concern is to observe editorial technique in action. To this end the pss-headings are closely scrutinized to determine their function in the arrangement of the pss. Numerous concerns are explicitly expressed in the terminology of the s/ss: authorship, genre, type of instrumentation, manner of performance, etc. However, it is not certain what role these terms play (if any) in the shaping of the pss collections. The s/ss are carefully analyzed in regards to the combination and arrangement of these terms within individual s/ss and patterns observed in the consecutive arrangement of pss bearing similar s/ss are noted. The cumulative data of author groupings, genre groupings and others are correlated to determine whether such groupings as do emerge are isolated instances or part of a larger, purposeful arrangement of the whole.

2. Tacit Indications of Purposeful Editorial Activity. After the study of the s/ss is complete, I turn to the consideration of tacit indications of editorial arrangement of the pss. Here are included those groupings of pss and signs of editorial activity not heralded by explicit editorial statements. The five-fold "book" division is considered in detail and correlated with the data of the s/ss (author and genre groupings in particular) to determine whether they are real, editorial divisions or merely accidental segmentation. The function of the *hllwyh* pss-groupings is discussed along with the related question of the function of pss beginning with the characteristic phrase: *hwdw lyhwh ky ṭwb ky lʿwlm ḥsdw*. In addition, numerous thematic groupings of pss are marked out and other techniques of arrangement related to those isolated in the Mesopotamian materials are indicated.

---

[21]H. M. I. Gevaryahu, "Biblical Colophons: A Source for the 'Biography' of Authors, Texts, and Books," *SVT* 28 (1975) 42-59. A complete bibliography of Gevaryahu's work on this subject is to be found below, p. 145 n. 9. See also Hermann Hunger, *Babylonische und assyrische Kolophone* (Neukirchen: Neukirchener Verlag, 1968) (hereafter cited as *BAK*); Brevard S. Childs, "Psalms Titles and Midrashic Exegesis," *JSS* 16 (1971) 137-50 (hereafter cited as "Psalm Titles").

THE FINAL "SHAPE" OF THE HEBREW PSALTER

The chief purpose of the final chapter (chapter 7) is to offer an explanation of the editorial motivation behind the canonical arrangement of the pss. This explanation must be based on the data derived from the previous study and avoid the temptation to import structure to the Psalter which does not exist there. The discussion in chapter 7 seeks to draw together such disparate data as (1) the use of author and genre categories in the s/ss to group pss; (2) the function of Ps One as an introduction to the whole Psalter; (3) the place of early collections in the final form; (4) the five-fold division of the pss into "books"; (5) the thematic grouping of pss, into a coherent picture of editorial motivation.

As will become increasingly clear as the study progresses, I am convinced by the data that there are clear indications of editorial activity throughout MT 150. These are not isolated examples of limited editorial concern, but are part of a broader editorial movement to unify the 150 pss into a coherent whole. Further, while this movement is not a totally new rearrangement of all 150 pss, it does move consistently and purposefully and so joins and arranges early collections, individual pss and later groupings, that the final product speaks the message intended by the final editor(s); a message which is distinct from and which intends to supersede that of the earlier pss-collections on which it is partly based.

With these brief explanations of the character and methodology of the project at hand as a guide, I will now turn to the examination of the comparative literature as outlined above. As I indicated in the previous discussion, the cuneiform hymnic texts will serve as the starting point, and, among these, I will first focus attention on the Sumerian Temple Hymn Collection.

2

The Collection of Sumerian Temple Hymns

This text (as the heading above suggests) consists of a collection of 42 hymns directed to as many different Temples, compiled by Enheduanna the En-Priestess, daughter of Sargon of Akkad (2334-2279 B.C.).[1] The

[1]First discovered in Nippur and now collated from fragments of 37 tablets. For relevant publications see: Åke Sjöberg and E. Bergmann, *The Collection of Sumerian Temple Hymns* (Texts from Cuneiform Sources, 3; Locust Valley, NY: J. J. Augustin, 1960) (hereafter cited as *TCS* 3); Claus Wilcke, "Der aktuelle Bezug der Sammlung der sumerischer Tempelhymnen und ein Fragment eines Klagelieds," *ZA* 63 (1972) 35-61; H. Zimmern, "Ein Zyklus altsumerischer Lieder auf die Haupttempel Babyloniens," *ZA* 5 (1930) 245-76. Enheduanna is well known from historical (inscriptions), archaeological (cylinder seals mentioning her name and a fragmentary disc bearing her likeness along with her name), and literary (the products of her own strongly marked style) sources. She was an immensely talented woman, a princess by birth, priestess by appointment of Sargon and a poetess in her own right. Having assumed the office of high priestess to the moon god Nanna of Ur in the reign of her father, she is known to have continued in that capacity until the reign of her nephew Naram-Sin (2254-2218 B.C.) at least twenty-five years later. In her capacity as poetess, she is known to be responsible for the creation of at least two cycles of literature of major importance: (1) that composed of Inanna and Ebih plus the cycle called The Exaltation of Inanna; and (2) the collection of temple hymns at hand. She enjoyed such prestige because of the standards she set in her various offices that she was virtually "deified" by succeeding generations of her countrymen. Further discussion of Enheduanna and the works attributed to her is found in William W. Hallo and J. J. A. van Dijk, *The Exaltation of Inanna* (Yale Near Eastern Researches, 3; New Haven: Yale University Press, 1968) (hereafter cited as *Exaltation*); and William W. Hallo, "Toward a History of Sumerian Literature," *Sumeriological Studies in Honor of Thorkild Jacobsen* (Chicago:

collection is characterized by a high degree of formal congruence. That is, the first 41 hymns share a common literary structure, while the last hymn (TH 42)[2] is an anomalous case and must be discussed separately. The basic structure of the hymns can be outlined in the following way:[3]

ADDRESS TO TEMPLE	é	O, House,[4]
DESCRIPTION OF DEITY	nun/nin-zu DN	your prince(ss), DN,
REFRAIN	mùš-za é bí-in-gub bára-za dúr bí-in-gar	has placed the house upon your m u š has taken his/her place on your dais.

The first two elements of this form are regularly expanded by the addition of hymnic epithets describing and honoring the Temple or deity indicated.[5] The Refrain, except for the occasional vocative insertion of the Temple Name, does not vary and concludes each composition. It is generally accepted that the cultural matrix of the "basic form" of these hymns is the ceremonial institution (or *re*institution) of temple worship for the

---

University of Chicago Press, 1976) 181-203 (hereafter cited as "History").

Dates used here and elsewhere in chapters 2 and 3 are taken, for convenience, from J. A. Brinkman, "Mesopotamian Chronology of the Historical Period," an appendix in A. Leo Oppenheim, *Ancient Mesopotamia* (rev. ed.; Chicago: University of Chicago Press, 1977) 335-48.

[2] This designation for the Temple Hymns (TH 1-42) has generally been accepted since the publication of *TCS* 3 (see above, n. 1).

[3] Transliteration and translation are taken from *TCS* 3 with slight modifications to allow for the generalization of the example. The descriptions of the formal elements are my own revisions of those suggested in *TCS* 3, p. 5. (All translations and transliterations, unless otherwise noted, are from the principal edition, *TCS* 3.)

[4] Alternative forms of address used here are: uru—city; Temple Name; City Name.

[5] Examples of such expansions are: TH 4, lines 48-50: "House with awe-inspiring radiance, laden with splendour, Lofty shrine (to which) the princely me's have been sent forth from heaven, storehouse of Enlil, founded for the primeval me's. . . ." TH 7, lines 96-98: "Your princess, the lady who 'causes silence,' the true and great lady of heaven, When she talks, heaven trembles, when she opens her mouth, there is clamour, Aruru, the sister of Enlil. . . ."

various deities described, as well as the construction (or *re*construction) of the temples addressed.[6]

Besides the close agreement of internal form, almost all students of the hymn collection have recognized a purposeful intent at work in the arrangement of the individual units in relation to one another. H. Zimmern notes a geographically conditioned movement in the text.

> Wir erhalten auf diese Weise, ähnlich wie in der Sammlung des Kodex Hammurabi, eine übersichtliche Liste der wichtigsten Kultstäde von Sumer und Akkad mit ihren Haupttempeln und Hauptgottheiten . . . (in grossen und ganzen geographisch in allgemein von Süden nach Norden verlaufend. . . .[7]

A brief survey of the list of the hymns provided in *TCS* 3, p. 13 is sufficient to lend some credence to the idea of geographical concern in the collection. While in the list of deities (column one) there is no discernible principle of organization (DN's are repeated and never grouped), the list of City Names exhibits obvious groupings according to geographical regions. For example, TH 2-6 are directed to temples in Nippur or its environs; TH 8-9 address temples of Ur; TH 20-22 concern the Lagaš district; and TH 40-41 are to temples in Akkad.

C. Wilcke also affirms a general South-East to North-West orientation for the Temple Hymns. He compares several texts listing a number of Mesopotamian cities and notes that some of these lists evidence similar geographical organization. Thus, the arrangement of the latter half of the second Ur lament reflects the advance of the Elamites against Ur, while the first half describes from North to South the deterioration of power in the Ur III kingdom. Similarly, the field-movements of Sargon's troops against Lugalzaggesi follow a general South to North orientation.[8]

In answer to occasional deviations in the Temple Hymns from the pattern of South-North movement, Wilcke feels most can be explained by the realization that regions are at times taken together as a unit, with the major cult site for that region given priority and less significant cities

---

[6]Wilcke, "Der aktuelle Bezug der Sammlung der sumerischer Tempelhymnen . . . ," *ZA* 62 (1972) 39, 48-49 (hereafter cited as "Bezug"); William W. Hallo, "The Cultic Setting of Sumerian Poetry," *CRRA* 17 (1969) 119-20.

[7]Zimmern, "Ein Zyklus altsumerischer Lieder auf die Haupttempel Babyloniens," *ZA* 5 (1930) 247.

[8]Wilcke, "Bezug," 39-46.

listed afterwards, regardless of the actual geographical locations. The regions themselves do conform to the South-North geographical arrangement. Wilcke further suggests that such regional groupings can explain those exemplars of the Temple Hymns in which certain cities were omitted. In those cases, the major cultic centers were listed without the minor sites.[9]

While TH 1-41 share an identical basic form, TH 42 diverges from this norm and must be treated as a special case. This deviation is most noticeable in that TH 42 alone entirely omits the stereotyped refrain: mùš-za é bí-in-gub bára-za dúr bí-in-gar, "has placed the house upon your m u š, has taken his/her place on your dais." Moreover, the characteristic phrase nun/nin-zu "your prince(ss)" is absent as well.[10] In addition to these omissions, the hymn contains between its body and its summary line (TH 42:542-545) two elements not found in the rest of the corpus of hymns:

DOXOLOGY	^{d}nisaba zà-mí	Praise Nisaba!
COLOPHON	lú-dub-KA-kéš-da en-ḫé-du$_7$-an-na	The compiler of the tablet (is) Enheduanna.
	lugal-mu-nì ù-tu na-me lú nam-mu-un-ùtu	My Lord, that which has been created (here) no one has created (before).
SUMMARY	14 é-^{d}nisaba ereš^{ki}-a	14. The house of Nisaba in Ereš.

While the inclusion of a doxology to Nisaba has no parallel in the rest of this text, a very similar doxology (DN zà-mì "Praise DN") is known as a standard feature of an earlier collection of temple hymns discovered at Abū Ṣalābīkh and considered a possible prototype of the Nippur collection (see below). There the doxology regularly follows each of sixty-eight brief hymns to temples and their deities.[11]

---

[9]Wilcke, "Bezug," 43-46.

[10]Wilcke, "Bezug," 39; *TCS* 3, 149-50.

[11]R. D. Biggs, "The Abū Ṣalābīkh Tablets. A Preliminary Survey," *JCS* 20 (1966) 80-81; idem, *Inscriptions from Tell Abū Ṣalābīkh* (University

> Seine [Sargon's] Tochter Enḫedu'anna [*sic*], die er als Enpriesterin des Nanna in Ur, der wichtigsten Stadt des sumerischen Südens, einsetzte, erscheint als die geeignete Person, diese Tat zum Preis des Königs in einer Hymnensammlung zu feieren.[21]

As a result, in this reconstruction, Enheduanna honors her father, the king (lugal-mu, TH 42, line 544), for facilitating the restitution of temple worship following his defeat of Lugalzaggesi and produces in his honor this series of hymns.[22]

Hallo would reconstruct the circumstances somewhat differently while holding to the same historical connections. He sees Enheduanna's appointment as En-Priestess and the subsequent edition of hymns in honor of Sargon as part of Sargon's attempt to weld together from the loose federation which had previously been Sumer and Akkad a strongly centralized kingdom. To this end, following the defeat of his rival Lugalzaggesi, Sargon assumed those titles by which his opponent had claimed rulership over Ur and Uruk, thus consolidating his control over both Sumer and Akkad. He further effected the union of the most important priestly offices of the two states by appointing his daughter, Enheduanna, En-Priestess of Nanna in the subjugated city of Ur. Besides these bureaucratic innovations, there is evidence that Sargon "equated the Sumerian Inanna with the Akkadian Ištar to lay the theological foundations for a united empire of Sumer and Akkad."[23]

It is this background against which Hallo views the production of the Temple Hymn collection:

> . . . the temples of Sumer and Akkad are apostrophized in a manner calculated to put royal solicitude for them in the best possible light; having triumphed in war and crushed Sumerian political aspirations, the Sargonic kings are nevertheless depicted as defenders of the traditional Sumerian faith.[24]

By her praise of Sargon for his reinstitution of temple worship and by her concern for temples both of Sumer and of Akkad, Enheduanna, through

---

[21]Wilcke, "Bezug," 48.
[22]Wilcke, "Bezug," 47-48.
[23]Hallo, *Exaltation*, 7-9.
[24]Hallo, "History," 186.

The position of the colophonic materials *before* the summary line for TH 42 would seem to indicate an integral relationship between the colophon and this particular hymn. Its inclusion, along with the doxology to Nisaba, sets this final composition apart from the first forty-one hymns and raises the question whether or not the divergent form signals a corresponding divergence of purpose and function.

Wilcke notes that this whole composition is to be considered a concluding doxology to Nisaba (the patron deity of the scribal art), in praise for the success of the work, and is to be distinguished from the preceding hymn collection. According to Wilcke, this concluding hymn of praise has been adapted to the form of the Temple Hymn collection, but not to such an extent as to obscure the fact that the actual collection ended with TH 41.[12] Here then, we have an explanation of the variations in TH 42 as opposed to the other forty-one hymns. The variation in form (the omission of the refrain and the nun/nin-zu phrase, the addition of the doxology to Nisaba and the inclusion of the colophon) signals a variation in *function* as well. This is not simply another temple hymn, but a doxology which serves to complete and conclude the whole collection. The shift from the collection to this concluding hymn is subtle, obscured by the similar introductory words which closely parallel those of the other hymns. But the breaking of the form and the inclusion of the colophon are conclusive. The collection is ended. "Praise Nisaba!"

Regarding the colophonic materials, it is striking that here, contrary to normal usage in cuneiform tablets, the colophon has become a fixed part of the literary composition and is no longer a variable document appended by each successive copyist-scribe and containing the data necessary for his own particular situation.[13] While one would expect the text of a literary tablet to remain essentially the same during the history of its transmission, one would also expect it to bear a number of different colophons, depending on the period in which it was copied, the particular scribe who did the copying, and other factors pertinent to the particular copy made rather than to the text in general (owner, commissioner, origin and condition of the original). Here, despite the fact that the *TCS 3* edition is collated from fragments of thirty-seven tablets, there is no

---

of Chicago Oriental Institute Publications, 99; Chicago: University of Chicago Press, 1974) 45-56.
[12]Wilcke, "Bezug," 39.
[13]"Eine Kolophon ist eine vom Text getrennte Notiz des Schreibers am ende einer Tafel literarischen Inhalts, die Aussagen über Personen, die mit dieser Tafel zu tun haben, enthält" (Hermann Hunger, *BAK*, 1).

indication of other copyist-scribes subsequent to the original author/compiler, Enheduanna.[14] The colophon has been "frozen" in its original form and transmitted as a part of the literary text.

This "frozen" colophonic material leads one to inquire more closely as to the role of Enheduanna in the composition/compilation of the Temple Hymn collection. The term used here (lú-dub-KA-keš-da) does not carry any necessary implications of "authorship" but rather has the meaning "compiler." Its Akkadian equivalent, kāṣir ṭuppi, connotes literally "one who binds (has bound, has joined) the tablet"; "compiler."[15] Perhaps the image invoked is that of the Mesopotamian librarian/archivist who, on occasion, bound related tablets together with cord for storage in the appropriate receptacle.[16]

Most have drawn upon Enheduanna's known literary activity, the dedication of the collection to her father, Sargon of Akkad, and the high degree of uniformity among the hymns to affirm the En-Priestess's right as "author" as well as "compiler."[17] Certainly, in light of her known productivity, it is doubtful that she exercised no individual, creative influence on the production of the Temple Hymn collection. Hallo, while not denying any individual contribution, views Enheduanna's role largely as the adaptor and incorporator of previously existing temple hymns into a completely new cycle of hymns which constitutes the collection we now know (at least in its original form). In Hallo's view, the Kesh Temple Hymn[18] and the Abū Ṣalābīkh Temple Hymn collection are evidence for

---

[14] *TCS* 3, p. 49, lines 543-45.

[15] *TCS* 3, p. 150, note to line 543. Hallo also notes the equivalency of these terms in "History," p. 187, n. 39. *CAD*, vol. K—kaṣāru, gives only the related meaning: "to compose a text," which does not sufficiently clarify the issue of authorship versus compilership.

[16] Ernst Posner, *Archives in the Ancient World* (Cambridge, MA: Harvard University Press, 1972) 56-58, speaks of this practice in the storage of tablets that "were flat on both sides" and mentions the discovery in Ugarit of tablets "in piles or packages [bound together] of sometimes more than ten." He later discusses a perhaps related practice of attaching supplementary documents to the primary document by means of strings (pp. 122-23).

[17] *TCS* 3, p. 5; p. 150, note to line 544; Wilcke, "Bezug," 46-47.

[18] The history of this individual hymn to the temple in Kesh is now known to extend back at least as far as the time of the Fara-Abū Ṣalābīkh tablets (ca. 2600 B.C.; Biggs, *Inscriptions*, pp. 24, 26, 30). The most recent and complete edition of the text (Gene B. Gragg, *The Keš Temple Hymn*, *TCS* 3, pp. 157-88) must now be updated by a fragment discovered

the existence of a body of similar literature which would have b
and available to Enheduanna as models or raw materials for
creative productions. While it is impossible to prove a lineal c
between these earlier collections and that of Enheduanna,[1
suggestion does serve to explain the tension in the "frozen"
between the description of the priestess as "compiler" and her s
statement (TH 42, line 544): lugal-mu nì ù-tu na-me lú nam-m
"My Lord, that which has been created (here) no one has created
By its emlphasis on Enheduanna's poetic originality, this stateme
takes on the function of a claim to "authorship" of this corpus.
new works, it seems to say, not older works adapted and brought
However, in view of the title "compiler" applied to the prieste
known availability of similar hymnic materials, Hallo is most
correct when he concludes, "presumably, it was the compositi
cycle as a whole (not each individual hymn) that represented he
contribution."[20]

C. Wilcke ties Enheduanna's "authorship" of these hymns
with the geographical movement evidenced in the arrangeme
collection. From his comparison of the Temple Hymns with a
lists of Sumerian cultic cities (see above), he concludes that th
Hymn collection emphasizes the region most affected by S
Akkad's campaign against Lugalzaggesi and the Sumerian So
collection must, he feels, stem from that period and specific
brates the restitution of temple worship which had been disrup
the hostilities. On the basis of such a background for the Tem
collection, Wilcke concludes that:

---

at Tell Abū Ṣalābīkh (Biggs, "An Archaic Sumerian Version of
Temple Hymn from Tell Abū Ṣalābīkh," *ZA* 61 [1971] 193-207 (
cited as *ZA* 61 [1971]. This fragment, though considerably ol
eight hundred years) than any previous exemplar, evidences v
deviation from the later versions.

[19] To my knowledge, no one has yet cited any conclusive
for direct links between these texts and the Temple Hymn c
Biggs (*ZA* 61 [1971] 196 n. 13) mentions the similarity of one e
the Kesh Temple, but this cannot function as evidence of th
dependence of the texts. My own examination of the texts
reveals no real relation of vocabulary or phraseology. The most
be said is that these earlier texts provide evidence of a previous
of such temple hymns which may have served as models for the
lection of hymns.

[20] Hallo, "History," 187.

this hymn collection, lends her support to the politico-theological reformation of her father and his ambitions for Sumero-Akkadian unity which underlay it.

We have seen how the colophon and the cultural matrix suggested by Wilcke and Hallo indicate an origin for the Temple Hymn collection in the time of Enheduanna and her father, Sargon of Akkad, subsequent to his defeat of Lugalzaggesi of Ur. The witness of the Kesh Temple Hymn and the Abū Ṣalābīkh temple hymn collection further indicates that the origin of individual temple hymns and even of collections of such hymns must be pushed even further back in time, at least to the Fara period (ca. 2600 B.C.). In contrast, Sjöberg-Bergman's study of the Temple Hymn fragments has uncovered no exemplar of any hymn which was inscribed any earlier than the Ur III period.[25] In fact, internal considerations indicate that certain hymns could not have originated prior to the Ur III period, or some 250 to 300 years after the presumed origin of the collection at the hands of Enheduanna. TH 9 is dedicated to the temple of Shulgi at Ur and must, therefore, be subsequent to that deified Ur III monarch (2094-2047 B.C.). This hymn bears "the subtitle daḫ-ḫu-um 'addition, additional hymn' which clearly shows that this hymn . . . did not belong to the 'canonic' [original?] collection."[26] In addition, TH 12 mentions the Giparu in Gaesh and cannot therefore have attained its final form until after this building was constructed by Shulgi's successor Amar-Suen (2046-2038 B.C.). These and other examples of less merit are cited in Sjöberg-Bergman's discussion (*TCS 3*, pp. 7-12).

As a consequence of these indications of later addition and edition, the Temple Hymn collection appears to evidence a longer period of transmission than might have been believed from its extreme formal unity. The Ur III date for the earliest exemplars and the inclusion of hymns which could not have formed part of the original indicate continued use of the collection at least as late as the Ur III period. This has led Wilcke to suggest a shift in function for the hymn collection which allowed it to retain its contemporary significance long after the original object of its praise and honor (Sargon of Akkad) had passed from the scene.

All dies spricht dafür, dass die TH in diesem Zeitraum

[25] *TCS 3*, pp. 6, 7; Hallo, "History," 187.
[26] *TCS 3*, pp. 8f.

> ihre Aktualität nicht verloren haben und nicht nur als Literaturwerk tradiert wurden.[27]

In Wilcke's opinion, the Temple Hymn collection ceased to function simply as praise for Sargon of Akkad and began to serve as incentive and commendation for later rulers to provide for the maintenance and reconstruction of the holy places. As a result, these hymns were able to outlive the time of their specific historical reference and make themselves available for continued use by later generations.[28]

Hallo speaks of such adaptability as a prime factor in the continued transmission and usage of Sumerian literary works.

> Although the original creative impulse most often arose out of and in response to a specific historical situation, the long process of canonization (that is, incorporation of the text in fixed form in the generally accepted curriculum of the scribal schools) tended to suppress allusions to these situations. If a composition resisted such sublimation or ideological updating, it tended to disappear from the canon.[29]

So, for subsequent generations, the Temple Hymn collection was sufficiently loosed from its specific historical reference to Sargon to become available for repeated use in very different historical circumstances. This initial adaptability did not apparently continue beyond the Old Babylonian period since this cycle of hymns (along with Enheduanna's other major literary work—her cycle of hymns to Inanna) completely disappear from the scribal curriculum, presumably because "they failed to sublimate their historical particulars sufficiently to qualify for enduring and universal interest in the cuneiform curriculum."[30]

We have in these hymns, then, a collection of compositions conceived and compiled by Enheduanna in response to a particular historical event and honoring Sargon of Akkad for his part in that event. This collection now shows evidence of subsequent additions and editing which have loosened these hymns from specific reference to a single event and adapted them for continued use in a different context.

---

[27]Wilcke, "Bezug," 49.
[28]Wilcke, "Bezug," 48-49; Hallo, "History," 186, n. 35.
[29]Hallo, "History," 194.
[30]Hallo, "History," 187.

The implications of the editing and transmission of the Temple Hymn collection are varied and significant for this study. Perhaps an initial inference may be drawn simply from the fact of the collection's existence in its current form. The collection indicates that at a very early date (2334-2279 B.C., if not earlier) it was possible to enter into a complex arrangement of individual literary compositions (each maintaining its own integrity) on the basis of a larger schema (in this case the campaign of Sargon of Akkad). We cannot, therefore, assume that all hymnic collections are haphazard arrangements of compositions devoid of any organizational intent.

Moreover, certain techniques employed in the organization of the collection should not be ignored. Two stand out in particular in relation to the Hebrew Psalter. The use of an explicit doxology to Nisaba at the conclusion of TH 42 (line 542), along with the corroborating data of the earlier collection from Abu Salabikh (in which each composition is concluded by the same doxology zà-mi "Praise") affirms a similarity of practice when compared with the frequent use of concluding doxology in the Hebrew Psalter.[31] The use of the TH 42 as an expanded doxology concluding the whole Temple Hymn collection is, likewise comparable to the use of Psalm 150, in the absence of a fifth explicit doxology, as a final, expanded doxology concluding the last book of the Psalter as well as the Psalter as a whole.[32]

The second technique—the retention of the colophonic material as a "frozen" part of a literary composition, even after subsequent additions and editing had skewed the function of the work from that of the original—is comparable to the retention in the biblical pss-headings of data referring to the cultic background and function of these pss which have been adapted to function in a far different and later context.

---

[31] The practice of ending a hymnic composition with a doxology is common in the Hebrew Psalter. Cf. the "Halleluyah" psalms: 104-106, 111, 113, 115-118, 135, 146-150; the psalms at the conclusions of the "books" of the Psalter: 41:14; 72:19; 89:53; 106:48. Other doxologies are found scattered throughout the Psalter: 7:18; 30:13; 66:20; 68:36; 99:9; 103:20-22; 115:18; 118:29; 135:21.

[32] The use of Ps 150 as the concluding "doxology" of the fifth book and of the whole Psalter is mentioned in most commentaries and Introductions (see Franz Delitzsch, *The Psalms* [Grand Rapids: Eerdmans, 1871] 1. 15; and Artur Weiser, *The Psalms* [Philadelphia: Westminster, 1962] 21 for two examples).

This adaptability of which I have spoken is perhaps the most important implication to be derived from the study of the Sumerian Temple Hymn collection. That later generations could utilize the Temple Hymns with such confidence and after such minor adjustments to the original work composed for an event long past is evidence of the adaptability of such a corpus to new situations beyond the bounds of its original intent. Later editions, by loosening the document from its original, specific reference, have made it applicable to later historical contexts. This is of great importance for our understanding of the Hebrew Psalter, where we find a similar adaptation process active in the transmission of the canonical pss.

Further questions of organizational technique and motivation, applicable to the study of the Hebrew Psalter, are raised by the politico-geographical motif which underlies the framework of the Temple Hymn collection. Might MT 150 also be subject to some similar, externally applied schema of arrangement, which while not necessarily *geographical* in character might be equally far removed from the accepted original matrix of the pss in the worship of the cult? Is it possible that such a framework (if it does exist) might be politically as well as theologically and cultically motivated? These are questions which have infrequently been asked of the biblical Psalter and which must be considered at a later point.

3

The Catalogues of Hymnic Incipits

The cuneiform literature of Mesopotamia provides a further source of comparative information about the arrangement and organization of hymnic compositions in the group of tablets which I have here styled "Catalogues of Hymnic Incipits." These texts, which date from the Ur III period (2112-2004 B.C.) to the Neo-Babylonian period (625-539 B.C.), afford an excellent opportunity to study the organizational principles involved in the collection and arrangement of a number of originally unrelated hymnic compositions. The catalogues differ from the Sumerian Temple Hymns in that, whereas the Hymn collection presents actual, complete compositions in their literary setting, related to one another according to a specific plan and purpose, the catalogues contain only incipits (the first lines of hymnic compositions) which have been brought together for a variety of reasons. One may then ask how such collections of hymnic incipits are of significance to an investigation of organizational techniques and principles. Might not these lists record incipits of compositions with no real connection with one another? I readily admit that possibility for some of the catalogues. However, most of these texts are not to be construed as lists of titles brought together out of a vacuum. No, most are related to actual collections of tablets, or at least portions of such collections, which they serve to catalogue. As Heinrich Otten has shown, many catalogues contain references which can only be control data necessary for the organization and prompt retrieval of tablets from an extensive collection. Such statements note the absence of particular tablets of certain series and, in several instances, indicate particulars regarding the physical circumstances of individual tablets. Thus, for example, one catalogue states that certain tablets do not "stand upright" (presumably on the library storage shelves).[1] This practice of noting the physical properties of a tablet is comparable to the modern librarian's practice of designating certain volumes as "folio" or "oversize" and housing them in a special location. Comments of this nature are not necessary for the listing of unrelated incipits but are vital in a catalogue to enable the prompt location and retrieval of materials of an actual collection.

Similar statements of "control data" emphasize clearly that many of the catalogues of hymnic incipits with which I am concerned are closely connected with actual tablet collections. Catalogue 1, line 45 indicates that the list records the incipits of 42 tablets "recovered by Ni'urum." Catalogue 2 refers to tablets which "have not been found," as well as others which were found or hidden "in a well." Catalogue 4 divides its incipits into two groups according to the "tablet container" (upper or lower) in which a tablet was stored. These and other indications show that many, if not all, of the catalogues must be viewed as reflections of actual collections of tablets and should be considered part of the highly organized system of libraries and archives which are known to have existed in the ancient Near East.[2]

Whereas with the Sumerian Temple Hymn collection we are dealing with the juxtaposition of complete literary compositions, here in the

---

[1]Heinrich Otten, "Bibliotheken im Altenorient," *Das Altertum* 1 (1955) 74.

[2]Libraries and archives of the ancient Near East have been the subject of considerable research. Some of the more interesting and important works in this regard are: A. A. Kampman, "Archiven en bibliotheken in het Oude Nabije Oosten," *Handelingen van het zeed Weteschapplijk Vlaamsch Congres voor Boek- en Bibliotheekwezen* (Schoten-Antwerpen: Lombaerts, 1942); W. G. Lambert, "The Sultantepe Tablets: a review article," *RA* 53 (1959) 117-38; Fritz Milkau, *Geschichte der Bibliotheken im alten Orient*, ed. Bruno Meissner (Leipzig: O. Harrassowitz, 1935); J. Papritz, "Archive in Altmesopotamien: Theorie und Tatsachen," *Archivalischen Zeitschrift* 55 (1959) 11-50; A. Pohl, "Der Archivar und die Keilschriftforscher," *Or* 29 (1960) 230-32; Ernst Posner, *Archives in the Ancient World* (Cambridge, MA: Harvard University Press, 1972) (especially Chap. one "The Clay Tablet Archives"); J. M. Sasson, "Some Comments on Archive Keeping at Mari," *Iraq* 34 (1972) 55-67; Josef Schawe, "Der alten Vorderorient," *Handbuch der Bibliothekswissenschaft*, ed. Georg Leyh (Wiesbaden: O. Harrassowitz, 1955); J. W. Thompson, *Ancient Libraries* (Hamden, CT: Archon Books, 1940); Morgens Weitemeyer, "Archive and Library Technique in Ancient Mesopotamia," *Libri* 6 (1956) 217-38.

catalogues we have only incipits of compositions, many of which no longer exist or have not yet been identified.[3] For this reason it is much more difficult to determine the systematic purpose or plan which governs the collection, and our conclusions on the basis of the catalogues must necessarily remain tentative. With the added caution that the catalogues may not contain the incipits of works currently in use but may instead reflect antiquarian interest in compositions long out of currency,[4] an investigation of the organization and arrangement of the various catalogues should prove fruitful for this discussion.

Twenty-two catalogues have been included in this study (table 1). Of these, two are from the Ur III period (*CATS.* 1 and 2); ten are Old Babylonian (*CATS.* 3-8, *CAT.* 18 and *CATS.* 20-22); seven are Neo-Assyrian (*CATS.* 11-16 and *CAT.* 19); while the Middle Babylonian, Middle Assyrian and Neo-Babylonian periods are each represented by one catalogue (*CATS.* 9, 10 and 17 respectively).[5] Almost all of these catalogues evidence some overt attempt to organize the material they contain.[6] The methods employed to this end range from the use of horizontal dividers to mark off groups within the whole to a complex combination of dividing

---

[3]While a great many of the incipits given in the catalogues have been identified with compositions known from other tablets, many more have not yet been identified, and many of the proposed identifications are disputed.

[4]I am indebted for this suggestion to William W. Hallo, who mentioned it in a conversation in November of 1977. While caution is needed, I cannot believe that such antiquarian interest obliterated organizational interest altogether.

[5]The numbering system used here for the catalogues follows that introduced by William W. Hallo ("On the Antiquity of Sumerian Literature," *JAOS* 83 [1963] 167-76 [hereafter cited as "Antiquity"]), where the first seventeen catalogues are listed. Catalogues 18-22 have been added on the basis of Hallo's comments in "Another Sumerian Literary Catalogue?" *StudOr* 46 (1976) 77-80. Two possible catalogues mentioned there and published in transcription in *UET/6:* 197 and 198, have not been included here.

Several of the catalogues fall together as duplicates so that the actual number of distinct catalogues is nineteen. There are two groups of duplicates: *CATS.* 11, 12, 13, and *CATS.* 15, 16. Hallo cites these duplicates as evidence that the transmitting scribes had "apparently arrived at a canonical version of the catalogues themselves" ("Antiquity," 168).

[6]*CATS.* 4, 8 and 20 show no evidence of overt organizational activity.

lines, headings, summary lines and benedictions (see table 2).[7] Perhaps a description of each tablet and its overt organizational structure is now in order.

CAT. 1.[8] A brief tablet of 45 lines (28 obverse and 17 reverse) containing 42 incipits in two distinct groupings. Dividing lines separate the incipits between the 32nd and 33rd lines and between the 43rd and 44th lines.[9] Immediately following each dividing line, a numerical/category summary line is given for the preceding section. The two segments are thus characterized:

:33	šu-nigín 32 ša-du-lugal	"Sub-total: 32 royal hymns"
	. . . .	
:44	šu-nigín 10 ša-du-igi-šè-àm	"Sub-total: 10 hymns which are 'out of use'"

The final line (l. 45) serves as the colophon of the tablet.

:45	pà-da nì-ú-rum	"Recovered by Ni'urum"[10]

[7]*Dividing lines,* in texts otherwise unlined, are usually a single horizontal line made by pressing the stylus across the width of the column. If the tablet is one in which each incipit is boxed in with impressed lines, the divider may be either a double line between entries or a larger, blank space.

Headings are statements apart from the incipits themselves, which stand prior to the section to which they refer.

Summary lines follow the incipits to which they refer and are of two types: (1) *numerical,* in which the preceding incipits are merely subtotaled with a number; (2) *category,* in which the type/genre of the preceding incipits is stated. It is of course possible to have a mixed summary line which both enumerates and types the incipits it summarizes.

[8]William W. Hallo, "Antiquity," 167-76.

[9]In Hallo's transliteration and translation, he has numbered the first summary line (following line 32) as 32a, so that the final line is numbered 44 instead of 45 as I have numbered it here.

[10]Transliteration and translation from Hallo, "Antiquity," 170.

TABLE 1

The Catalogues of Hymnic Incipits

CATALOGUE	MUSEUM NO.	DATE	PROVENANCE
Cat. 1	YBC 3654	Ur-III	?
Cat. 2	HS 1360	Ur-III	Nippur
Cat. 3	?	O. Bab.	Ur
Cat. 4	?	O. Bab.	Ur
Cat. 5	HS 1504	O. Bab.	Nippur
Cat. 6	CBS 29.15.155	O. Bab.	Nippur
Cat. 7	AO 5393	O. Bab.	?
Cat. 8	VAT 6481	O. Bab.	?
Cat. 9	HS 1477	Mid-Bab.	Nippur
Cat. 10	VAT 10101	Mid-Assyr.	Assur
Cat. 11	K2539+3276	Neo-Assyr.	Nineveh
Cat. 12	K2	Neo-Assyr.	Nineveh
Cat. 13	BM 82-3-23,5220	Neo-Assyr.	Nineveh
Cat. 14	K9618	Neo-Assyr.	Nineveh
Cat. 15	K3141	Neo-Assyr.	Nineveh
Cat. 16	K3482	Neo-Assyr.	Nineveh
Cat. 17	Herb. Clark Cyl.	Neo-Bab.	?
Cat. 18	CBS 14077	O. Bab.	?
Cat. 19	Rm. 2,220	Neo-Assyr.	?
Cat. 20	?	O. Bab.	Ur
Cat. 21	BM 23771	O. Bab.	?
Cat. 22	BM 23701	O. Bab.	?

TABLE 2

Organizational Elements Contained in the Catalogues

Catalogue	Dividing Lines	Heading	Numerical Summary	Category Summary	Series Title	Benediction
Cat. 1	X		X	X		
Cat. 2	X			X	X	
Cat. 3			X			
Cat. 4						
Cat. 5			X			
Cat. 6	X					
Cat. 7			X?	X?		
Cat. 8						
Cat. 9	X			X		
Cat. 10	X		X	X		X
Cat. 11-13	X	X	X	X		
Cat. 14			X	X		
Cat. 15-16			X	X		
Cat. 17		X				
Cat. 18	X		X			
Cat. 19			X	X		
Cat. 20						
Cat. 21			X	X		
Cat. 22	X		X	X		

CAT. 2.[11] A tablet of 21 lines, divided into four sections by means of horizontal dividers. These sections correspond with four "series" of tablets which this catalogue enumerates. The first two sections follow a common form, which is illustrated below on the basis of lines 1-9.

HEADING: dub-sag-ta[12]

FIRST TABLET
(SERIES TITLE): ^{d}en-ki unú-gal im-e_{11}

FINAL TABLET: an-zag-še[13]

INTERVENING
TABLETS an-ku_{10}-zu ama-tu_6-zu-ke_4
giš-gi-bu_5-e
dingir-KAS_4-dingir-KAS_4-mè-ke
maš-maš-erim-kúr-kúr

SUMMARY gir-gin-na-^{d}en-ki-unú-gal-im-e_{11}-kam
šà-PU-dili-kam

TRANSLATION:[14] From the first tablet
"Enki has ascended to the dining-hall"
To "The Zenith of Heaven"
"The one who knows the eclipses, the mother of he who knows the incantation"
"In the swaying cane thicket"
"The . . . gods of the Battle"
"The hostile, struggling Twins"

---

[11] Pohl, *TMH* n.F. 1/2 (1937) 360; S. N. Kramer, *TMH* n.F. 3 (1961) 19-20 and no. 55.

[12] The -ta here and in line 10 is equivalent to the preposition ištu/ultu "from."

[13] The final -še used here and at the end of line 11 corresponds to the preposition ana "to, upto."

[14] Transliteration is taken from Kramer, *TMH* n.F. 3 (1961) 19. The translation is my own translation and adaptation of Kramer's original German.

> Successive sections of "Enki has ascended to the dining-hall
> In a well.

Lines 1-3 indicate that the incipits enumerated here are from the "series" of tablets which extends from the "first tablet" (whose first line determines the title of the whole series: ^{d}en-ki unú-gal im-e$_{11}$) to the tablet entitled an-zag "The Zenith of Heaven" (line 3). The following four lines (4-7) contain the incipits of the tablets included within this "series." So, in all, there are six incipits and six tablets included. The summary line (line 8) repeats the title of the "series" and indicates that the preceding incipits are successive tablets in that series.

After the conclusion of the first two sections in line 17, the catalogue continues with a brief statement regarding a third "series" whose successive sections "have not been found" (lu nu-da-pad). This statement in turn is followed by a blank space of several lines, after which the tablet is concluded with two lines which appear to be another summary line.[15]

:20	gir-gin-na	Successive sections of
:21	uru-bal-a-áš-di-da-kam	"He who advances against the hostile city"

It appears from the information in lines 9 and 17 that these tablets were at some time concealed "in a well," possibly to preserve them from some danger. The displacement of tablets from their normal storage places for their preservation during times of danger is known from archaeological evidence.[16] In *CAT*. 2, this comment may account for the tablets which "have not been found," as well as for the blank space preceding the last summary line. Kramer (*TMH* n.s. 3, p. 20) makes no attempt to explain this vacant space or the final lines:

> Zeilen 20-21 (vgl. Zeilen 8 und 17 als korrespondierenden Kontext) scheinen in der Luft zu hängen und man weiss nicht was der alte Schreiber bei dieser Bemerkung im Sinn hatte.

I suggest that, perhaps, the blank space was left for the later insertion of the expected incipits in the still wet clay in the event the tablets were

[15]Kramer, *TMH* n.F. 3 (1961) 20.

[16]Heinrich Otten, "Bibliotheken im alten Orient," *Das Altertum* 1 (1955) 68.

subsequently uncovered. *CAT.* 2 then is an inventory of *actual* texts as they were recovered from hiding, not merely a list of tablets known to be part of a certain "series."

CAT. 3.[17] An unlined tablet of 55 lines, bearing incipits of 67 compositions. No dividing lines are present. At the foot of the Obverse (25 lines), a summary line indicates that 25 incipits precede. On the left edge of the tablet, a numerical summary for the Reverse (42 incipits) and the total of all compositions (67) are given. On two lines groups of tablets are enumerated by generic classification.

:33	3 dumu-é-dub-ba	"3 son of the tablet house"
:43	11 lugal	"11 royal compositions"

CAT. 4.[18] A tablet of 25 lines (Obverse 14, Reverse 11) containing 23 incipits. The incipits are divided into two groups by means of category summary lines (lines 12 and 25). No horizontal dividing lines are used. Line 12 is indented to call attention to its summary function. Line 25 is set off only by its final position and similarity to line 12. Division of the incipits is based on which of two "tablet containers" the tablets listed were assigned to or discovered in. There is no further classification on the basis of genre or the deity addressed.

:12 šà-^{gi}GÁ-MEZEM ša-ap-lu-um
"In the lower tablet container"

:25 šà-^{gi}GÁ-MEZEM e(!)-lu-um
"In the upper tablet container"

---

[17]Transliteration and partial translation are included in S. N. Kramer, "New Literary Catalogue from Ur," *RA* 55 (1961) 169-76 (hereafter cited as *RA* 55 [1961]). A copy of the cuneiform text is provided in Gadd-Kramer, *UET 6/1* (1963) 123.

[18]H. H. Figulla and W. J. Martin, *UET* 5 (1953) 86, contains a transcription of the cuneiform. Pertinent comments are found in Inez Bernhardt and S. N. Kramer, "Götter-Hymnen und Kult-Gesänge der Sumerer auf zwei Keilschrift- 'Katalogen' in der Hilprecht-Sammlung," *WZJ* 6 (1956/57) 394 (hereafter cited as Bernhardt-Kramer) and H. Kraus, *OLZ* 50 (1955) 518.

CAT. 5.[19] An unlined tablet containing 33 incipits in two columns. The second column is concluded by a numerical summary for the whole catalogue.

CAT. 6.[20] An unlined tablet of 62 lines. Dividing lines occur following lines 10, 20, 30, 49 and 62, but no summary lines are evident, nor is there any other indication of overt organization.

CAT. 7.[21] This tablet contains 68 lines, the contents of which are very similar to that of *CAT.* 6.[22] The erasure following line 18 may function as a dividing line. This blank line and the uneven distribution of incipits over the four columns of the tablet (col. I—22 incipits; col. II—24; col. III—7; col. IV—14) suggest intentional division of the incipits into four sections. The final summary in line 68: 4 na-rú-a "4 lists" is thought to refer to this division.[23]

---

[19]For a photo, transcription, transliteration and German translation, see Bernhardt-Kramer, pp. 389-91.

[20]S. N. Kramer ("The Oldest Literary Catalogue," *BASOR* 88 [1942] 10-19) provides a photo, transcription and transliteration of *CAT.* 6 (hereafter cited as *BASOR* 88).

[21]For transliteration and translation of all of *CAT.* 7, see Kramer, *BASOR* 88 (1942) 10-19. A copy of the cuneiform text is available in Henri de Genouillac, *TCL* 15 (1930) 28. Important comments regarding the structure of the tablet are given in Bernhardt-Kramer, pp. 393-94.

[22]The first ten lines of both catalogues are thought to be identical in content and arrangement. "Of [*CAT.* 7's] 68 titles, 43 are identical with those of [*CAT.* 6] though the order frequently varies" (Kramer, *BASOR* 88, 17).

[23]The erasure obliterates a line of signs which, in turn covers a horizontal line. "Ausserdem befindet sich auf der Originaltafel unter dem ausgekratzten Text von 'Nr. 19' eine mit dem Lineal gezogene horizontal Linie. Dies mag anzeigen, dass der Schreiber die beiden Titel-Gruppen vor und hinter der horizontal Linie getrennt hat, und rechtfertigt so die Vermutung, dass er die Kompositionen, die in diesem 'Katalog' aufgeführt sind, in vier Gruppen einteilte: 1-18, 19-46, 47-53 und 54-67. Vielleicht bezieht sich die sumarische Übersicht 4 na-rú-a genau am Ende der Tafel irgendwie auf diese Einteilung" (Bernhardt-Kramer, p. 393).

CAT. 8.[24] A very fragmentary tablet containing parts of 34 lines. Of these, only 30 are capable of significant reading. The tablet consists of groupings of incipits followed by indented, numerical/category summary lines. Classification is by type as well as by deity addressed. Thus only incipits of the same genre are grouped together, but genre types are repeated when addressed to different deities (see figure 1 below).

OBVERSE	REVERSE
1 tigi to Ningal	3 ír-šem to [?]
2 tigi to Sin	1 sìr-nam-šu-ub to [?]
1 sìr-nam-šu-ub to ?	3 sìr-nam-šu-ub to Dingir-mah
[2 illegible summary lines without incipits]	6 ír-šem to Ninurta
1 [?] to Enlil	2 ír-šem to Dingir-mah

Figure 1. Categories of Hymns and Deities Addressed in Catalogue 8

CAT. 9.[25] An unlined tablet containing approximately 50 incipits of varied hymn types, divided into five groups by category summary lines followed by horizontal dividers. Classification is by genre, with no apparent repetition of genre groups. Song types catalogued are:

[24]Heinrich Zimmern (*VS* 10 [1913] xii and plate 216) provides a transcription of the text. A transliteration and discussion of the tablet are to be found in Bernhardt-Kramer, p. 394.

[25]Bernhardt-Kramer (pp. 389-94) provides photo, transcription, transliteration, and German translation.

:25 [sìr . . . .] -me-eš
:43 sìr-nam-gala-me-eš
:48 sìr-nam-sipad-da dINANNA-meš
:61 tigi-me-eš
:82 a-da-ab-me-eš[26]

Within each of the genre categories, incipits are identified by the deity they address. This is accomplished by adding the name of the deity after an individual incipit or group of incipits (cf. Obv. 1-5; Rv. 80-81) either on the same line or on a line of its own. There is no consistent attempt to group all incipits to a single deity together, even within the same genre classification, with the result that the names of the deities are frequently repeated.

CAT. 10.[27] An extensive catalogue of eight columns and over 300 lines. In columns I-IV of the Obverse and I-III of the Reverse, some 180-

---

[26]There is no connection, so far as I can tell, between the adapa-song type represented here and the apkallu sage of the same name. According to *CAD*, A, p. 102, the adapa-song derives its name from the adapu-instrument by which it was accompanied. While *CAD* does not offer an identification for the adapa-instrument, others have suggested the timbrel or tambourine (cf. S. N. Langdon, "Babylonian and Hebrew Musical Terms," *JRAS* [1921] 169-91 [hereafter cited as "Musical Terms"]; Francis W. Galpin, *The Music of the Sumerians and their immediate Successors the Babylonians and Assyrians* [Cambridge: Cambridge University Press, 1937]9). A list of compositions designated as adapa-songs has been compiled by Adam Falkenstein ("Sumerische religiöse Texte," *ZA* 49 [1949] 87), where he also suggests a close connection of the adapa-song with the royal cult (pp. 87, 101).

[27]Transcription of a few lines from Reverse, cols. I and II may be found in *KAR:* 158. A discussion of the text as well as a complete transliteration and German translation is available in Erich Ebeling, *Ein Hymnen Katalog aus Assur* (Berliner Beiträge zur Keilinschriftforschung, vol. I/3; Berlin: Erich Ebeling, 1923) (hereafter cited as *Hymnen Katalog*). The following offer transliteration, translation and/or discussion of various portions of the catalogue: E. Ebeling, "Aus den Keilinschrifttexten aus Assur religiöse Inhalts," *MDOG* 58 (1917) 48-50; S. N. Langdon, "Musical Terms"; Heinrich Zimmern, "Zum Liederkatalog aus Assur," *ZA* 34 (1922) 90f.; Theophile James Meek, "Babylonian Parallels to the Song of Songs," *JBL* 43 (1924) 245-52; Adam Falkenstein, "Sumerian religiöse Texte," pp. 87, 91, 103.

plus incipits are arranged into at least 31 separate groupings by means of numerical/category summary lines, double dividing lines and benedictions.

OBVERSE, COLUMNS I-IV. For the Obverse, several factors are at work in the arrangement of the incipits. First, all the incipits on this side of the tablet are divided into one of at least four "types" of songs (other types may have been lost in the lacunae): (1) akkadita (col. I, 1-48); (2) ištarūta (col. II, 1-53); (3) tege šumera (col. III, 1-31); (4) adapa (col. III, 32-46+). Column IV is too fragmentary to determine the type of its contents. Within these large divisions, the incipits are grouped according to "series" (iškarātu). It is thought that each series was addressed to a particular deity (Ištar, Ira, Adad, Enlil).[28] For each series, the songs (zamāru) are listed by incipits, and each series is concluded by a formalized numerical/category summary line which contains the following information.

a. A running account of series and songs listed for this "type" grouping. The account takes the form:

X iškarātu X zamāru[meš]

b. A description of the type of songs the scribe has listed (amnu) in this series grouping. Types enumerated are:

1. akkadita
2. ištarūta
3. tege šumera
4. adapa šumera

c. A benediction invoking the blessing of the deity Ea, most probably on the patron of the scribe.

[d]E-a ba-la-aṭ-ka li-iq-bi
"May Ea command good health for you!"

At the end of a complete grouping of series containing a certain type of songs, a final summary line is offered which enumerates the number of zamāru listed in all the preceding series of that type. This

[28]Erich Ebeling, *Hymnen Katalog*, p. 9.

summary line regularly indicates the language of the songs, whether or not such information was provided in the individual series summaries (see figure 2).

Apparently the following organizational principles are at work in the four columns of *CAT*. 10.

1. *Type of song* is probably the most basic division of the Obverse. As far as can be determined from the extant portions of the tablet, all compositions of the same type were consistently grouped together.

2. *Language*. This concern pervades the whole catalogue as well. Within the larger "type" groupings, dialect was an important factor of arrangement.

3. *Series* to which an incipit belonged determined its position within the larger linguistic framework.

4. *Size*. The number of compositions in a completed collection of series may also have affected the arrangement of these larger units in relation to one another. The movement is from longer to shorter collections. However, because of the fragmentary nature of the catalogue, it is difficult to make a definitive analysis. The extant collections of series occur in the following order:

akkadita	(at least) 7 series	(probably) 36 songs
ištarūta	6 series	31 songs
tege šumēra	4 series	23 songs
adapa	? series	? songs

On the Reverse, columns I-III, however, size of the individual groups apparently plays no part in the arrangement. For example:

Rv. II,			Rv. II,		
1-5	11	širḫunga	19-21	2	elilu šadrûtu
6-11	5	kirretu	22-24	2	inḫu^{meš}
12-15	2	gangiṭṭu	25-30	5	pûru akkadû
16-18	2	nûru^{meš}			

REVERSE, COLUMNS I-III. The first three columns of the Reverse contain a continuation of the listing of incipits, but in a slightly different format. In the individual series summary lines, there is no longer any

Obverse, col. II

:18 3 iš-ka-ra-a-tu 15 za-ma-ru^{meš}
3 series, 15 songs

:19 ^{d}ištar-ú-ta am-nu
Ištarūta songs I have listed

:20 ^{d}E-a ba-la-aṭ-ka li-iq-bi
May Ea command good health for you!

:27 4 iš-ka-ra-a-tu 20 za-ma-ru^{meš}

:28 ^{d}ištar-ú-ta am-nu

:29 ^{d}E-a ba-la-aṭ-ka li-iq-bi

:48 naphar 33 za-ma-ru ak-ka-du-ú
Altogether, 33 Akkadian songs

Obverse, col. III

:16 3 iš-ka-ra-a-tu 15 za-ma-ru^{meš}

:17 te-gi-e šú-me-ra
Sumerian tigi-songs

:18 ^{d}E-a ba-la-aṭ-ka li-iq-bi

:31 naphar 23 te-gu-ú šú-me-ru
Altogether, 23 Sumerian tigi-songs

Figure 2. Examples of Individual and Final Series Summary Lines in Catalogue 10.

mention of iškarātu "series." Rather, the type of song becomes the primary ordering principle, with language serving as a secondary division.[29]

Rv. col. II, 4-5
napḫar 8 šumeru 3 akkadū
napḫaruma 11 širḫunga

S. Langdon believes that many of the song types are further defined by the instruments used in accompaniment.[30] David Wulstan, however, has shown that these terms most likely describe various tuning intervals of the Babylonian harp.[31]

Rv. col. IV, 45ff.
23 iratu ša e-šir-te Akkadi KI
17 iratu ša ki-it-me
24 iratu ša eb-bu-be
4 iratu ša pi-i-te[32]
[ ] iratu ša ni it/d $MURUB_4$
[ ] iratu ša ni-*iš GAB.RI
[ ] iratu ša $MURUB_4$-te (= qablite)

---

[29]In some instances the language is not indicated in Rv. cols. I-III, however, this omission is rectified in the summary record given in Rv. IV.
Rv. II, 11
napḫar 5 kirrētu
but Rv. IV, 28
5 kirretu akkadû

Rv. III, 6
23 irâti ša eširte
but Rv. IV, 45
23 irâti[meš] ša eširte akkadū[ki]

[30]S. N. Langdon, "Musical Terms."

[31]David Wulstan, "The Tuning of the Babylonian Harp," *Iraq* 30 (1980-81) 215-28. See also O. R. Gurney, "An Old Babylonian Treatise on the Tuning of the Harp," *Iraq* 30 (1980-81) 229-33.

[32]While Langdon considers the pîtu an instrument, he does not further define it. Others have seen in it a wind instrument or pipe (*Grove's Dictionary of Music and Musicians,* [ed. Eric Blom; 5th ed.; New York: St. Martin's Press, 1960] 1. 282-83).

Translation:

"23 love songs of the 'normal' (type), Akkadian"
"17 love songs of the 'cover' (type)"
"24 love songs of the 'flute/pipe' (type)"
" 4 love songs of the . . . (type)"
"... love songs, of the . . . (type)"
"... love songs, of the . . . (type)"
"... love songs, of the 'middle' (type)"

Regardless of their interpretation, these terms serve to distinguish otherwise identical song types.

REVERSE, COLUMN IV. Column IV of the Reverse of Catalogue 10 apparently contained a complete summary of the contents of Obv. I-Rv. III. Sufficient connections remain between the notations in Rv. IV and the various summary lines in the rest of the tablet to confirm the reliability of this assumption.[33] Except for Rv. IV, 1-2, which are so fragmentary as to raise doubt as to their contents, an important organizing factor for the rest of the summary record presented in this column appears to be language. Where all the songs of a particular type are in the same language, the description of "type" is simply followed by the word indicating the appropriate dialect.

Rv. IV, 8	. . . .] tegu šumeru
Rv. IV, 13	. . .] sirdingirgallašu šumeru
Rv. IV, 16	5 pâru akkadû
Rv. IV, 24	12 zamar šarri akkadû

Where, however, the songs of a certain type are of varied origin, the number of songs in each language is enumerated separately and then totaled at the last.

Rv. IV, 21-23
9 šumeru^{meš}

[33]It is difficult to determine exactly which portions of Obv. I-Rv. III correspond with the summary record in Rv. IV. However, it is possible to reconstruct much of the arrangement by using those correspondences which do occur (see above, n. 9) to fix the relative positions of the groups of incipits in Obv. I-Rv. III to the summary record. To see how I have worked this out, see n. 34.

1 akkadû^{meš}
napḫar 10 zamar ^{d}ningišzida

There is no attempt to group all collections of Akkadian or Sumerian songs into separate groups. Rather, the song types seem to "out rank" language as the regnant organizational principle. Only in one possible instance are series of different song types grouped together by dialect. The exact description of the contents of these series is still somewhat in doubt.[34]

---

[34]These lines provide a starting point for the reconstruction of the correspondences between the catalogue and the summary record of Rv. IV. I would offer the following observations:

a. The tegû Šumerū noted in Rv. IV, 8 and followed there immediately by an uncertain number of Sumerian and Akkadian zamāru^{meš} adapū^{meš} must correspond to Obv. III, 1-31 (tegû šumerū) and Obv. III, 32-46 (adapu šumeru [adapu akkadû presumably followed in the lacuna]).

b. The nambal egi šumeru recorded in Rv. IV, 7 must lie in the lacunae at the end of Obv. II and the beginning of Obv. III.

c. The first half of the expanded version of the description of the ištarūta which occurs in Obv. II, 46:

iškaru ri'i ri'i ^{d}ištarūta amnu

almost certainly corresponds with the last category of songs listed in Rv. IV, 3-6:

. . . .] iškaru re'u " re'u

indicating that at least these songs listed in Obv. II, 38-47 (if not all the ištarūta-songs) correspond with the description in Rv. IV, 5.

d. The final summary line for all the incipits of Obv. II occurs at Obv. II, 48 and categorizes the incipits only as: napḫar 33 zamāru akkadû. This agrees with Rv. IV, 6, where the preceding compositions are all called . . . .] akkadû. Further, the occurrence of the final summary line indicates that the otherwise unidentified incipits following in Obv. II, 49-53, must be the nambal egi šumeru recorded in Rv. IV, 7. How many of these songs have been lost we have no way of knowing.

e. The descriptive summary of Obv. I, 43:

. . . .] imni akkadita

may correspond to the category of songs listed in Rv. IV, 3:

. . . .] iškaru maru mara imni

f. If the preceding is true, we must find the iškaru murtami of Rv. IV, 4 in the incipits at the end of Obv. I or the lacuna which follows.

g. There is evidence that both these groups of songs (Obv. I, 1-44; Obv. II, 1-48) are Akkadian. The term akkadita constantly reoccurs in Obv. I, 1-44 while, in the final summary line of Obv. II, 48, the songs of

Rv. IV, 3-6

. . . .] iškaru maru mara imni
. . . .] iškaru murtami
. . . .] iškaru re'u " re'u
. . . .] akkadû

CAT. 11.[35] Another long catalogue of approximately 230 lines. The tablet is divided into nine sections by the use of category headings coupled with numerical/category summary lines (see figure 3 below).[36] The Obverse and Reverse differ slightly in format (as is the case with *CAT.* 10).

OBVERSE. The four segments of the Obverse actually form one tightly unified whole. The correspondences between Obv. col. I and col. II

---

this column are described as naphar 33 zamāru akkadû. This accords well with the description in Rv. IV, 6: . . . .] akkadû.

[35]*CAT.* 11 is supported by the partial duplicates *CATS.* 12 and 13. For a transcription of the whole of *CAT.* 11, see *IVR*^{2}: 53 [60]. C. Bezold (*Catalogue of the Cuneiform Tablets in the Kounyunjik Collection of the British Museum* [London: Harrisons and Sons, 1891] 2. 1 and 451; hereafter cited as *Catalogue*) gives a brief description of *CAT.* 11. For the restoration of *CAT.* 11 (K.2529) by the fragment K.3276, see S. Langdon, "The Assyrian Catalogue of Liturgical Texts. A Restoration of the Tablet," *RA* 18 (1921) 157-59 (hereafter cited as "Restoration"). A Hebrew transliteration is available in Joseph Halévy, *Documents religeux de l'Assyrie à de la Babylonie* (Paris: Maisonneuve et Cie., 1882), 170-75. Further comments are to be found in Arthur Ungnad, "Sumerische Handerhebungsgebete," *OLZ* 21 (1918) cols. 116-19 and S. Langdon, "Unidentified Duplicates of the Sumerian Liturgy 'e-lum-gud-sun'. The Titular Litany," *AnOr* 12 (1935) 202-6 (hereafter cited as "Duplicates").

[36]In my opinion, on the Obverse these headings and numerical/category summary lines were intended to be read across both columns continuously. In this case, the initial heading (building on the reconstruction of Langdon) probably read:

BALAG-meš dingir-ri-e-ne
Balag-liturgies to the gods

The later summary lines were:

:42 ŠU-NIGIN 39 BALAG ^{d}En-lil-là-ge
Sub-total: 39 Balag-liturgies to Enlil
:61 ŠU-NIGIN 18 BALAG ^{d}INANNA-ge
Sub-total: 18 Balag-liturgies to INANNA

are exact.[37] Both contain the same number of lines (61), all the breaks (headings, dividing lines, summary lines) occur at the same places (see figure 3). These as well as other significant correspondences between the incipits of the two columns have led S. Langdon to suggest a liturgical motive for this presentation. According to Langdon, "*the titles in Col. II go with the corresponding titles in Col. I.* Col. I carries the official titles of the LITURGIES." The liturgy listed in Obv. I, 2 is known to have been completed by the composition given in Obv. II, 2, and the same is true of the incipits in Obv. I, 4 and Obv. II, 4. The scribe has listed the titles of these liturgical works in Col. I and the concluding composition of each liturgy in the corresponding line of Col. II.[38]

The arrangement of the Obverse, then, is as follows. The first line of both columns is broken. In column one, only a plural sign (-meš) remains, while for column two -ne stands written at the far right (restored from K.3276). These two lines are probably to be restored:[39]

---

[37]There is some ambiguity about the treatment of line 16 (of both columns). Obv. I, 16 is apparently a blank line with no signs written. According to Langdon's proposal that Col. II carries the corresponding Balag-compositions for the liturgies whose titles are listed in Col. I, one would expect Obv. II, 16 to be correspondingly blank. But all transcriptions clearly show the presence of the BALAG sign at the beginning of the line. As this sign elsewhere in *CAT.* 11 is used only in summary lines to indicate the category balag (cf. Obv II, 42, 61) or in headings (Obv. I, 1), its presence here should also indicate a summary line. In view of the summary line in Obv. I, 42 enumerating the first thirty-nine incipits, this seems less likely. However, it is possible that the scribe has divided this first section of incipits into two groups according to the deity addressed, without numerically distinguishing them. In such a case, I would expect the BALAG sign of Obv. II, 16 to have been followed by the name of a particular deity and to have concluded with the sign -ge (cf. Obv. II, 42, 61). This is precisely the case in Langdon's restoration of this column on the basis of K.3276 (*RA* 18 [1921] 158), where he completes the line with . . .] LÁL-SAR. This group of signs, when preceded by the A-sign, are read as the divine or geographical name A-šur$_4$ = Aššur (W. W. Hallo, "Zāriqum," *JNES* 15 [1956] 225). This would seem to confirm that this line was intended by the scribe to function as a category summary line for the first fourteen incipits which precede it. In lieu of a numerical summary in Obv. I, 16, then, the scribe has left a blank line to indicate the break and to assure that his lines would correspond.

[38]S. Langdon, "Duplicates," p. 202.

[39]S. Langdon, "Restoration," pp. 157-58: "Column I of the Catalogue is preceded by the rubric balag-meš [dingir-ri-e-ne], ... [Column

BALAG]-meš [dingir-ri-e]-ne
Balag-liturgies to the gods.

They function as a heading for the compositions subsequently listed. Fourteen incipits are then listed in each column (lines 2-15), marked off in Obv. II, 16 by a category summary line.

Obv. II, 16
BALAG [. . .a (?)] -šur$_4$-ge
Balag-liturgies to Aššur

Twenty-five incipits follow this summary line in both columns before the next break occurs with the numerical/category summary line (line 42 of both columns).

Obv. I and II, 42
ŠU-NIGIN 39 BALAG ^{d}En-lil-lá-ge
Sub-total: 39 Balag-liturgies to Enlil

Eighteen more lines follow (in both columns) before the final numerical/category summary line (line 61).

Obv. I and II, 61
[ŠU-NIGIN 18(?)] [40] BALAG ^{d}Inanna-ge
Sub-total: 18(?) Balag-liturgies to Inanna

Among the important considerations involved in the arrangement of the Obverse are the following:

1. All compositions are BALAG-meš dingir-ri-e-ne "Balag-liturgies to the gods."

II] also has a heading which ended [. . . . .]-ne; from the contents the restoration balag-meš dingir-ri-e-ne is apparently required but the traces before the NE do not indicate the sign E."

[40] I am not certain whether the numerical summary here should be considered a running account of all incipits or just an enumeration of those occurring in the last section. Since the summary in Obv. I, 42 obviously enumerates all previous incipits regardless of the presence of the category summary of Obv. II, 16, perhaps a running account is called for. In this case, I wonder if Obv. I, 16 was not originally a numerical summary line [SU-NIGIN 14] which has subsequently perished.

Obv. Col. I	Obv. Col. II	Rv. Col. IV	Rv. Col. III
:1 [BALAG] -meš	:1 [dingir-ri-e] -ne	:1	:1 ER-ŠEM-MA-meš KI-DU- [DU]
:2	:2 [restored by K.3276]	[first third of column badly broken]	:2
15 incipits	15 incipits	13 incipits	25 incipits
		:13	
		:14	
:16 blank	:16 BALAG [sub-total?]		
		15 incipits	:26
			:27
25 incipits	25 incipits	:28	
		:29 ŠU-NIGIN 47 ŠU-IL-LÁ-GAN-meš	15 incipits
		:30	
:41	:41	PROSE EPILOGUE AND COLOPHON	:41
:42 ŠU-NIGIN 39	:42 BALAG ^{d}En-lil-lá-ge		:42 ŠU-NIGIN 40 [ER] -ŠEM-MA-meš
:43	:43 [col. broken]		:43 ŠU-IL-LÁ-GAN-meš [. .] -ne
18 incipits	18 (?) incipits	:55	:44 [restored by K.3276]
:60	:60		19 incipits
:61 [. . . . .]	:61 BALAG ^{d}Inanna-ge		:62

Figure 3. Schematic Presentation of Catalogue 11

2. The liturgical correspondences of the incipits in col. II determined their positions relative to those of col. I.

3. The incipits are strictly divided by deity addressed.

REVERSE. Of the three sections distinguished on the Reverse of *CAT.* 11, only two (Rv. III, 1-42 and Rv. III, 43-IV, 29) contain listings of incipits. Each of these two groups is introduced by a category heading and concluded by a numerical/category summary line.

Rv. III, 1
ER-ŠEM-MA-meš KI-DU- [DU]
Lamentations (for?) ceremonies

Rv. III, 42
ŠU-NIGIN 40 [ER] -ŠEM-MA-meš
Sub-total: 40 Lamentations

Rv. III, 43
ŠU-IL-LÁ-GAN-meš [........] -ne
Prayers for the Raising of the Hand . . . .

Rv. IV, 29
ŠU-NIGIN 47 ŠU-IL-LÁ-GAN-meš
Sub-total: 47 Prayers for the Raising of the Hand.

The explicit division of these incipits is by genre classification (iršemma and šuilla). The first group (Rv. III, 1-42) is divided into two groups of 25 and 15 incipits by a dividing line inserted after Rv. III, 26 and before Rv. III, 27. This division does not seem to reflect any internal classification of the material and is probably only an editorial marking of lines at regular intervals. The second group includes the remainder of Rv. col. III, 43—-IV,29. The 47 incipits[41] in this division are grouped according to the deity they address and each incipit is concluded by the formalized expression ša DN "to (or for) the god DN." The compositions to particular deities are arranged together and grouped in the following sequence.

[41] Only 40 of these incipits are now extant, the bottom of Rv. III having been broken away. The numerical summary line in Rv. IV, 29 totals the complete number as 47 and shows that 7 incipits have been lost in the lacunae between Col. III and Col. IV.

Anu	1	incipit	Ninurta	6	incipits
Enlil	2	"	Nergal	1	"
Ea	1	"	Papsukkal	1	"
Sin	3	"	Nusku	3	"
Šamaš	2	"	*Tammuz*	*2*	*"*
Adad	1	"	Ninlil	1	"
Marduk	2	"	Belet-ili	1	"
Amurru	1	"	Ningal	2	"
[12 incipits lost]			Inanna	10	"
		^{d}NA-NA-A	1		"

These incipits are further separated into two groups by a dividing line between Rv. IV, 13 and 14. This irregular grouping of 32 and 15 incipits defies any simple strophic explanation. It is interesting to note that this division serves to separate the deities listed into masculine and feminine groups, with the feminine group placed at the last of the list.[42]

The Reverse is concerned first to group incipits according to genre classification and shows a secondary interest in the deity addressed (Rv. III, 43—IV, 29). This is somewhat comparable to the Obverse where only one genre is cited throughout and the incipits are distributed among the three deities they address.

The third and final section of the Reverse (Rv. IV, 30-55) consists of the epilogue/colophon, which can be divided generally into four parts.

1. Rv. IV, 30-32—the description of the corpus of texts catalogued.
2. Rv. IV, 33-44—in praise of the god Nabû and of King Assurbanipal.
3. Rv. IV, 45-50—the description of the transmission process.

[42]The first of the male deities follow an order which may well reflect a standard (Anu, Enlil, Ea, Sin, Šamaš, Adad, Marduk). Oppenheim observes virtually the same order in his discussion (*Ancient Mesopotamia*, pp. 194-96): the ancient deities Anu, Enlil, Ea; the astral deities Sin (moon) and Šamaš (sun); the storm god Adad. The same order may be observed in several texts recorded in J. B. Pritchard, *ANET* vol. 2 (Princeton, NJ: Princeton University Press, 1975): The Treaty between Ashurnirari of Assyria and Mati'ili of Arpad (p. 51) (Aššur . . . Anu . . . Enlil . . . Ea . . . Sin . . . Šamaš . . . Adad . . . Marduk. . . .); The vassal treaties of Esarhaddon (p. 54): (Aššur, Anu, Enlil, Ea, Sin, Samas, Adad, Marduk). The initial group (Anu, Enlil, Ea) is much more frequent.

4. Rv. IV, 51-55—final invocations in behalf of the library of Assurbanipal.[43]

CAT. 12.[44] Duplicates *CAT.* 11, Rv. III, 27-41.

CAT. 13.[45] Duplicates *CAT.* 11, Rv. III, 1-5.

CAT. 14.[46] A fragmentary tablet bearing parts of fourteen lines from a larger catalogue of incipits. Two indented numerical/category summary lines are preserved:

line 4	13 ér-šà-ḫun-gá	"13 Penitential Psalms"
line 7	2 ér-šà-ḫun-gá	"2 Penitential Psalms"

The catalogue is too fragmentary to determine what principle occasioned the division into separate groups of compositions of the same genre classification.

CAT. 15.[47] A fragmentary tablet with 23 partial lines from a

---

[43]A transliteration and German translation of the last 23 lines may be found in Hermann Hunger, *BAK,* pp. 102-3. I offer here the translation and transliteration of the first three lines:

:30 DUB-SAG-meš EŠ-GAR NAM-US-KU IGI-LÁ-meš <u>ša ina šu-su-u</u>
Titles of the series: Lamentation Priests' corpus. Collated. Those which were available.

:31 <u>ma [-'-du-tum ul amru ina lib-bi la ru-ud-du-u</u>
Many were not seen nor included [added].

:32 <u>..............................r] u-ud-di</u>

[44]Bezold, *Catalogue,* Vol. II, pp. 1, 451, gives a brief description of this catalogue and its correspondences and variations from *CAT.* 11.

[45]A transcription of *CAT.* 13 (BM 82-3-23, 5220 = K.2529, Rv. col. III, 1-5) is to be found in S. Langdon, *Babylonian Liturgies. Sumerian Texts from the early Period and from the library of Ashurbanipal, For the most part transliterated and translated, with introduction and Index* (Paris: Paul Geuthner, 1913) (hereafter cited as *BL*), no. 151.

[46]Transcription is available in Langdon, *BL,* Pl. XLI, no. 115.

[47]Langdon, *BL,* Pl. XLVI, no. 139 provides transcription. His transliteration and translation are to be found in the same volume, pp. 58-59. A later transcription and partial transliteration are offered in Langdon, "A

catalogue similar to *CAT.* 14 in that both preserve indented numerical/category summary lines. As in *CAT.* 14, both summary lines preserved here cite ér-šà-ḫun-gá as the genre of the contents.

CAT. 16[48] A small fragment of 21 lines. The Obverse duplicates *CAT.* 15, lines 9-19. The Reverse adds eight more partial lines not known from *CAT.* 15. Again, one extant indented numerical/category summary line divides the incipits and declares the contents to be ér-šà-ḫun-gá.

CAT. 17.[49] Known as the Herbert Clark Cylinder, this tablet "is a catalogue of the tablets found in the library of some temple or individual. The small number of texts catalogued makes the latter alternative more probable. The collection consisted of twenty-one texts belonging to seventeen different series. There were two texts from each of two series, three from another series, and one apiece from fourteen other series."[50] These compositions are not listed by individual incipits (as has been the custom in the previous catalogues), but are enumerated in genre categories much as in a numerical/category summary line.[51]

2 u-mu-un-e an-na-ra
1 e-zid-dè dug-ga-àm

The list (lines 3-19) was preceded by a double heading (lines 1-2).

line 1	enim-dingir-ri-e ad(?)	Prayer (word?) to god
line 2	dubba-enim-meš	Tablet of the prayers

List of the Known Titles of Sumerian Penitential Psalms (ERŠAḪUNGA)," *RA* 22 (1925) 119-25 (hereafter cited as "List").

[48]Transcriptions are found in Langdon, *BL,* Pl. XLV, no. 138 and in Langdon, "List," 119-25 along with a partial transliteration and translation.

[49]Transcription, transliteration and translation may be found in D. D. Luckenbill, "A Neo-Babylonian Catalogue of Hymns," *AJSL* 26 (1909) 27-32 (hereafter cited as *AJSL* 26). A photo of the cylinder and very brief physical description were published in S. Levy and P. Artzi, *Sumerian and Akkadian Documents in Israel.* Atiqot, English series 4 (1965) No. 99.

[50]Luckenbill, *AJSL* 26, pp. 28-29.

[51]Could these brief entries have been taken from the summary lines of a more extensive catalogue?

The tendency was to group the tablets in this collection according to the series to which they belong. I am not able to determine any additional attempt to organize the series thus listed.

CAT. 18.[52] This fragmentary catalogue preserves 23 lines from two partial columns of a tablet which may have contained as many as six columns originally. There are no signs of headings or summary lines, but double dividing lines are in evidence following Obv. lines 2 and 12 as well as Rv. line 10. W. W. Hallo indicates that the divider of Obv. line 12 "is followed by the 10-mark to indicate, evidently, that ten compositions were included between the two double dividing lines. . . . Since these dividing lines do not seem to reflect any generic grouping . . . , the guess may be ventured that they were drawn mechanically after every tenth entry."[53]

CAT. 19.[54] Another fragmentary catalogue containing compositions of the ér-šà-ḫun-gá type, *Cat.* 19 is closely related to *CATS.* 14, 15 and 16. The same type of indented numerical/category summary lines occur twice here.

:4   27 ér-šà-ḫun-gá
:7   2 ér-šà-ḫun-gá

CAT. 20.[55] This fragmentary text containing parts of 22 lines demonstrates no evidence of headings or summary lines. The only horizontal line occurs after the final line on the Reverse.

CAT.21.[56] Kramer describes this catalogue as "a 4-column tablet . . . that lists the incipits of 83 compositions designated by the scribe as ír-šem-ma-dingir-re-e-ne, 'iršemma of the gods.'" According to the

---

[52] Transcription published in E. Chiera, *STVC:* 41. William W. Hallo provides a partial transliteration and translation in "Another Sumerian Literary Catalogue?" *StudOr* 46 (1975) 77-80 (hereafter cited as "Another Catalogue?").

[53] Hallo, "Another Catalogue?" p. 78.

[54] Transcription, transliteration and translation (almost complete) are available in Langdon, "List," pp. 119-25.

[55] Only a transcription is available to my knowledge. It is found in Gadd-Kramer, *UET 6/2,* Pl. CCXXXII, no. 196.

[56] Transcription, transliteration and translation published in S. N. Kramer, "Two British Museum irsemma 'Catalogues,'" *StudOr* 46 (1975) 141-66 (hereafter cited as *StudOr 46*).

indented, numerical summary lines, these 83 incipits were taken from nine separate tablets where the compositions they introduced were inscribed. Thus the overall governing factor of organization was the tablet on which the composition was written. The incipits from different tablets are set apart by indented numerical summary lines of the following type.

:3	[..] šà-l [one]-dub tablet	[..], the contents of one
:13	10 šà-l [one] -dub tablet	10, the contents of one

Within these tablet divisions, the compositions were listed by incipits preceded by a number, apparently indicating the number of compositions of that type on the tablet under consideration.[57] Some of the incipits are repeated as many as three times in the course of the nine tablets catalogued.[58] At the end of the catalogue, the scribe has categorized the contents of the catalogue as:

ír-šem-ma-dingir-re-e-ne
"iršemma of the gods"[59]

CAT. 22.[60] A small, five-sided prism inscribed with incipits of 76 iršemma compositions, *CAT.* 22 is divided into two sections based on the deity to which its compositions are addressed. The incipits are preceded by a number indicating the number of compositions of this type catalogued (as in *CAT.* 21 above). There is no indication of different tablets involved here. Two indented numerical/category summary lines are set off from the incipits they enumerate by a horizontal dividing line:

---

[57]Just what this means I am not certain. Are these "series" titles containing a number of tablets? This seems unlikely in the case of iršemma's. Or are these duplicate copies of tablets introduced by the incipit listed? Again, if these are compositions inscribed on a single tablet, it seems unlikely that duplicates of the same irsemma would be included.

[58]Kramer, *StudOr 46*, pp. 142 and 159, note 5.

[59]Kramer, *StudOr 46*, p. 158, note 2, concludes: "the 'gods' in this rubric are no doubt Inanna and Ninšubur, as is evident from the fact that at least 22 of the incipits in [*CAT.* 21], are identical with those in [*CAT.* 22], where they are designated as 'irsemma of Inanna' and 'iršemma of Ninšubur'. . . ."

[60]Transcription, transliteration and translation also published in Kramer, *StudOr 46*, pp. 141-66.

(following line 67)

76 šid-bi ír-šèm-ma-^{d}inanna	"Its number is 76 iršemma of Inanna"

(following line 74)

7 ír-šèm-ma-^{d}nin-šubur	7 iršemma of Ninšubur

This last summary line is followed by another dividing line which sets it apart from the concluding summary of the whole prism:

ír-šèm-ma-^{d}inanna-ù-^{d}nin-šubur
"iršemma of Inanna and Ninšubur"

The basic overt division of these incipits is, therefore, the deity addressed. Since all compositions catalogued are iršemma there can be no genre distinction.

ANALYSIS OF ORGANIZATIONAL CONCERNS AND PRINCIPLES

This survey has brought out a number of organizational concerns which the ancient scribes embodied as overt characteristics and features of these catalogues. Of these, by far the most important (and therefore widespread) is genre. Sixteen of twenty-two catalogues use some form of genre classification for their incipits. Such classification is not surprising in view of its importance in the cultic milieu from which these compositions stemmed and in which they continued to function. Genre classification made these hymns more readily available for the cultic functions they were intended to perform.

Besides this major principle, other important concerns have been shown to be at work in the overt organization of the incipits. Deity addressed is not as widespread as genre (7 and 22 catalogues), but is an important factor, even the dominant one in several catalogues (*CATS.* 8-13, 22). Liturgical correspondences affect the arrangement of incipits in *CAT.* 11. Currency of usage is significant in *CAT* 1. All these and more are evident from the explicit organizational structure of the catalogues of incipits. A further look at the catalogues shows these concerns cannot be restricted to such obvious attempts to organize, but must be recognized as active even when no *explicit* indications are in evidence.

I now intend to reexamine these twenty-two catalogues for evidence of organizational technique and concern which cannot be derived solely from overt indications of intent (headings, colophons, summary lines, etc.). To this end I will need to look within those larger groupings which are so delineated, as well as those catalogues and segments of catalogues which are devoid (or practically devoid) of any explicit indications. It should prove interesting to see if the same or different organizational concerns are active here (albeit *implicitly*). I shall group the material according to type of organizational concern reflected, rather than by catalogue.

1. *Genre Groupings.* Explicit grouping of incipits by genres is an important organizational method in the catalogues. Such arrangement is only logical in a culture which so prizes its cultic literature. Similar organization of incipits according to genre by less explicit means is also a feature of these tablets. It is necessary to look at those examples where genre does not already play a part in the overt structure of the catalogue. Such genre interest is in evidence when the scribes "lumped" incipits together into category lines preceded by numbers (cf. *CAT.* 3, Rv. 33 dumu-é-dub-ba "Three son of the tablet house"), but it is also at work in the simple juxtaposition of successive incipits.

Kramer has called attention to such a grouping in *CAT.* 6. "An excellent example of arrangement according to content [genre] is that of the last 13 titles of [*CAT.* 6] . . .; to judge from their titles, these are all 'wisdom' compositions."[61] Other evidence of genre arrangement is forthcoming in this catalogue. In lines 32-35, four incipits of compositions which are ostensibly lamentations over the destruction of certain cities (Ur, Nippur, Sumer and an unknown site) are written successively.[62]

:32 tùr-ra-na :34 u_4-šu-bala ag-dè
:33 tùr-me-nun-e :35 uru-me-zi-da

[61]Kramer, *BASOR* 88 (1942) 18, note 45. These compositions are explicitly marked off from the rest of the incipits by the horizontal line between lines 49 and 50. At first glance this line may appear to be a misplaced dividing line which should have followed ten compositions (as those after lines 10, 20, 30 and 40). The "wisdom" genre grouping which follows this line, however, reveals its true nature.

[62]In the parallel passage (*CAT.* 7, 27-30), these incipits are repeated consecutively, but in a slightly different order:

:27 tùr-ra-na :29 uru-me-zi-da
:28 tùr-me-nun-na :30 u_4-šu-bala(!) ag-de

Note how the inversion of the last two incipits strongly suggests that line 29 is also part of this group of laments over cities (which its initial sign—uru "city" tends to support).

W. W. Hallo was earlier of the opinion that the Old Babylonian catalogues (*CATS.* 3-8; 18; 20-22)

> differ formally from all the later ones in that they seem to exhibit no single consistent sequence or system of classification; the later lists not only classify the texts by genre but, as is shown by the existence of duplicate copies in an least two cases . . . , apparently arrived at a canonical version of the catalogues themselves. . . .[63]

He has since revised his opinion and feels that concern with genre was active in the production of catalogues even in the Old Babylonian period, especially as indicated by the genre oriented catalogues 21 and 22. Whereas in these two catalogues genre classification is a part of the *overt* organizational structure, *CAT.* 18 (in its present extant condition) evidences genre arrangement without overt structure. "Granted the above identifications, the order of entries in *CAT.* 18 would be: ("obverse?") individual lament, congregational laments; ("reverse?") disputation, royal hymn, divine hymns."[64] Genre interests seem, therefore, to exert important influence on the organization of the catalogues whether in overt or implicit terms.

2. *Arrangement by Deity Addressed.* Among the explicit organizational methods employed, deity addressed is a strong secondary interest in a number of catalogues. In *CAT.* 18, deity considerations are operative in the juxtaposition of three incipits beginning with ^{d}UTU = Sin (*CAT.* 18, Obv. 11-13). Deity (or "series") may also be a factor in the grouping of four incipits in *CAT.* 21, lines 72-75:

1 su_8-ba ....
1 su_8-ba ....
1 su_8-b [a].................
1 su_8-[ba].................

[63]Hallo, "Antiquity," 168.
[64]Hallo, "Another Catalogue?" 80.

Here, in each case, su_8-ba is translated "The Shepherd" and points to "compositions concerned with Dumuzi that belong to the Dumuzi-Inanna or Dumuzi-Geštinanna cycle of laments."[65] One must include here the two Šulgi hymns which appear together in *CAT.* 1, Obv. 14-15.

3. *Juxtaposition by Similar Phraseology.* There is a tendency evident in many of the catalogues to group together incipits on the basis of similar wording or phraseology. This is most noticeable when the incipits so arranged begin with the same sign or word. An interesting example of this phenomenon is found in *CAT.* 1, where the following groupings occur:

:3	lugal	:16	en
:4	lugal	:17	lugal
:5	en	:18	lugal
	.....	:19	ur-sag
:8	en	:20	lugal
:9	ur-sag	:21	lugal
:10	ur-sag	:22	ur-sag
:11	lugal	:23	en
:12	nin	:24	lugal
:13	en	:25	lugal
:14	^{d}šul-gi	:26	ur-sag
:15	^{d}šul-gi	:27	nin

The arrangement is very tantalizing and strongly suggests a purposeful patternism to me. However, since Hallo[66] is only able to identify ten of these incipits with any certainty, any further analysis is extremely difficult.

Many examples of juxtaposition by similar phraseology are in reality occasioned by other considerations, as in the case of the first two of the four incipits of lamentations over the destruction of cities from *CAT.* 6 (see above, pp. 54-55), where both begin with tùr, and the two self-laudatory hymns to Šulgi and Lipit-Ištar (*CAT.* 3, Obv. 4-5) whose incipits both begin lugal-me. Other cases are not so easily explained in this way. In *CAT.* 3, three consecutive incipits beginning with the sign nam occur.

---

[65]Kramer, *StudOr 46*, p. 152.
[66]Hallo, "Antiquity," 169.

Obv. 23-25

nam-nun-e
nam-nun-e sag na-il (?)-(?)
nam-lugal

While, according to Kramer, the first two incipits are probably hymns to Nanna-Sin, the last can hardly be such, since it is the "Sumerian King List."[67] It seems that similar initial signs or words have led to the grouping of otherwise unrelated incipits.

In other instances it is not possible to determine whether additional factors were at work in the juxtaposition of incipits with similar phraseology. This uncertainty is due, for the most part, to insufficient information regarding the incipits or the compositions to which they refer. In several catalogues, compositions beginning with u_4-ri-a are grouped together (*CAT.* 3, Rv. 28-30; *CAT.* 6, Obv. 20-21 = *CAT.* 7, Obv. 14-15). It is possible that these compositions are myths or epics as Kramer suggests,[68] but this is far from certain, especially since the three incipits of *CAT.* 3 are followed by a fourth (u_4 ma-da dam na-na) which Kramer describes as Wisdom. It seems, at least for the fourth incipit in *CAT.* 3, that the determining factor was the similarity of the initial phraseology and not the genre.

Some further examples may be mentioned. *CAT.* 11, in the initial section of the Reverse, evidences three such groupings (Rv. III, 7-9 umun; Rv. III, 10-11 é; Rv. III, 12-13 ur-sag). In *CAT.* 17, three consecutive "series" begin with the same sign combinations:

:16 1 im-gid-da ki-el KASKAL za-e(?)-(?)-giš
:17 3 im-gid-da ab-ba ^{d}NUSKU(?)-
:18 1 im-gid-da ŠÊŠ dim-ma-(?)-sun(?)

Perhaps the most extreme case is that of *CAT.* 15, lines 12-17 = *CAT.* 16, lines 4-9, where no less than six consecutive incipits begin with the phrase me-e dìm-me-ir-mu.[69] Even *internal* phraseology can figure in the juxtaposition of incipits in a case such as *CAT.* 11, Rv. III, 17-19.

---

[67]Kramer, *RA* 55 (1961) 174.

[68]Kramer, *RA* 55 (1961) 174-75.

[69]The phrase dìm-me-ir-mu occurs frequently in these catalogues, being found in 12 of 20 incipits in *CAT.* 15 and 9 of 17 in *CAT.* 16.

:17 UR-SAG GAL me-ni še-ir-ma-al-la-íl-la
:18 me-ni še-ir-ma-al-la e-ne ram-mal-lí gú-ud-du
:19 UR-SAG ni-gal-me še-ir-ma-al-la e-ne ram-mal-lí

Some of the more strongly structured catalogues (such as *CATS.* 2, 9, 10, 11, 12, 13), in which series or genre concerns define the relation of the incipits to one another, seem to resist this type of juxtaposition due to the control exercised by the major organizational features. The exceptions cited for *CAT.* 11 above occur in the one section of the catalogue devoted to a single category of hymn (ir-šemma) in which no other strong organizational force (deity, series) is at work.

In all these cases, the impeding factors are (1) the dearth of information about so many of the incipits concerned, and (2) the inconsistency of the phenomenon. While such groupings occur with sufficient regularity to belie mere hazard, there is never any clear attempt to bring total consistency to the endeavor. There seems to be always some stray incipit which could have better been related to some other group and yet was not. There is always the possibility that, given better understanding of the compositions themselves, other factors would emerge which condition the apparently simple phraseological connections.

THE "CANONIZATION" OF SUMERIAN LITERATURE

William W. Hallo has discussed elsewhere the stages involved in the gradual fixation or "canonization" of a standard corpus of Sumerian literature at various points in its history of transmission.[70] He describes the development of four such "canons" (Old Sumerian, neo-Sumerian, Old Babylonian and post-Sumerian), each of which enshrines the creative products of a particular period, which have survived a long period of transmission and adaptation, in a literary corpus characterized by a standard text and a standard order. As indication of this process of standardization, Hallo cites such features as (1) catch-lines to indicate the proper sequence of tablets within a series; (2) colophons concerned with data necessary for the classification of texts and describing elements of the transmission process; (3) the existence of duplicate texts evidencing identical order and near-identical text; (4) the production of catalogues of incipits such as these at hand.

---

[70]Hallo, "Individual Prayer in Sumerian: The Continuity of a Tradition," *JAOS* 88 (1968) 71-89. His most thorough treatment is found in "History," pp. 181-203.

Hallo further suggests that the catalogues themselves were subject to the same standardization process which marks the texts they enumerate.[71] A close examination of these catalogues does reveal evidence of such a move toward standardization, at least in some instances. Some of these have already been mentioned above. The discovery of fragments duplicating portions of other catalogues exactly with regard to content and order (*CATS.* 11, 12, 13 and *CATS.* 15, 16) indicates a high degree of fixity for those compositions. For other catalogues exact duplicates are not known. However, in several instances, partial correspondences (of a surprisingly extensive nature) in content and order do occur. These partial correspondences, while not evidence for the final stage of "canonization," do indicate the on-going process which has not yet reached its conclusion; a process of classification, arrangement, standardization, with the ultimate purpose of establishing a fixed body of literature with a fixed, "canonical" arrangement. The comparison of the contents of three of the Old Babylonian catalogues mentioned above (*CATS.* 3, 6 and 7) yields a good example of a "canon" in the making. As may be seen from figure 4 (p. 61), the first ten incipits of *CATS.* 6 and 7 correspond exactly in content and order.[72] In addition, four of these ten incipits (1 and 2; 8 and 9) are confirmed in their order relative to one another by their occurrence in identical order in *CAT.* 3 (incipits 4 and 5; 13 and 14 respectively). There are several more correspondences of lesser extent between *CAT.* 6 and *CAT.* 7 (*CAT.* 6:17-21 = *CAT.* 7:11-15; *CAT.* 6:32-35 = *CAT.* 7:27,28,30,29; and *CAT.* 6:41,42,44 = *CAT.* 7:34,33,35).

Numerous correspondences of two incipits in identical order occur in addition to these and receive further support from *CAT.* 3. These extensive correspondences (especially in the case of *CATS.* 6 and 7) can hardly be laid to chance. On the contrary, it does seem to indicate an awareness of or development of a standard grouping and ordering of these incipits. This concern to standardize the catalogues themselves lends even more credence to the organizational intent expressed toward the incipits they contain.

In summary, the scribes who prepared these catalogues were most frequently concerned to arrange the compositions by genre category

---

[71] Hallo, "Antiquity," 168-69.

[72] There is some question about the first four lines of *CAT.* 7 which have, unfortunately, been largely broken away. However, the remaining signs lead Kramer, *BASOR* 88 (1942) 17, note 26, to affirm that these ten incipits exactly reproduce those of *CAT.* 6.

groups. They accomplished this by various means: (1) a catalogue might be restricted to compositions of one type (*CATS.* 14, 15, 16, 21, 22—all irsemma); (2) a catalogue might be divided into sections, each containing one genre grouping (especially *CATS.* 10 and 11); still it was possible (3) to group compositions of the same category together with little or no overt indication (*CAT.* 6 where the last 13 incipits are "wisdom" compositions); or (4) to "lump" them together in a single summary line without listing the incipits at all (*CAT.* 3, lines 33 and 43).

This chief principle of organization could be modified by a number of other concerns. Evidence has been adduced for divisions and groupings (within genre groupings or, indeed, on some occasions, overriding them) based on (1) liturgical correspondences (*CAT.* 11); (2) series (*CATS.* 2 and 10); (3) deity addressed (*CATS.* 8-13, 22). On other, less frequent occasions, groupings are made according to such varied considerations as (1) the tablet on which a composition was written (*CAT.* 21); (2) the container in which a tablet was kept (*CAT.* 4); (3) currency of usage (*CAT.* 1); or (4) the language of the composition (*CAT.* 10). What emerges is an extremely flexible system of classification capable of sufficient modification to accommodate the various purposes for which individual catalogues were produced.

CAT. 6	CAT. 7	CAT. 3
1	1	4
2	2	5
3	3	
4	4	
5	5	
6	6	
7	7	
8	8	13
9	9	14
10	10	
11		11
12		12
17	11	
18	12	
19	13	
20	14	29
21	15	30
25	16	
26	17	
27	21	19
28	22	20
32	27	44
33	28	
34	30	45
35	29	
36	53	46
37	52	
38	23	37
39	24	39
40	26	
41	34	
42	33	
43		
44	35	

Figure 4. Correspondences of Incipits of Three Old Babylonian Catalogues

4

The Qumran Psalm Manuscripts and the Hebrew Psalter I. Preliminary Questions

Thus far I have dealt with groups of hymnic compositions and incipits which are, at best, distantly related to the Hebrew Psalter. Their role here has been viewed largely as one of inference and control, rather than direct contact or observable influence. Now, however, I intend to extend the study to a group of texts which are integrally related to the canonical Psalter, since they are themselves Hebrew psalm texts. I am speaking, of course, of the numerous psalm manuscripts (Mss) found among the Dead Sea Scrolls (DSS). These documents vary considerably in extent (from a few words to thirty-five columns) as well as in date of origin (from 175 B.C. to A.D. 68; see table 3, p. 122). Of the eleven Mss-bearing caves at Qumran, seven have yielded a total of 30-plus distinct Ps texts. By far the most numerous are the collections of cave four (18 distinct PssMss) and cave eleven (5 distinct Mss).

I have already stressed the importance of these texts for the study of the canonical Hebrew Psalter. In the first place, they represent the earliest known exemplars of canonical pss (almost 1,000 years earlier than any Hebrew Psalter text previously known).[1] For this reason they are invaluable for this study as corroboration, at an early date, of the existence and/or position of such important editorial/organizational elements as (1) the pss-headings; (2) the postscripts; (3) doxologies; (4) known groupings of pss (such as the Qorahite and Asaphite pss and the Psalms of Ascents). Further, the tendency of the Qumran scribes to present the canonical pss in arrangements other than that preserved for us in the "standard" Masoretic Text (MT) and even to intersperse non-biblical, apocryphal compositions with them, clearly raises important questions

---

[1] James A. Sanders, *The Dead Sea Psalms Scroll* (Ithaca, NY: Cornell University Press, 1967) 9-10 (hereafter cited as *Psalms Scroll*).

regarding the place of these Mss in the transmission-history of the Hebrew Psalter and may yield significant data concerning the state of its text at this early date.

The relation of these texts to the development of the "canonical" Psalter as we now know it has been much debated and must be considered before the data derived from these texts can be viewed in the proper perspective. I will begin first to attack the "canonical" question, after which I will present the information which I have gathered concerning the more obvious editorial/organizational elements mentioned above. Finally, I will consider the significance of the variant Qumran tradition for an understanding of the editing and organization of the canonical Psalter.

When one comes to consider the literature concerning the "canonicity" of the variant Qumran psalms material, one is faced from the outset by two conflicting viewpoints. The one, which finds its strongest proponent in James A. Sanders, sees in the QPssMss a variant Psalter tradition which was as authoritative for its adherents as the MT Psalter was and still is for its own community. The opposing viewpoint, most thoroughly represented by the late Patrick W. Skehan, would deny that the variant pss material at Qumran constitute an authoritative "canon" and affirms further that it is secondarily dependent on the canonical MT 150 Psalter as we now know it.

Before discussing these two alternative viewpoints, let us first consider two important questions which greatly affect how one approaches the matter at hand. First, just how much of the Qumran pss data actually gives evidence of variation from the MT norm, and second, is it really possible to speak of *the* Qumran Psalter, a consistent (while variant) tradition which is "all-of-a-piece"? The first question is readily answered, as Patrick Skehan shows in an article prepared for publication in *Journées biblique*. "There are . . . at least 7 off-beat Psalm Mss from Qumran, 4 of which include noncanonical texts."[2]

What Skehan describes as "off-beat Mss" are those pss texts which exhibit variation from the MT 150 Psalter either in content (omission of canonical pss; addition of non-canonical pss) or in arrangement (variant order of canonical pss) or a combination of both. The seven Mss which fall into this category are: 11QPs[a] (the large pss scroll edited by

[2]Patrick W. Skehan, "Qumran and Old Testament Criticism," *Qumrân: sa piété, sa théologie et son milieu*, edited by M. Delcor; Bibliotheca ephemeridum theologicarum Lovaniensium 46 (Louvain: Duculot, 1978) 163-82 (hereafter cited as "Criticism").

Sanders); 11QPs[b] (a small scroll with only three columns extant which reduplicates part of 11QPs[a]); 11QPsAp[a] (a fragmentary scroll containing Ps 91 preceded by three otherwise unknown apocryphal compositions); 4QPs[d] (a fragment attesting the variant order of Ps 147 followed by Ps 104); 4QPs[f] (containing Pss 107-109 followed by the *Apostrophe to Zion* known from 11QPs[a] and two other unknown apocryphal hymns); 4QPs[k] (a very fragmentary text which Skehan feels contains Ps 135 followed by Ps 99); and 4QPs[n] (a fragment of Ps 135:6-12 with the addition of a portion of Ps 136 and its characteristic refrain).[3] Sanders himself adduces the

---

[3] *11QPs[b]*—J. P. M. van der Ploeg, "Fragments d'un manuscrit de psaumes de Qumran (11QPs[b])," *RB* 74 (1967) 408-12 (hereafter cited as "Fragments").

11QPsAp[a]—J. P. M. van der Ploeg, "Le Psaume XCI dans une recension de Qumran," *RB* 72 (1965) 210-17 (hereafter cited as "Psaume XCI"); "Un petit rouleau de psaumes apocryphes (11QPsAp[a])," *Tradition und Glaube* (K. G. Kuhn Festschrift; Göttingen: Vandenhoeck and Ruprecht, 1971) 128-39 and Tafeln II-VII (hereafter cited as "Petit rouleau"); Otto Eissfeldt, "Eine Qumran Textform des 91. Psalms," *Bibel und Qumran* (Festschrift Bardtke; Berlin: Evangelische Haupt-Bibelgesellschaft, 1968) 82-88 (hereafter cited as "Textform").

4QPs[a]—Professor Skehan has provided me with a transcription of all the 4QPss materials entrusted to him. For descriptions of this text, see Patrick W. Skehan, "The Qumran Manuscripts and Textual Criticism," *SVT* 4 (1957) 154 (reprinted in *Qumran and the History of the Biblical Text*, edited by F. M. Cross and Shemaryahu Talmon [Cambridge, MA: Harvard University Press, 1975] 212-25); also E.-M. Laperrousaz, "Publication, en Israël, d'un fragment du 'Rouleau des Psaumes' provenant de la grotte 11Q de Qumran . . . ," *RHR* 169 (1966) 235-37.

4QPs[f]—J. Starcky, "Psaumes Apocryphes de la Grotte 4 de Qumran," RB 73 (1966) 353-71 (hereafter cited as "Psaumes Apocryphes"); E.-M. Laperrousaz, "Publication de fragments de psaumes apocryphes provenant de la grotte 4 de Qumran," *RHR* 173 (1968) 108-10; Shemaryahu Talmon, "Mizmôrîm Hîṣônîm ballāšôn hā'ibrît miqqûmrân," Tarbiz 35 (1966) 214-34 (an English translation of this article appeared as "Pisqah beʾemṣaʿ Pasuq and 11QPs[a]," *Textus* 5 [1966] 11-21).

4QPs[k]—This text is included in Skehan's transcriptions while its contents are catalogued in *Psalms Scroll*, pp. 143-55.

4QPs[n]—In a private communication in February 1978, Professor Skehan, in reference to 4QPs[n] stated: "4QPs[n] in frgt. 1 clearly has Ps 135, 6-8, without the refrain of Ps 136, frgts. 2-3 continue this for vs. 11-12A. . . . I am in a position to reconstruct the width of the line. . . . There was no room for a refrain after Ps 135, 11; whereas there *must*

first five of these texts in support of his concept of *the* Qumran Psalter, while the latter two are added by Skehan in an effort to complete the data.[4]

Of the seven, the last two should probably be omitted from consideration: 4QPs^k because of its extremely fragmentary condition which calls Skehan's identification of Ps 99 into question and renders interpretation of the whole fragment doubtful; 4QPs^n because the confusion of Ps 136:20-23 with Ps 135:11-12 might well be a scribal error whose value should not be overrated. In regard to the five remaining texts, a few remarks are warranted. Sanders, with good reason, adduced 11QPs^b as evidence of an established Qumran Psalter tradition. This brief text confirms exactly three instances of 11QPs^a's variation from the MT 150 norm: (1) it duplicates much of the apocryphal "Plea for Deliverance" which occurs in 11QPs^a col. 19; (2) it reduplicates precisely the variant order of the canonical Pss 141, 133, 147 found in 11QPs^a col. 23; (3) it confirms the non-canonical composition based on Ps 118 which is found in 11QPs^a col. 16. Such exact correspondences lend credit to Sanders's affirmation "the sum of it is that our surprising Cave 11 contained two copies of the one really imposing witness to the Hebrew Psalter in pre-Masoretic times."[5]

Sanders uses the other three texts (11QPsAp^a, 4QPs^d and 4QPs^f) with their variant order and apocryphal compositions to support his idea of an atmosphere of great freedom at Qumran in the organization and

---

have been a refrain after 135:12a. . . . So it is after 12A that the refrain is introduced, and it is from that point that the pattern of Ps 136 is followed."

[4]Sanders has espoused his view (as has Skehan) in a number of articles. On this subject, see particularly *Psalms Scroll*, p. 12; "The Qumran Psalms Scroll (11QPs^a) Reviewed," *On Language, Culture, and Religion: In Honor of Eugene A. Nida* (The Hague: Mouton, 1974) 95-96 (hereafter cited as "Reviewed"); "Variorum in the Psalms Scroll (11QPs^a)," *HTR* 59 (1966) 86-87 (hereafter cited as "Variorum"); Skehan, "Criticism," pp. 165-67.

[5]Sanders, "Cave 11 Surprises and the Question of Canon," *McCormick Quarterly Review* 21 (1968) 288 (hereafter cited as "Surprises"). This important article has been reprinted a number of times including: *New Directions in Biblical Archaeology*, edited by D. N. Freedman and J. C. Greenfield (New York: Doubleday, 1969/1971) 101-16; *Nosaḥ ham-miqraʾ be-qumran*, edited by R. Weis and I. Tov (Jerusalem: Hebrew University, 1972) 104-13; and *The Canon and Masorah of the Hebrew Bible*, edited by Sid Z. Leiman (New York: KTAV, 1974) 37-51.

arrangement of pss materials, especially in relation to the rigid form of the MT 150.[6] He is less convincing here, as Skehan shows by using these same texts in his attempt to *invalidate* Sanders's claims for a consistent Psalter tradition at Qumran. While these texts, as Skehan admits, may offer some support for a free use of the biblical pss in arrangements not attested in the canon and in conjunction with apocryphal compositions, they do *not* support the idea of a consistent Psalter tradition at Qumran. Their various departures from 11QPs^{a} itself as well as from MT 150 indicate a variety of pss arrangements of which 11QPs^{a}/11QPs^{b} would appear to be only one. Skehan, accordingly, would deny the existence of a single, consistent, Qumran tradition of pss arrangement which could and should be recognized as *the* Qumran Psalter.[7]

A quick survey of these three Mss should clarify the arguments put forward by these two men. As noted above, 11QPsAp^{a} is a Mss of five columns which contain a number of apocryphal compositions (three?) and conclude with the canonical Ps 91. Sanders cites this Mss as an example of "a more ancient stage of Psalter tradition than that of the Masoretic Psalter" and proposes the Mss be resignaled 11QPs^{e} to indicate its Psalter character.[8] Skehan, on the other hand, plays down any relationship which might exist between this text and 11QPs^{a}. With some justification, he refers to the suggestion of van der Ploeg that this "small scroll" may well represent the "four songs for string music to be sung over the stricken" mentioned in the prose segment cataloguing David's compositions in 11QPs^{a} col. 27.[9] While Skehan is probably correct in saying "there is no evidence these texts themselves ever occupied a place in [11QPs^{a}]" (something Sanders has never claimed to my knowledge), he fails to note that, if this scroll *is* to be equated with the "Songs over the Stricken," it is a text of a fundamentally different type than a Psalter collection. It is primarily a very limited collection of compositions (possibly no more than the four mentioned in 11QPs^{a}) used specifically to drive out demons and should not be used to support or negate claims concerning the authenticity of 11QPs^{a} as a Psalter.[10]

One must be careful when making judgments based on fragmentary texts. Such is certainly the case with 4QPs^{d}, a text of five fragmentary

---

[6]"Surprises," 296-98; "Variorum," 86-87; "Reviewed," 95-96, 98; *Psalms Scroll*, 11-12.

[7]Skehan, "Criticism," 165-66.

[8]Sanders, "Surprises," 296.

[9]Skehan, "Criticism," 166.

[10]Van der Ploeg, "Petit rouleau," 128-29.

columns containing only Pss 147:1-104:35, in that order. Ps 147 is apparently preceded by some unknown ps whose concluding hllwyh is now all that remains extant. While Skehan correctly notes that this conjunction of Pss 147 and 104 is precisely the reverse of what occurs in 11QPs^{a}, fragment E, cols. I-III, and does not, therefore, lend direct confirmation to that variant arrangement of pss, he does not observe that the association of these two pss here (4QPs^{d}) may well reflect an awareness on the part of the editor/scribe of a relationship beyond mere chance.[11] Without a broader context it is impossible to evaluate correctly the import of this text. Admittedly it does not precisely confirm Sanders's idea of a single, consistently ordered Qumran Psalter, but it does (along with 11QPs^{a}) possibly admit an awareness of a relation of these two pss which may have resulted in their having been intentionally juxtaposed in both instances.

Finally, with 4QPs^{f} we must exercise equal caution. Originally a scroll containing both canonical and apocryphal pss (as the writing, spacing and leather apparently indicate) 4QPs^{f} was cut apart in antiquity by a dagger or similar instrument, precisely at the point where the canonical and apocryphal compositions met. Due to this accidental separation, it was some time before scholars Skehan and John Starcky, to whom the canonical and apocryphal segments were respectively allotted, with the assistance of J. Strugnell were able to make the connection of these two fragments. One must realize, however, that there is no actual join represented, only a highly probable positioning of two separate fragments. The impression given by the whole Mss is of a group of consecutive canonical pss (106-109) followed by a group of three (or perhaps four) apocryphal pss (led by the "Apostrophe to Zion" known from 11QPs^{a}, but in a different context).[12] One must be cautious in his evaluation due to the limitations of the text. We do not know what preceded or what followed this extant portion, and there must remain some question as to the certainty of the connection of the two fragments. Whatever the final conclusion, one must admit that the placement here of the "Apostrophe to Zion" immediately preceding other apocryphal compositions does not confirm the order of 11QPs^{a} where this work was followed immediately by the canonical Ps 93 and then eight other canonical pss. So, what data we are able to derive from 4QPs^{f} does not enhance the picture of a single consistent Qumran Psalter against which Skehan militates. At the same time it does reflect

---

[11]Skehan, "Criticism," 166-67.

[12]Starcky, "Psaumes apocryphes," 353.

a freedom in the conjunction of "canonical" and "apocryphal" pss which is uncharacteristic of the MT 150 tradition of exclusivity.

In regard to the two questions with which I began, it is possible now to demonstrate that only a small number of the 30-plus QPssMss discovered near the Dead Sea evidence an arrangement other than that of the MT 150. Further, considering all the known variant pss material, it is not possible to demonstrate the existence of a single consistent Psalter tradition at Qumran. The evidence for variation from MT 150, though limited in scope, is certainly not consistent within itself. There is however evidence of at least one extensive PssMs which does exhibit considerable variation from MT 150 in content and arrangement and which, in addition, is apparently more than a single, isolated case since it existed in at least two copies ($11QPs^a$ and $11QPs^b$). In light of the extent of this document and the number and significance of its variations in order and content from MT 150, it would be unthinkable to omit a discussion of its relation to the canonical Hebrew Psalter. The other variant texts are much more fragmentary, so that it is correspondingly difficult to determine whether they are severely limited collections for very specific purposes (the expulsion of demons as in $11QPsAp^a$) or fragments of true psalters which were originally more extensive.

As I have said previously, we are faced with two opposing views of the "canonicity" of the Qumran pss materials, primarily as represented by $11QPs^a$. Ever since the unrolling and subsequent publication of the Qumran Psalm Scroll, James A. Sanders (and others of like mind) has pushed to understand the scroll as a representative of the Hebrew Psalter at a point in time prior to the fixation of its content and arrangement in the form currently evidenced in the MT 150. Since $11QPs^a$ is dated on paleographical as well as archaeological grounds to the first half of the first century A.D., Sanders's view has raised serious questions regarding the previously accepted thesis that the Psalter was "canonized," "fixed" by the fourth century B.C. (or certainly no later than the Maccabean period).[13] On the other hand, Skehan (and his supporters) views the Qumran Psalm Scroll as a "library edition" of pss which were arranged after the fixation of the canonical Psalter as we now know it (Skehan prefers the fourth century

---

[13]Skehan has most recently and persuasively argued for the earlier date in "Criticism." Otto Eissfeldt discusses the various dating options in *The Old Testament* (New York: Harper and Row, 1965) 450-51. Mitchell Dahood, on the basis of Ugaritic data, indicates "a preexilic date for most of the Psalms" with some possibly "composed in the Davidic period" (*Psalms I* [Anchor Bible; Garden City, NY: Doubleday, 1965] xxx).

B.C. date for that fixation). This Qumran "Psalter," according to Skehan, is not only subsequent to MT 150, but evidences an awareness of and dependence on that collection.[14] It is important to analyze the arguments for and against both of these positions in order to assess the value of 11QPs[a] for our understanding of the arangement of the present MT 150 collection.

James A. Sanders

Through the years since his first articles mentioning 11QPs[a], Sanders has advanced an argument in support of the "canonicity" of the scroll which consists of a number of points. First among these is the strong Davidic framework discernible in the Ms. In a 1963 article concerning the 11QPs[a] version of Ps 151, Sanders draws upon numerous elements in the final two columns of the scroll (The Last Words of David from 2 Sam 23:7; the prose work called David's Compositions; the climactic position of Pss 151 A,B as well as the absence in the superscript to Ps 151 of the LXX terms ἰδιόγραφος and ἔξωθεν τοῦ ἀριθμοῦ) as evidence that "at Qumran . . . there was little or no doubt that [David] was the author of the psalter as they knew it."[15] The presence of such strong Davidic elements in this climactic position leads Sanders to believe, not only that the Qumran sectarians thought David to be the author of the psalter, but also that "these last columns of the scroll clearly demonstrate the belief that David composed . . . all the psalms in the scroll."[16] Sanders goes even further to suggest the evidence shows 11QPs[a] "was clearly considered a portion of the Davidic psalter."[17] The Davidic character of the scroll is further enhanced by the addition of superscriptions attributing authorship to David for canonical Pss 104 and 123 (contrary to MT 150); the apparently Davidic superscription to Ps 151 B; and also the

---

[14] Skehan, "Criticism," 172.

[15] Sanders, "Ps 151 in 11QPss," *ZAW* 75 (1963) 77-78 (hereafter cited as "Ps 151"). While it might be argued that the presence of this qualifying phrase in the LXX suggests the contents of the psalter was already fixed when the Greek translation was made, a recent study by A. Pietersma ("David in the Greek Psalms," *VT* 30 1980 213-26) indicates this superscript is a later addition *after* the LXX translation was accomplished.

[16] Sanders, "Variorum," 84.

[17] Sanders, "Variorum," 84, 90. See also *Psalms Scroll,* 10-11; "The Dead Sea Scrolls—A Quarter Century of Study," *BA* 36 (1973) 140; and "Two Non-canonical Psalms in 11QPs[a]," *ZAW* 76 (1964) 67 (hereafter cited as "Non-canonical Psalms").

totally different nature of the superscription to Ps 151 A, in which no doubt of Davidic authorship is admitted (contrary to LXX).[18]

This pervasive aura of Davidic authority is not marred by any attempt to distinguish externally between "canonical" and "non-canonical" pss in the scroll itself. Non-canonical pss stand next to canonical ones with no distinguishing remarks or characteristics. The ordinary scribal conventions of script and layout are observed in both cases.[19] Internally, the apocryphal pss admit no evidence which *demands* a late date or which is *necessarily* Essenian or Qumranian in origin. Indeed, Sanders, in his analysis of all the apocryphal compositions in 11QPs^{a}, repeatedly uses the term "biblical" to describe each one. The "Plea for Deliverance" is "biblical in vocabulary, style, form and ideas." "Apostrophe to Zion" is "beautifully biblical." Sirach 51:13ff. is as "completely biblical . . . as any psalm in the scroll." Only one of these compositions (Ps 154) "lends itself to thoughts about the Qumran sect," but even these similarities are in no sense necessarily Essenian or Qumranian.[20]

An article by D. Lührmann provides support for Sanders in his opposition to a necessarily late date for these apocryphal compositions and also rejects the idea of their origin at Qumran. Lührmann feels these documents (and the structure of the scroll as a whole) can best be explained as the product of "late wisdom" originating by the end of the third century B.C. The theology of the apocryphal pss is closer to that of "late wisdom" as reflected in *Sirach* than the thought of Qumran. Lührmann even questions how much interest these works held for the Qumran sectarians.[21]

Sanders insists that the inclusion of these works in 11QPs^{a} is indicative of their acceptance as Davidic. Inclusion would not have been possible for a composition whose roots were so contemporaneous as to have been known.[22] This distinction is clear when one compares these apocryphal pss with the Hodayot. The style and vocabulary are drastically different.

> The remarkable difference between the Cave 1 hymns and our apocryphal psalms, aside from some question of style, is that the latter are contained in a scroll of biblical psalms. And

---

[18]"Ps 151," 77-78.

[19]"Non-canonical Psalms," 73; *Psalms Scroll*, 11.

[20]*Psalms Scroll*, 108-9, 116, 119, 123. See also "Non-canonical Psalms," 66-67, 73.

[21]Dieter Lührmann, "Ein Weisheitspsalm aus Qumran (11QPs^{a}xviii)," *ZAW* 80 (1968) 87-98 (hereafter cited as "Weisheitspsalm").

[22]"Non-canonical Psalms," 67, 73.

> this must not be lost sight of. The Psalms Scroll was believed, by its scribe and by those who read and appreciated it, supposedly the sectarians at Qumran, to have been Davidic in original authorship. No such claim is made for the Thanksgiving Hymns: on the contrary, there is some basis for thinking that they were composed by the leader of the Qumran sect, who was called the Teacher of Righteousness. . . . These apocryphal psalms must be treated independently of the Cave 1 Thanksgiving Hymns.[23]

Ultimately Sanders concludes that, in view of the scroll's strong Davidic character, the lack of any evidence of necessary sectarian origin and the absence from the scroll of any clearly sectarian theological or liturgical bias, 11QPs^a should be considered "not as a deviation from a rigidly fixed canon of the latter third of the Psalter but rather as a signpost in the multi-faceted history of the canonization of the Psalter."[24]

While this statement falls short of the affirmation of "canonicity" one would expect, Sanders has elsewhere stated the case more clearly.

> I think that the field is moving toward affirming that the Qumran Psalter, represented by 11QPs^a but also by other more fragmentary Psalter manuscripts from cave 4 and 11, was revered at Qumran as authoritative as any other Psalter present there: it was "canonical" at Qumran though by no means closed; on the contrary, it was, while authoritative, still open-ended.[25]

Sanders draws on further data in 11QPs^a to conclude that the "canon" represented here was not yet fixed, but could still receive additional material. He does not suggest that the Psalter as a whole is fluid, but limits this "open-ended" character to the "last third" of the book (i.e., Pss 101-150). By contrast, he feels the stability of Pss 1-100 at Qumran is "remarkable." There is little evidence of deviation from the MT 150 norm. He cites only the omission of Ps 32 in both 4QPs^a and 4QPs^q and the juxtaposition of Pss 38 and 71 (in that order) in 4QPs^a as variations in the first two-thirds of the Psalter.[26] He further notes that:

> All the other variations in order of psalms at Qumran, even in Cave 11, appear in the last third of the Psalter, and all the

[23] *Psalms Scroll*, 11. See also "Variorum," 85-86.

[24] *Psalms Scroll*, 13; "Variorum," 90-91; "Surprises," 42.

[25] "Reviewed," 98.

[26] "Surprises," 292.

> non-Masoretic psalms in the Qumran Psalter show up in the same last third.[27]

This data requires a new view of the stabilization process of the Psalter, in which stabilization occurred gradually from beginning to end with Pss 1-100 assuming relative fixity at a time when Pss 101-150 were still susceptible to rearrangement and supplementation.

Sanders points to the work of Avi Hurvitz, who concludes that the ten post-exilic Masoretic pss (by his standards) are all in the last third of the Psalter, as confirmation of this gradual process of stabilization.[28] While books I-III of the Psalter had stabilized by the time of 11QPs[a] and were no longer subject to alteration, books IV-V were still "open-ended" and permitted further expansion in obedience to the compiler's "desire to be faithful to the Davidic corpus or heritage" evidenced in the prose epilogue of the Scroll.

As a tentative hypothesis Sanders advances the following points:

1. The process of stabilization was arrested when the Qumran sectarians left Jerusalem to pursue an independent existence. (It was stable in the first two-thirds.)

2. The fluid final portion was expanded at Qumran by "Hasidic and proto-Essene" hymns which were considered "Davidic."

3. The Jerusalem group were pushed towards early stabilization to preserve their own position. This resulted in the MT 150 collection.[29]

Reaction to Sanders's claims has come from several quarters and I will look first at the criticism of Shemaryahu Talmon.

Shemaryahu Talmon

In his article "Mizmôrîm hîṣônîm ballāšôn hāʿibrît miqqûmrân," the Israeli scholar Shemaryahu Talmon argues against viewing 11QPs[a] as a "copy of the Biblical Book of Psalms." He tends to present it instead as a collection of compositions for homiletical and liturgical purposes. Talmon practically dismisses the question of canon out of hand, pointing to the "numerous non-canonical interpolations" and the "unorthodox arrangement of the canonical psalms" as clear indications of the scroll's non-canonical nature. To this he adds the "surprising inclusion . . . of a prose piece

---

[27]"Surprises," 292.

[28]"Surprises," 294.

[29]"Surprises," 294-95.

[David's Compositions]" which he finds incompatible with a canonical collection.[30]

In the second half of his article, Talmon rather obliquely supports his evaluation of 11QPs[a] as non-canonical in his discussion of the *pisqah be*ʾ*emṣa*ʿ *pasuq* (p.b.p.) blank spaces left within a verse in the ancient Mss of the Hebrew Bible and preserved by the copyist scribes throughout the centuries. According to Talmon, the p.b.p. are intended to call the attention of the reader to "missing" text units. However, these units are not omissions of original canonical text materials, but are "extra-textual elaborations of and expolations on given passages in scripture, especially in the Books of Samuel, to which the early tradents wished to direct" attention. In other words, the p.b.p. in the Pentateuch introduce extra expansions of the scriptural accounts which immediately precede them. Talmon feels that Ps 151 A of 11QPs[a] was intended to expand poetically on the account of David's election in 1 Samuel 16 and was "introduced" or "indicated" by the p.b.p. which is found in 1 Sam 16:12. Similarly, Ps 151 B is introduced by the p.b.p. in 1 Sam 17:37 and expands on the story of David's battle with Goliath. Talmon suggests that Pss 154 and 155 of 11QPs[a] "share the theme of David's rescue from the lion and the bear" and may well have served to expand some other incidents in the canonical account of David's life.

Talmon seems to suggest that the use of these "apocryphal" pss to expand on the scriptural texts marked by p.b.p. supports a non-canonical evaluation of their character. He says,

> In concluding we wish to stress that there can be no doubt that the men who introduced the *p.b.p.* into the MT never considered the extraneous expansions to which they point as integral components of the Bible. They were intended to remain outside the authoritative canon, as some kind of appendices to the original Scripture version.[31]

---

[30]Shemaryahu Talmon, "Mizmôrîm Hîṣônîm ballāšôn hāʿibrît miqqûmrân," *Tarbiz* 35 (1966) 214-34 and Summaries, pp. II-III (hereafter cited as "Mizmôrîm,"). An English translation is available in "Pisqah beʾemṣaʿ pasuq and 11QPs[a]," *Textus* 5 (1966) 11-21 (hereafter cited as "Pisqah").

[31]"Pisqah," 21. See also "Mizmôrîm," Summaries, p. III.

However, one must be clear that what Talmon must mean is that the expansive texts were not intended to be included in the canonical text *at the place where the p.b.p. occurs.* This is not to say that these texts could not find their place *elsewhere* in scripture. In fact, Talmon indicates some p.b.p. *do* apparently refer to *canonical* texts, including some of the canonical pss (Ps 132 expands the p.b.p. in 2 Sam 7:4; Ps 51 expands the p.b.p. in 2 Sam 12:12; Ps 3 expands the p.b.p. in 2 Sam 16:13).

Far from precluding the possibility of "canonicity" for these apocryphal compositions in 11QPs[a], this use of canonical texts (including pss) to expand p.b.p. elsewhere in scripture seems to enhance that possibility. At the least, the association of these "apocryphal" texts with the scriptural accounts they are thought to expand would serve to lend them a certain degree of authority which could explain their inclusion in a "canonical" collection, even if not the MT 150.

M. H. Goshen-Gottstein

In his article "The Psalms Scroll (11QPs[a]): A Problem of Canon and Text," M. H. Goshen-Gottstein rejects Sanders's claim that the prose "epilogue" in 11QPs[a], col. 27, (David's Compositions) serves as proof that the compiler attributed all these compositions to David and, thus, considered them all equally authoritative and, ultimately "canonical."[32] Goshen-Gottstein argues that attribution of authorship to David does not necessitate canonicity. The epilogue, then, yields no conclusive evidence of the canonicity of 11QPs[a]. To the contrary, the presence of this prose piece is an indication that the scroll was considered *non*-canonical. According to Goshen-Gottstein, the prose epilogue derives from the desire to exalt David above his son Solomon by attributing to David more compositions (4,050) than is elsewhere recorded for Solomon (4,005—1 Kings 5:12). Furthermore, Goshen-Gottstein points out that the epilogue stresses the "liturgical" uses of these 4,050 pss of David, which indicates 11QPs[a] is not a "canonical" Psalter at all, but a selection of canonical pss for liturgical purposes. This juxtaposition of "canonical" and "apocryphal" further serves to "ensure future use" of the non-canonical pss by association with their canonical counterparts.[33]

---

[32]M. H. Goshen-Gottstein, "The Psalms Scroll (11QPs[a]): A Problem of Canon and Text," *Textus* 5 (1966) 22-33 (hereafter cited as "Canon and Text").

[33]"Canon and Text," 27.

Pointing to other examples of "liturgical" concern in 11QPs[a] Goshen-Gottstein cites the variant form of Ps 145 (cols. 16-17) which varies from MT 145 by the addition of the continuous refrain "Blessed be the LORD and blessed be his name forever and ever" following each bicolon and taking its lead from the initial verse "I will extol thee, my God and King, and bless thy name forever and ever." This is a liturgical expansion of the canonical ps and not a ps in its own right.

The "Catena" in col. 16 using parts of the canonical Ps 118 is further evidence of liturgical adaptation of canonical pss as is the variant version of Ps 146 found in col. 2. Goshen-Gottstein views the latter ps as a liturgical hymn "based on themes from the psalms" rather than an adaptation of Ps 146.

Further, Goshen-Gottstein declares, if 11QPs[a] were proven "canonical," several difficulties would result. First, it would mean that there would be "two (out of more?) different canons, current at Qumran." Secondly, as a result, "our whole picture of the completion of the growth of the various books of the Bible accepted as 'canonical' may be wrong," a possibility Goshen-Gottstein is not willing to admit.[34] Finally, if 11QPs[a] is a "canon," it is only a *sectarian* canon because of its dependence on a sectarian calendar evident in the prose epilogue. Such a sectarian canon would have been very limited in influence and scope and would have little import for our understanding of the Hebrew Psalter.

In summary, Goshen-Gottstein feels (1) the prose epilogue and its claims of Davidic authorship present no compelling evidence of the *canonicity* of 11QPs[a]; (2) that the *obviously* liturgical interests of the epilogue along with the liturgical concern reflected in the scroll compositions themselves are not consonant with a scroll of canonical nature; (3) a variant "canonical" Psalms scroll would call into question accepted theories of the canonization of the Hebrew Bible and would only be of limited, sectarian significance.

Patrick W. Skehan

The foremost opponent of the canonicity of 11QPs[a], Skehan objects to what he views as contradictions and inconsistencies in Sanders's claim that the Psalms Scroll is at once "canonical" and "authoritative." Such terminology, says Skehan, can only lead to confusion. "A canon is a closed

---

[34]"Canon and Text," 26.

list of books. There is no reason to suppose the people of Qumran had any such thing."[35] The terms "canonical" and "open-ended" which Sanders uses to characterize 11QPs[a] also seem mutually exclusive to Skehan. "Canonical" implies closed, exclusive, marking off what alone is acceptable. "Open-ended," on the other hand, emphasizes the tentative nature of the collection and the possibility of future addition and/or deletion of items. Sanders cannot have it both ways according to Skehan. Either 11QPs[a] is "open-ended" or it is "canonical"—it cannot be both.

Skehan initially limits his discussion to the last "book" (Pss 107-150) of the Psalter by adducing evidence from the Chronicler to prove that the Psalter was already fixed through Ps 106 by the fourth century B.C. Referring to the use in 1 Chr 16:8-36 of hymnic compositions known to us now as portions of canonical pss (Ps 105:1-15; Ps 96:1-13; Ps 106:1, 47-48), Skehan concludes that the Chronicler is quoting from those Psalms in their fixed Psalter positions. The chief datum on which he bases his conclusion is the apparent use in 1 Chr 16:36 of an adaptation of the concluding benediction and hllwyh of Ps 106:48, which is one of the doxologies thought to conclude the first four books of the Psalter. Skehan summarizes:

> Now everyone is aware that the verse just quoted is not properly a verse from *Ps* 106 at all; but is a compiler's addition to the end of the 4th book of the canonical Psalter, comparable to what occurs at the ends of *Pss* 41, 72 and 89. In other words, by about 400 B.C., the Chronicler was borrowing from a fixed place not merely the first and last verses of *Ps* 106, as he did, but also, in the added vs. 48, a benchmark in the structuring of the Psalter as we know it.[36]

Skehan goes on to say that this data does not prove that the fifth book was closed at that time, but does indicate the relative priority of MT 150 over 11QPs[a] and allows him to limit his discussion to the last book which is still open to question.

Skehan develops his own understanding of the nature of 11QPs[a] in a number of articles and, in doing so, bases his rejection of its canonicity on several factors. The argument is multi-pronged and must be considered carefully. Skehan's conclusions can be separated into two groups. First,

---

[35]"Criticism," 164.
[36]"Criticism," 167-68.

the nature of the scroll as a "liturgical" composition precludes its canonicity. Second, evidence of the priority of MT 150 and of the dependence of 11QPs[a] on it indicates the sectarians' recognition of the authority of the text in its MT 150 arrangement and denies canonicity to 11QPs[a]. According to Skehan:

> The question has been raised whether the full canonical collection in the usual arrangement [MT150] was known there. The present writer [Skehan] thinks there are adequate indications that it was and that the standard arrangement is presupposed by the liturgical adaptations and by a subsequent "library" edition honoring David as the sponsor and author of Psalm materials.[37]

Skehan first turns his attention to the liturgical nature of the scroll. He agrees with Goshen-Gottstein that the prose epilogue "David's Compositions" is a clear indication of the scroll's liturgical interest. The catalogue stresses the liturgical function of all of these compositions of David. According to Skehan, everything mentioned in this passage (with the exception of the four songs for the stricken) is liturgical. There are:

Psalms (line 5)[38]		3,600
Songs for daily offerings (1.6)	364	
Songs for Sabbath offerings (1.7)	52	
Songs for festivals, holy days (1.8)	30	
"Songs for the stricken" (1.10)		
Total number of songs	450	
Grand total		4,050

Skehan further claims "there is nothing in the catalogue that can be construed as a reference to any of the non-canonical pieces in the scroll."[39] Since there is no clear reference in the catalogue to any apocryphal composition, it cannot be certain that they were ever considered the products of Davidic authorship.

---

[37]Skehan, "The Scrolls and the Old Testament Text," *McCQ* 21 (1968) 272-83. References are to the reprint of this article in D. N. Freedman and J. C. Greenfield, *New Directions in Biblical Archaeology* (Garden City, NY: Doubleday, 1969) 89-100 (hereafter cited as "Scrolls and Text").

[38]This chart is taken from Sanders, *Psalms Scroll,* 134.

[39]"Criticism," 169.

Noting that no apocryphal ps is introduced before the 23rd column of 11QPs[a], Skehan concludes this is evidence of their secondary insertion among the canonical compositions. In the last twelve columns, eight non-canonical pss are mixed with eleven of the last fourteen pss of the MT 150 arrangement. The three canonical pss omitted in these columns (Pss 146, 147 and 148) had already appeared at an earlier point in a liturgical grouping. For Skehan, this fact can only be explained by the dependence of 11QPs[a] on the MT 150 arrangement in which all fourteen of these pss (137-150) were already grouped in the canonical arrangement.[40] Besides their position which, he believes, shows their dependence, Skehan affirms that the non-canonical compositions are, in all cases, later than the canonical pss among which they are dispersed. This further emphasizes the secondary nature of these apocryphal pss.[41]

Skehan's analysis of the structure and content of the scroll leads him to the conclusion that Ps 101 (the first composition extant in the collection) began at the top of a column (the only composition in the scroll to do so). Since this ps does not correspond with one of the "Book" divisions of the MT 150 Psalter (the closest is at the end of Ps 106) but is the first of the last fifty pss of the canonical arrangement, he concludes that the Qumran Psalter never included a more extensive collection. The purpose of 11QPs[a] was merely to expand liturgically these last fifty pss of the canonical collection to the honor of David.[42]

The conclusion of this honorary "library edition" is marked by the climactic position of the "Last Words of David" quoted from 2 Sam 23:7, and followed here by the catalogue of "David's Compositions." Skehan finds in this latter work a number of variations on the number 150 which he feels prove an awareness of the canonical limitation of the Psalter to 150 compositions. It is for this reason that Ps 151 A and B is added *after* the climactic statement. It was known to be "outside the number" of accepted Davidic compositions as explicitly expressed in the LXX s/s to Ps 151.[43]

Further evidence of the dependence of 11QPs[a] on the MT 150 arrangement is to be seen in:

1. The inclusion of 13 of 15 of the šyr hm ᶜlwt pss in their expected MT 150 order (cols. 3-6).

---

[40] "Criticism," 169.
[41] "Criticism," 169.
[42] "Criticism," 169-70.
[43] "Criticism," 170.

2. While the last two of this group of pss (Pss 133 and 134) are detached from the rest and introduced singly, Ps 133 still retains the characteristic šyr hmʿlwt s/s indicating its displacement from its original position (Ps 134 is defective at its beginning so no conclusions can be made).

3. While Pss 145 and 146 are separated from each other in 11QPs^{a}, the expansion of Ps 146:9 based on 145:9 and 12 is viewed by Skehan as evidence of a memory of their original juxtaposition.

4. The acrostic Ps 145 in MT 150 is defective in the nûn verse. This defect is supplied in 11QPs^{a} in a clumsy addition in which the divine name ĕlōhîm is used instead of *YHWH* as elsewhere in the ps. Skehan concludes the ps was taken from MT 150 and clumsily repaired.[44]

5. Skehan originally felt the "Hymn to the Creator" (col. 26) was composed as a "pendant" to Pss 149-150 and, as such, was a sectarian document of the Qumran community. His view of the "Hymn" rests chiefly on its use of three Hebrew words which Skehan feels bind these three compositions together as a single unit. The opening phrase of the "Hymn" (gdwl wqdwš YHWH . . .) brings together two attributes of YHWH expressly mentioned in 150:1-2 (his "holiness" qwdšw and his "greatness" gwdlw). Psalm 149 is connected with the "Hymn" by the addition to 149:9 of the phrase lbny yśrʾl ʿm qwdšw (reminiscent of 148:14) which ties in with the *holiness* theme expressed in 150:1-2 and the first line of the "Hymn." The author of the "Hymn" further emphasizes the connection with Ps 149 with his phrase in the second line lpny hdr ylk which picks up on the word hdr "glory" used also in 149:9 (hdr hwʾ lkwl ḥsydyw). This obvious liturgical arrangement (149-150—Hymn) stands opposed to Ps 101 as "end to beginning."[45]

Skehan has subsequently modified his opinion of the Qumran origin of this liturgical grouping. He now admits that it is most likely much earlier (second century B.C.). However, he still claims that this arrangement is only understandable, if at that time Ps 150 was the end of "an established Psalm collection which was even then not open-ended."[46]

Briefly summarized, Skehan's argument would seem to consist of the following points.

---

[44]"Criticism," 170-71.

[45]Skehan, "A Liturgical Complex in 11QPs^{a}," *CBQ* 35 (1973) 202-5 (hereafter cited as "Liturgical Complex").

[46]"Criticism," 171-72.

a. From internal considerations it is possible to show that 11QPs[a] is a liturgical collection in honor of David and therefore cannot be a "canonical" Psalter.

b. Evidence indicates 11QPs[a] is temporally subsequent to MT 150.

c. 11QPs[a] is not only subsequent to MT 150, but is also aware of and dependent on the canonical arrangement of the pss.

d. By its dependence on the MT 150 pss arrangement 11QPs[a] admits the authority of the canonical collection and is subject to it. Skehan's evaluation of 11QPs[a] is not without its difficulties. Some criticism of his viewpoint is appropriate at this stage.

In regards to Skehan's use of 1 Chr 16:8-36 to "prove" the fixation of "books" I-IV of the Psalter by the fourth century B.C., several comments are in order. First, Skehan's assumption that this passage represents "selections" of canonical pss is not satisfactorily verifiable. As Sanders mentions elsewhere, this could be an independent composition which is "a pastiche of Psalms 105:1-15; 96:1-13; 106:1 and 47-48."[47] Sanders suggests that the combination of "floating bits of liturgical material" was a viable means of creating new pss for different situations or occasions. Canonical evidence of such technique is found in Ps 70 which is virtually identical with Ps 40:13-17 and Ps 108 which reproduces parts of two other canonical pss (108:1-5 = 57:7-11; 108:6-13 = 60:5-12). The assumption that the Chronicler was quoting from a fixed group or even fixed individual pss is not necessarily supported here.

If, however, one does assume that these are selections from those canonical pss we now know, one is still not compelled to accept the fixation of the fourth book of the Psalter at that date. Skehan overstates his case when he says "everyone is aware" that Ps 106:48 is not a part of the ps, but an addition to mark the close of the fourth book. "Everyone" certainly does *not* agree that these doxologies were *intended* to break up the Psalter into five books.[48] Some view the present five-fold division as a late move to relate the Psalter to the five books of Moses which drew

---

[47]Sanders, "Surprises," 287.

[48]While Mowinckel admits the possibility that pss bearing such doxologies were seized upon by the editor(s) of the Psalter as indications of book divisions, he denies that the original conjunction of doxology and ps came about for this purpose. "The concluding doxologies . . . are connected with the use of each psalm in the temple service . . . and were not added by the collectors as 'concluding formulas' for the separate collections. . . ." (*PIW*[2], p. 193, 197). See also the comments of Dahood, *Psalms I*, p. xxx.

on doxologies already present in the text. The lack of a comparable doxology at the end of the fifth book is sometimes mentioned in this regard.[49] Further, even if one assumes the validity of the five-fold division, the "doxologies" are not *necessarily* to be considered "additions" to their respective pss. These particular pss could have been selected for their particular positions because they already possessed a suitable doxology. This might explain the considerable degree of variation in the form and content of the doxologies from book to book of the Psalter. Such variation could easily have been eliminated had the doxologies been mere editorial additions without a previous history. Finally, if these doxologies *were* integral parts of the pss to which they are appended, the use of 106:48 in 1 Chr 16:36 would have nothing to tell us about the date of fixation of the fourth book of the MT 150 Psalter. It seems then that Skehan's insights, while suggestive, are not ultimately compelling.

Skehan places a great deal of weight on the liturgical nature of the Psalms Scroll and the incompatibility which he assumes between liturgical interest and canonicity. Sanders himself comments on this tendency in his article "Cave 11 Surprises and the Question of Canon."

> What is more than abundantly clear is that all Psalters are liturgical collections, Masoretic and non-Masoretic. . . . The real question is whether the Qumran Psalter as we now have it is a variant form of that liturgical collection which came to be called Masoretic or is it an aberration from it, perhaps the earliest Jewish prayer book. Does it reflect on its past or anticipate its future?[50]

Elsewhere Sanders expresses his appreciation for Skehan's work on the liturgical aspects of $11QPs^a$ and concludes "some of his work is extremely helpful: it is the sort that should be applied to that other liturgical collection of psalms, the MT-150 collection!"[51] Certainly Skehan never clearly states why liturgical interest and arrangement precludes canonicity (for that matter, neither has Goshen-Gottstein who depends on much the same argument). Clearly MT 150 is itself a liturgical collection and evidences many liturgical interests in the arrangement of its individual pss. As a single example, one needs only to recall the obviously liturgical

---

[49]See the comments of Heinrich Herkenne, *Das Buch der Psalmen*, Die Heilige Schrift des Altes Testaments (Bonn: Peter Hanstein, 1936).

[50]Sanders, "Surprises," 292.

[51]"Reviewed," 96.

arrangement of Pss 145-150 which concludes the whole Psalter with praise upon praise, in response to David's exhortation at the end of Ps 145 "My mouth will speak the praise of the Lord, and let all flesh bless his holy name forever and ever" (145:21). This and other examples of the liturgical interest and practice of MT 150 will be discussed at a later point.[52] It seems that liturgicality cannot of itself be used as evidence of the non-canonical nature of 11QPs^a.

Concerning Skehan's statement that nothing in "David's Compositions" can be regarded as a reference to any of the apocryphal compositions, one can only ask, how can he be sure? He gives no certain method of distinguishing canonical and non-canonical pss other than the obvious (and unhelpful) fact that the latter do not occur in the canon. If he is speaking of reference to specific, individual compositions, I would say there is no *certainty* that the epilogue refers to *any* of the pss—canonical or otherwise. The single possible exception is the four "Songs for the Stricken" which may well refer to the collection of apocryphal and canonical pss studied by J. van der Ploeg.[53] These pss, however, were never a part of 11QPs^a. Skehan's statement seems at once subjective and non-productive.

Skehan further claims the fact the non-canonical compositions do not appear until the 23rd column of 11QPs^a and are then interspersed with 11 of the last 14 pss of MT 150, indicates 11QPs^a is dependent on the canonical arrangement and the apocryphal pss are secondary insertions. There is no denying the facts of the scroll's arrangement. However, Skehan fails to take note of the severe disarrangement of the canonical pss included in 11QPs^a. Eleven are completely omitted (Pss 106-108; 110-117) while the position of at least thirteen others (Pss 109, 118, 147, 146, 148, 119, 145, 139, 93, 133, 144, 140 and 134) completely contradict the canonical order, as the schematic rendering of the contents of the scroll (see below, pp. 124-25) readily shows. Again, Skehan does not convincingly show that the late appearance of these apocryphal pss is evidence of the scroll's dependence on MT 150.

Skehan's belief that the apocryphal compositions are always "later" than the canonical pss is questionable on several grounds. First, there are many who support a late date (some as late as the Maccabean period) for at least some of the canonical pss.[54] While this is far from conclusive, it

---

[52]See below, pp. 187-94.

[53]Van der Ploeg, "Petit rouleau," 128-29.

[54]See Avi Hurvitz, *The Identification of Post-exilic Psalms by Means of Linguistic Criteria* (in Hebrew; Jerusalem: Magnes Press, 1966).

at least clouds the issue considerably. Secondly, Skehan offers little or no evidence for his claims, leaving us to *assume* it as "self-evident." Thirdly, D. Lührmann, in an article "Ein Weisheitspsalm aus Qumran 11QPs[a] XVIII)," argues persuasively that all these apocryphal texts are products of "late wisdom" and as such, were written down no later than the end of the third century B.C.—some forty years before the Maccabean period and almost 250 years before 11QPs[a] was written or copied in its present form.[55] There have long been disagreements over the dating of the individual pss. The historical allusions which they contain are not sufficiently precise in most instances to command universal agreement. (Indeed, it is this temporal freedom of the pss which grants ready access to the believer who finds his own estate addressed with such power!) Similarly, arguments based on stylistic, linguistic and grammatical considerations have shown themselves capable of conflicting interpretation.[56]

In a different direction, it is not the actual antiquity of these texts which is of primary importance here, but the *assumed* antiquity from the point of view of the compiler of 11QPs[a]. What Sanders has said, in a reference to the apocryphal Ps 154, is instructive for all these compositions.

> For it [Ps 154] to have been accepted in the Qumran psalter, it probably was considered ancient enough to merit a place alongside the 36 psalms in the scroll which later at Jamnia were deemed canonical. If its actual date were known, or if its author were remembered, it probably would not have been included in 11QPs[a] which at Qumran was clearly considered a portion of the Davidic psalter.[57]

Even if one disagrees with Sanders's final assessment of the "canonicity" of 11QPs[a], the basic truth of his point cannot be dismissed. The late date

---

[55] Lührmann, "Weisheitspsalm," 93, 97.

[56] Most introductions deal with the complexities of the dating issue. For a sample, see the discussions in Franz Delitzsch, *Biblical Commentary on the Psalms*, vol. I (Grand Rapids, MI: William B. Eerdmans, 1871) 7-19; Sigmund Mowinckel, "The Antiquity of Psalmography and the Psalms," *The Psalms in Israel's Worship*, vol. II (Oxford: Basil Blackwell, 1962) 146-58; Artur Weiser, *The Psalms* (Philadelphia: Westminster, 1962) 91-95; Mitchell Dahood, *Psalms I* (Garden City, NY: Doubleday, 1965) xxix-xxx; Otto Eissfeldt, *The Old Testament: An Introduction* (Oxford: Basil Blackwell, 1965) 446-51.

[57] Sanders, "Non-canonical Psalms," 67.

of a composition would not necessarily have excluded it from a canonical collection as long as (1) that collection was not yet closed (this is the matter at question here and should not be assumed) or (2) its origin was not so recent as to have been known by the collector. If, as Lührmann suggests, these apocryphal pss were composed by the end of the third century B.C. and 11QPs^a is to be dated on paleographical grounds to 30-50 A.D., there would seem to be sufficient time elapsed to allow the origins of these texts to have become obscured. In a discussion of the attribution of authorship in Sumero-Akkadian literary works, W. W. Hallo concludes that authority is indicated by antiquity of authorship, with the highest authority reflected by attribution to the deity. According to Hallo, there is an increasing tendency to ascribe authorship to authoritative works. This ascription may function (1) to indicate the actual author of the text when known or (2) to fix an anonymous text in the historical period to which the imputed author belongs.[58] The implications for 11QPs^a are obvious, especially if the intent of "David's Compositions" is to claim Davidic authorship for all the pss of the scroll as Sanders suggests. The effect would be to recognize the authority of these apocryphal compositions, whose own origins had become obscured by time, by relating them to the person David, indicating the *compiler's* conviction that they were ancient documents, regardless of our own subsequent evaluation.

There is little point in debating the suggestion that Ps 101 apparently began at the top of a column and *possibly* began the whole scroll. Again, one cannot deny the evidence of the scroll. Ps 101 apparently *did* begin the first column of fragment A of 11QPs^a and this fragment *may* possibly represent the first column of the scroll. However, there is no way to be certain whether or not there ever were additional scrolls which recorded the pss of the first two-thirds of the MT 150 Psalter and completed the collection represented here. The evidence of the scroll does not permit a decision either way.

If the position of the "Last Words of David" immediately following Pss 149-150 and preceding the catalogue "David's Compositions" is intended, as Skehan suggests, to represent the climax and conclusion of this "library edition," and if Ps 151 A,B was included after this catalogue because it was known to be "outside the number" of canonical compositions, two difficulties must be explained.

---

[58]W. W. Hallo, "New Viewpoints on Cuneiform Literature," *IEJ* 12 (1962) 13-26; "Antiquity," 167-76; "History," 181-203.

1. Why is this distinction of Ps 151 A,B as outside necessary in a collection which does not presume to be canonical and in which "apocryphal" compositions have already been included? Skehan makes no reply to this question.

2. Why are canonical Pss 140 and 134 also written after what Skehan views as the climax and conclusion of the work? In reply to this second question, Skehan has weakly suggested that they were "accidentally" omitted previously and the error was not discovered until after the "conclusion" was written. Consequently they had to be written immediately following the conclusion. But this explanation could apply equally as well to Ps 151 A,B which is in no way distinguished from these two canonical pss immediately preceding it. It also fails to explain why the two "omitted" canonical pss were not written in the proper canonical order in relation to one another if canonicity were such an issue here. Again Skehan's argument is not convincing unless one assumes from the first that which he is trying to prove: that these compositions are secondary "apocryphal" pss.

The following comments are directed to Skehan's discussion of internal indications of 11QPs^{a}'s dependence on the MT 150 Psalter tradition.

1. The šyr hm^{c}lwt pss. Skehan assumes that the occurrence of Pss 120-132 (the first 13 of the 15 šyr hm^{c}lwt pss) in consecutive MT 150 order, along with Ps 133's retention of the characteristic s/s of this group despite its separation from the rest, can only be explained by dependence on the MT 150 arrangement. At the most, however, this merely indicates the priority of this particular collection of pss and not of the whole MT 150. In fact, the detachment of Pss 133 and 134 (from the group and from one another) would seem to demand the conclusion that this group was not yet so firmly fixed that the compiler was constrained from any alteration. The presence of this arrangement of these pss in 11QPs^{a} might be evidence for the gradual development of individual groups of pss which only later came together to form the MT 150 Psalter.[59] That 11QPs^{a} and MT 150 both availed themselves of this collection can offer no solution to the question of priority and dependence.

2. The expansion of Ps 146:9 on the basis of Ps 145:9 and 12 indicates an awareness of the prior juxtaposition of these two pss (presumably

---

[59]Otto Eissfeldt, *The Old Testament: An Introduction*, (New York: Harper and Row, 1965) 293-94.

in MT 150). But the expansion is also based on Ps 33:8.[60] Does Skehan suggest Pss 146 and 33 were once juxtaposed? Without prior knowledge of the MT 150 arrangement, this suggestion would never have been made. Even if it could be shown beyond doubt that juxtaposition is indicated, there is no evidence that suggests *where* that juxtaposition took place, or that necessitates the prior existence of the *whole* MT 150.

3. 11QPs[a]'s "clumsy" substitution for the missing nûn verse of the acrostic Ps 145 affirms the dependence of the scroll on the MT version of the composition. There is still no necessary proof of dependence here. All that can be said with certainty is that LXX, 11QPs[a] and MT 150 all seem to know the same Hebrew *Vorlage* of this ps. Each has dealt with the defect in its own way. MT 150 has retained the defective ps. LXX has supplied the defective verse in a manner similar to 11QPs[a], but the Greek uses *kyrios* = *YHWH*, contrary to the Psalms Scroll and consonant with the rest of the ps itself. 11QPs[a] has supplied the defect, but uses ĕlōhîm which contrasts with the regular usage of *YHWH* throughout the rest of this ps and may have been intended to call attention to the secondary nature of the addition.

4. Regarding the liturgical arrangement of Pss 149-150—"Hymn to the Creator," one might accept Skehan's proposal of its second-century origin and its nature as a liturgical unit without feeling compelled to accept the existence of the fixed MT 150 Psalter at that date. Indeed, one might affirm the association of Pss 149 and 150 or even of the whole "final Hallel" (Pss 146-150) without affirming a closed Psalter. The existence of groups of pss (even extensive groupings such as Pss 120-132 and Pss 146-150) do not prove the existence of the MT 150 collection in which they were later embedded. In this light, Skehan's conclusions regarding the dependence of 11QPs[a] on the MT 150 are not ultimately convincing. If, as he suggests, this grouping *was* used during the second century B.C. for the purposes of public prayer, this proves nothing about the MT 150, but only of this limited liturgical unit.[61] The fact that this hymn could serve as the basis for an adaptation in the book of *Jubilees* would suggest that in the second century B.C. it must have possessed a certain degree of authority. Skehan must also resort to some "fancy footwork" to explain the presence of so many compositions *after* this climactic grouping. That Pss 140 and 134 were "misplaced" and Ps 151 A,B

---

[60]Sanders, *Psalms Scroll,* 37; Skehan, "Criticism," 171, omits any reference to Ps 33:8.

[61]Skehan, "Criticism," 171-72; "Liturgical Complex," 202-5.

was "excluded" is only convincing if one first accepts his argument that $11QPs^a$ is subsequent to and dependent on MT 150, and that "as a liturgical collection, $11QPs^a$ effectively terminates with Pss 149, 150 and the *Hymn to the Creator*,"[62] an assumption which is clearly debatable.

In retrospect, the review of these various arguments regarding the nature of the Qumran Psalms Scroll makes it clear that there are actually three separate issues involved: canonicity, authority and priority. The following comments would seem pertinent.

CANONICITY

1. "Canonical" implies "closed." Skehan's criticism of Sanders's description of $11QPs^a$ as at once "canonical" and "open-ended" is based on a view of canonicity not generally accepted today. He views the canon as the product of an authoritative decision made by a limited group of "scholars"; a decision which *then* becomes authoritative and binding for all believers. The recent works of Sid Z. Leiman, Brevard S. Childs and others (including Sanders himself) have emphasized the complex nature of the development of canon.[63] For them a "canon" can no longer be taken as an exclusive list of acceptable books with no possibility of deletion or addition. Leiman's definition is probably representative:

> A canonical book is a book accepted by Jews as authoritative for religious practice and/or doctrine, and whose authority is binding upon the Jewish people for all generations. Furthermore, such books are to be studied and expounded in private and in public.[64]

This view is consonant with that expressed by Childs in his *Introduction to the Old Testament as Scripture* and by Sanders in his *Torah and Canon* and would apply to the Christian canon as well as the Jewish. Noticeably

---

[62]"Criticism," 171.

[63]Brevard S. Childs, *Introduction to the Old Testament as Scripture* (Philadelphia: Fortress, 1979) (hereafter cited as *IOTS*). Sid Z. Leiman, *The Canonization of Hebrew Scripture* (Transactions of the American Academy of Arts and Sciences, vol. 47; Hamden, CT: Anchor Books, 1976) (hereafter cited as *Canonization*). James A. Sanders, *Torah and Canon* (Philadelphia: Fortress, 1972).

[64]Leiman, *Canonization*, 14.

absent is any reference to exclusivity or closure in the basic definition of canonicity. A "closed list of books" is not (for Leiman) simply a "canon," but a "*closed* canon."[65]

This recent view of canon emphasizes the *gradual* development of the canon over the "committee decision" type process and seems to me more realistically to reflect the complex growth of the Old Testament canon. It seems then that Sanders is correct in his affirmation of the possibility of an "open-ended canon."

2. "Fixation of form" does not *necessarily* imply "canonical." It is possible that a "canonical" work would have once existed (prior to its "canonization") in a fixed form, but without the *exclusive* authority conferred by the ultimate closure of the canon. One must distinguish the *fixation* of the MT 150 in its present (i.e., "canonical") form from the triumph of that particular arrangement of pss over all competing arrangements. Consequently, even if it were possible to *prove* that MT 150 assumed its final form in the fourth century B.C. (which is doubtful), that would be insufficient reason to *assume* its exclusive claim to authority after that date.

3. "Canonicity" of a document can be satisfactorily determined only by (a) statements to that effect or to the contrary (such statements are only authoritative for those making them and do not preclude the possibility of competing opinions, as, for example the "truncated canon" of Marcion and the reaction of the early church fathers); or by (b) evidence of usage consonant with such authority.[66] Neither of the above is available at Qumran for 11QPs^a. Consequently, it will be necessary to leave open the question whether or not 11QPs^a ever functioned with *exclusive* authority at Qumran or elsewhere.

AUTHORITY

1. "Authority does not imply ultimate inclusion in the "closed canon." This is clearly pointed out by the early church fathers' citation of

---

[65]Leiman, *Canonization*, 14-16, 23-24, 131-35.

[66]Leiman, *Canonization*, 15-16 and n. 35. Robert Gordis, "Quotations as a Literary usage in Biblical, Oriental and Rabbinic Literature," *HUCA* 22 (1949) 157-219; "Quotations in Wisdom Literature," *JQR* 30 (1939-40) 123-47. Joseph A. Fitzmyer, "The Use of Explicit Old Testament Quotations in Qumran Literature and in the New Testament," *NTS* 7 (1960-61) 297-333.

apocryphal texts as scripture. Obviously these texts were "authoritative" to those who cited them, but were not ultimately part of the closed canon.

2. "Authority" attributed to a single composition does not extend necessarily to a whole collection. In this regard, a collection of pss must be viewed differently from a work in which disparate elements have been edited into a consistent whole, obscuring the original boundaries of the units in the process (as in the Pentateuch).[67] For this reason the presence of "canonical" pss in 11QPs^a does not necessarily extend "authority" to the apocryphal compositions ranged alongside them.

3. "Authority" attributed to *all* the individual compositions of a collection does not necessitate one accept the authority of the arrangement demonstrated in that collection. As a result, even if all the "apocryphal" compositions of 11QPs^a could be shown to be "authoritative," one would still not be justified in declaring their *arrangement* (11QPs^a) "authoritative." Unless explicitly prohibited, it would seem feasible to alter the arrangement of the individual pss without necessarily affecting the authority of the individual items.

4. "Authority" can be determined only by direct statements to that effect or by evidence of usage consonant with such authority.[68]

PRIORITY

1. "Priority" of a collection does not preclude the "authority" of another, dependent collection. A clear example of this is the work of the Chronicler. While clearly subsequent to and dependent on the book of Kings, while containing materials not found in the earlier work and evidencing a different theological framework, the books of the Chronicler have also functioned with "authority" and have even found their way into the "closed canon." So it appears that different arrangement, content and even theological motivation would not prevent a collection such as 11QPs^a ultimately being considered "authoritative."

---

[67]Sanders, "Surprises," 294: "It must be remembered that the Psalter cannot be viewed in the same way other biblical books are viewed in the question of canonization. Each psalm is an independent entity and has its own existence in a way narratives, oracles, and even proverbs do not have within the book where they are located."

[68]Robert Gordis, "Quotations in Wisdom Literature," *JQR* 3 (1939-40) 123-47; "Quotations as a Literary Usage in Biblical, Oriental and Rabbinic Literature," *HUCA* 22 (1949) 157-219. Joseph A. Fitzmyer, "The Use of Explicit Old Testament Quotations in Qumran Literature and in the Old Testament," *NTS* 7 (1960-61) 297-333.

2. Evidence of priority is extremely difficult to ascertain, since much data can frequently work both ways.[69] For this reason Skehan cites the occurrence in 11QPs^a of Pss 120-132, 133, 134 as evidence of the priority of MT 150 and the dependence of the Qumran Scroll, while Sanders points to the same phenomenon as evidence that at this stage in the development of the Psalter, this group of pss had not settled into the "fixed" arrangement which is *subsequently* found in MT 150.

3. "Priority" of a single composition (or even a *group* of pss) does not necessarily imply the priority of the whole collection. Thus, if Pss 120-134 do represent a collection prior to 11QPs^a, this does not prove the prior existence of the whole MT 150.

CONCLUSION

It seems these three issues: "canonicity," "authority" and "priority" continue to defy final resolution. We are left then with several possible explanations of the relation of MT 150 and 11QPs^a. These options may be presented schematically as follows.

A. Direct-Sequential Linkage- [11QPs^a Prior] -Sanders

individual pss units →	gradual collection and stabilization (beginning to end) →	*11QPs^a* stable through Ps 100-fluid in last third →	*MT 150* final fixation- "leaner" canon

B. Parallel Collection

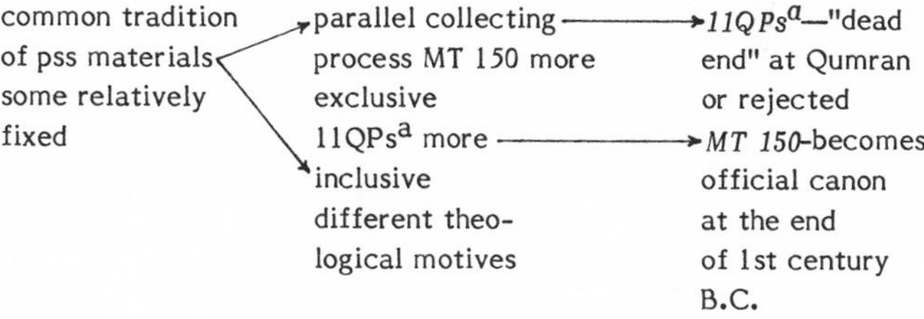

[69]Sanders, "Reviewed," 97.

C. Library Edition-[MT 150 prior-11QPs[a]] -dependent Skehan

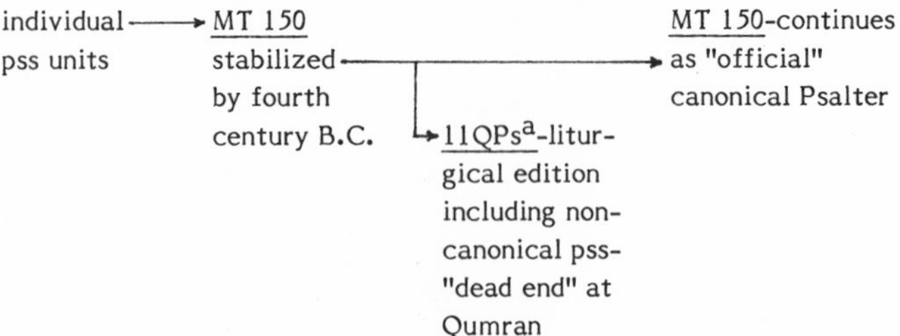

The importance of 11QPs[a] must not be underestimated. If either A or B above are true, it is an important witness to the fluidity of Psalter tradition at a relatively late date, at least among some groups. Of particular interest are Sanders's suggestions concerning the historical relationship between MT 150 and 11QPs[a]. If he is at all correct, it would seem that the departure of the sectarians from Jerusalem to Qumran (ca. 150 B.C.?) and the subsequent more inclusive expansion of the final third of the Psalter evident at Qumran may well have provided the impetus for the final stabilization process resulting, by the end of the first century A.D., in the closed canonical Psalter. It should be interesting to see what evidence of this interaction can be discovered in the present canonical shape of the MT 150 and its Qumran reflex.

Even if such evidence is not forthcoming and if 11QPs[a] is nothing more than Skehan's "library edition," it is still of interest as an example of theological/liturgical arrangement of Hebrew hymnic compositions at a very early date. For these reasons, an examination of 11QPs[a] remains a vital part of this study. I will proceed now to a survey of all the available QPssMss and the data they provide for our understanding of the editorial arrangement of the MT 150 Psalter.

5

The Qumran Psalm Manuscripts and the Hebrew Psalter II. Presentation and Analysis of the Texts

The section which follows immediately contains my detailed analysis of the QPssMss for data concerning the presence of editorial and organizational technique and concern which is applicable to the study of the canonical Hebrew Psalter. Of special interest are any indications of confirmation of or variation from the MT 150 arrangement in terms of explicit editorial statements (s/ss, p/ss, hllwyh's, doxologies); contents (deletion of canonical pss or addition of apocryphal pss); and order (variant arrangement of canonical pss). Where such evidence is extant, its relation to MT 150 is noted. Where data are lacking due to the fragmentary nature of the Mss, some attempt has been made to determine the likelihood of its presence by analysis of each scroll's structure and by making inferences from other matters of scribal convention. (Especially helpful here are questions of line length and methods of paragraph division within a text.)

For a detailed discussion of such matters, I defer to the extensive work on the subject by Malachi Martin, *The Scribal Character of the Dead Sea Scrolls.*[1] Since, however, Martin's work is limited to the 1QMss (1QS, 1QM, 1QH, 1QIs^{a}, 1QIs^{b}, 1QpHab), and since in the following analysis I draw frequently on the evidence of paragraphing to determine the connections and divisions between discrete ps units, some general statements of scribal techniques of paragraphing at Qumran are necessary. There are in the QPssMss five techniques employed to mark the points of juncture between pss. These are described below and accompanied by a schematic diagram.

---

[1]Malachi Martin, *The Scribal Character of the Dead Sea Scrolls*, 2 vols. (Louvain: Institut Orientaliste Université de Louvain, 1958) (hereafter cited as *Scribal Character*).

1. The preceding ps ends in a partial line (i.e., the final line does not reach to the lefthand margin of the column) and the new ps begins at the righthand margin of the next line.

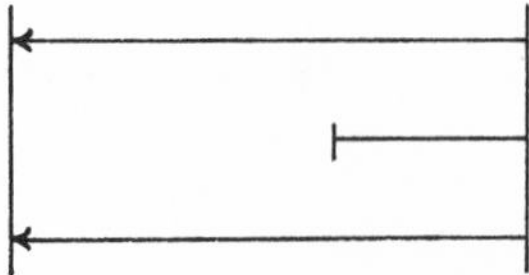

This is by far the most common method of paragraphing used in the QPssMss (32 of 49 determinable instances of juncture) and is equivalent to Martin's "marginal paragraph" which he likewise finds to be most common in the 1QMss.[2]

2. The preceding ps ends in a partial line and the new ps begins on the next line following an indentation.

The distinguishing feature here between methods 1 and 2 appears to be the length of the concluding line. When it occupies *less* than half the line, the new ps begins directly at the righthand margin (as in method 1). When however it exceeds the mid-point (yet does not fill it) the tendency is to *indent* the first line of the new ps (as in method 2). Method 2 is considerably less frequent than the first (only 4 of 49 instances) and is closely related to method 4 from which it is distinguished at times only with difficulty.

3. When the preceding ps concludes with a full line (i.e., it reaches or exceeds the lefthand margin), the new ps *sometimes* (in 5 out of 10 occurrences) begins at the righthand margin, but only after an intervening line has been left completely blank.

---

[2]Martin, *Scribal Character*, vol. 1, 142-43.

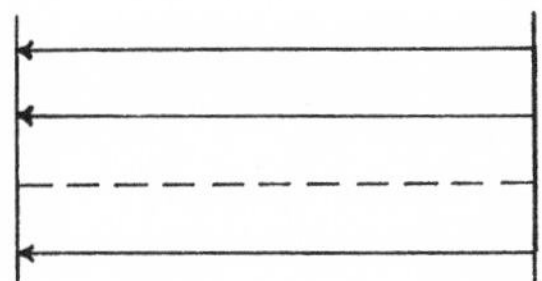

4. On other occasions, however, no blank line is introduced and the scribe is content to begin the new ps on the very next line after an indentation.

As one can see, there is very little difference between method 2 and method 4. It is frequently difficult to distinguish a completely filled line from a line which lacks but a few letters (particularly in the case of fragmentary texts). This is especially true when one must work from photographs (see Martin's comments)[3] or, even more distantly, from typed transcriptions. However, since the division is clear in any case, the study is not adversely affected by the difficulty.

5. Finally, on a few occasions (3 of the 49 determinable cases) the division between pss takes place *within* a single line marked by a brief blank space, after which the new ps begins and continues.

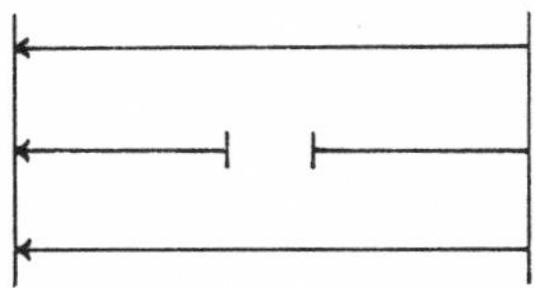

---

[3]Martin, *Scribal Character*, vol. 1, 98.

Martin refers to a similar method which he terms "sub-paragraphing" within larger divisions. The fragmentary nature of the texts here has rendered it practically impossible to determine whether similar intent can be attached to this phenomenon in the QPssMss.

With these preliminary comments, I will now begin the analysis of the individual pss texts from Qumran. I direct my attention here only to those portions of the texts which preserve the points of transition from one ps to another. (In some instances only the beginning or conclusion of a single ps is preserved.) I attempt to describe the physical circumstances of each text so that the basis of my judgment is clear. A summary of the data for the explicit editorial statements (s/ss, p/ss, hllwyh's, doxologies), in the form of a full listing of the QPss data compared (for each ps) with that of MT 150, is provided in Appendix A, pp. 231-35.

DESCRIPTION OF THE QUMRAN PSALMS MANUSCRIPTS

4QPs^{a}

fragment a (Pss 5:9-6:1)

At the point of juncture in this fragment, a blank line separates the extant portions of these two pss. Since the last word of Ps 5 appears at the left margin of the last line before the blank, the intervening line was completely blank (Method 3). The spacing required to complete the missing lines of Ps 5 as well as line two of Ps 6 (as determined from the extant words at the extreme left of the column) indicates that, in all probability, the s/s of Ps 6 was originally present and began at the right margin of the line following the blank.

fragments c-d

Col. I

Pss 31:23-25 + 33:1-12 (Ps 32 omitted)

At the left margin of this fragmentary column a blank line separates the extant portions of the two pss. However, since the last line before the blank ends with 31:24a, the remainder of this ps must have extended into the righthand portion of the "blank" and has been lost in the lacuna. The lacuna to the right of the first line of Ps 33 is not extensive enough to have contained the missing part of Ps 33 as well as a s/s. Apparently no s/s was written (in agreement with MT). (Method 1.)

Pss 34:22-35:2

In the extant portion of these two pss, a blank line intervenes. However, the fragment is too small to be placed conclusively in relation to the margins of the original column. Thus it is impossible to speculate as to how much text has been lost preceding the extant part of Ps 35:2. There is insufficient data to know whether or not a s/s was present or what method was employed to mark the division.

Col. II

Pss 35:26-36:9

Here the right margin of the column is extant. No blank line separates these pss. The s/s of Ps 36 is present beginning at the right margin and agrees with that of MT. The s/s must have been followed immediately in the same line by verse two. (Method 1?)

fragment g

Pss 38:16-23 + 71:1

No blank line separates these two pss. In fact, 71:1 follows immediately the end of 38:23, in the same line, with no indication of separation. This would seem to indicate that these pss were read together as one. As in MT, there is no evidence of a s/s for Ps 71.

fragment i

Pss 53:4-54:6

A blank space separates these pss at the extreme left of the column. Apparently the missing portion of 53:7 extended into this blank line from the right and has been lost in the lacuna. Thus this ps ended in a partial line. The s/s of Ps 54 has likewise fallen victim of the lacuna with only the last two words of the historical note preserved at the left. Spacing indicates the s/s must have begun at the right margin (Method 1) and extended some 59 spaces to the left. The amount of space agrees with the missing text of 53:7 and 54:1.

fragment k, Col. 1 + fragment l

Pss 62:13-63:4

The extant part of these pss is separated by a blank line at the far left of the column. The last word of 63:2 occurs at the left margin of the first line following the blank. Considerations of column width and line length indicate the lacuna to the right of this line could have contained the MT s/s *and* the missing portion of 63:2. Since the last word of Ps 62 is written at the extreme left margin of the last line above the blank, it is evident that a completely blank line was left to indicate the division. Thus the s/s of Ps 63 began at the right margin of the first line following this space. (Method 3.) Space available would have contained the s/s as known in MT.

fragment k, Col. II + fragments m, n, o

Pss 66:16–67:8

The fragments preserve both right and left margins of this column, giving some idea of its extent. No blank line separates the pss at the right margin. The last word of 66:20 is written at the right margin while the first word of the s/s of Ps 67 appears at the right margin of the next line. (Method 1.)

fragments p, q

Ps 69:1–19

A blank line precedes the first line of Ps 69 at the extreme left. It is uncertain, however, whether the line was completely blank or partially filled. The s/s of Ps 69 apparently began at the right margin of the first line after the "blank." The initial word of the s/s has been lost, but the remainder agrees with MT.

4QPs^{b}

This is a text of thirty-six fragmentary columns containing Pss 91-118 with the major omission of Ps 104-111. The extant pss follow the MT arrangement. Because of the fragmentary state of the Ms, data concerning s/ss and the connection of pss is frequently missing or inconclusive. The following observations are possible.

Col. III
Pss 91:16a-92:8a

Reconstruction indicates that either a blank line or a s/s separated Pss 91 and 92. Nothing more can be ascertained.

Col. V

Pss 92:16a-93:5c

Apparently Ps 92:16 occupied the first two lines of this column. Spacing indicates Ps 93 then followed immediately with no s/s or separating line. This may indicate these pss were read as one. The last line of this column was left entirely blank separating Ps 93 from 94 which begins at the top of Col. VI.

Col. VI

Pss 94:1-4, 8-9

Only the extreme left of the column is preserved. The ps is written stychometrically, one stych per line. There is no evidence of any s/s (in agreement with MT). The first line of Ps 94 is apparently the top of a column, so it is doubtful that any s/s has been lost, especially in view of the blank line at the bottom of Col. V.

Col. VIII

Pss 94:19a-95:4a

Reconstruction of Cols. VI-X on the basis of 18 lines per column (as indicated in Cols. VI and VII) would suggest that in Col. VIII, Pss 94 and 95 were written with no separating line or s/s. Perhaps these were read as one ps.

Col. XI-XIV

Pss 96:10a-99:4d

Since these columns are very fragmentary, little can be offered conclusively. Skehan indicates in his transcription that these columns each contained 18 lines. A reconstruction on this basis suggests blank lines separated Pss 96-97 (Col. XI); Pss 97-98 (Col. XIII); Pss 98-99 (Col. XIV). This reconstruction fits well with the preservation of Ps 99:5a at the top of Col. XV.

Cols. XV-XVI

Pss 99:5a-9c + 100 + 101:1-2a

Skehan's reconstruction of these two columns suggests that Ps 99 ended on line 15 of the 16-line Col. XV. Since Ps 100:1b begins on the first line of Col. XVI, we are left to surmise concerning the last line of Col. XV. Either it was left blank to separate the pss or it contained the s/s of 100:1a. Because the line in question has been entirely lost, the problem cannot be solved. However, it is clear that these pss were recognized as distinct compositions. The juncture of Pss 100 and 101 is not preserved and must remain obscure.

Cols. XVII-XIX

Pss 101:2b-102:9b?

These columns are too fragmentary for much comment. Skehan reconstructs on the basis of 16 lines per column. On this basis, it seems Pss 101 and 102 were separated in Col. XVIII by both a blank line and the s/s of Ps 102. This cannot be certain however.

Cols. XX-XXVII

Pss 102:10a + 103 + 112-113:1a

These columns can be fairly accurately reconstructed due to the continuous preservation of the tops of all eight columns. The reconstruction indicates all eight columns contained 16 lines each and confirms the variant arrangement of Pss 102-103 followed immediately by Pss 112-113. Discussion of pertinent columns follows immediately below.

Col. XXII

Pss 102:26-103:3

The transition from 102 to 103 comes at a fragmentary section of the scroll. Skehan indicates in his transcription that a blank line separates these pss. The s/s of Ps 103 is present on its own line before the body of the ps and slightly indented from the right margin. Possibly the s/s of Ps 100:1 occupied a similar position. If so, this may indicate a common practice in this scroll. The extant portion of the s/s agrees with MT.

Cols. XXV-XXVI

Pss 103:20a-112:10c

Col. XXV begins with Ps 103:20a while Col. XXVI begins with Ps 112:4a. Although the transition at the bottom of Col. XXV is lost in a lacuna, the reconstruction indicates that a blank line and the s/s of Ps 112:1a (hllwyh) probably intervened. Most important is the clear omission of Pss 104-111 of the MT arrangement which could not possibly have been included here. There seems to be no other explanation for such an omission than purposeful intent.

Col. XXVII

Ps 113(?):1

The only word preserved on this column is hllwyh. The position of this word at the top of a column at the right margin, suggests it is the s/s to the following ps rather than the p/s of a preceding ps. Since Ps 112 is contained in Col. XXVI and MT 114 has no hllwyh, Ps 113 is the logical choice. This is confirmed by the spacing considerations between Cols.

XXVI and XXVII. However, since this is the only word preserved, the identification must remain tentative.

Cols. XXVIII-XXXII
Pss 113-116

These columns are almost completely missing. Only one small fragment of Ps 115:2-3 (Col XXIX?) is extant. Skehan surmises that it would take this number of columns to contain the text of Pss 113-116 which are missing between Col. XXVII and the next fragments (Col. XXXII). Conclusive reconstruction is not feasible, however. Considering the omission of Pss 104-111 in this same Ms, the presence of Pss 113-116 must remain a question.

Cols. XXXIII-XXXVI
Pss 116:3a-119?

Here again the bottom of three consecutive columns and a fragment of a fourth are preserved permitting accurate reconstruction of the contents. Evidently each of these columns contained 17 lines. Only in Col. XXXIV are transitions between pss indicated. Skehan reconstructs the five missing lines at the top of this column as follows:

line 1—hllwyh
lines 2-3—Ps 117
line 4—blank
line 5—hllwyh

Ps 118 then appears at the right margin of line 6. One implication of this reconstruction is to present the hllwyh's as s/ss to the pss which follow them and not as p/ss as in many MT Mss (cf. *BHS*). However, since this is all reconstruction of a lacuna, it is conjectural and cannot be confirmed as certain. Clearly, though, these pss were viewed as distinct compositions and not read together.

4QPs^c

fragment b

Ps 17:1(?)

Although a s/s is present, context is broken to the right and left. The word which appears directly below in the very next line seems to be the first word of the third stychos of 17:1 (hʾzynh). If this ps was written stychometrically (two stychoi per line) as was Ps 18 of this Ms, it would seem that the s/s began at the right margin and stych one of the ps proper continued immediately to the left on the same line. This analysis cannot be certain due to the fragmentary condition of the text.

fragment e

Pss 27:12-28:3

A blank line separates these pss in the portion preserved. The s/s, if originally written, is no longer extant. Since the first extant line of Ps 28 begins with the second half of the first verse, verse 1a must have been lost in the lacuna to the left of the "blank" line. (Method 2 or 4.) It is not possible to determine whether the MT s/s was also part of the Qumran tradition for Ps 28.

fragments l, m, n, o, p

Col. I

Ps 49:1-17

A blank line precedes the first line of this ps. Skehan indicates it is *not* the top of a column. The s/s is partially preserved and originally began at the right margin of the first line. The first word has been lost. The s/s was followed immediately to the left by the next verse of the ps. The ps does not seem to have been written stychometrically.

fragments n, o

Col. II

Pss 50:14-51:5

No blank line separates the two pss. The final portion of 50:23 partially fills the last line immediately preceding 51:1. The s/s of Ps 51 is present and begins at the right margin. (Method 1.) The historical statement follows the s/s immediately to the left. Both s/s and statement agree with MT.

fragments n, p

Col. III

Pss 52:6-53:1

No blank line separates these pss. The last two words of Ps 52 occupy the line preceding the first line of Ps 53. The s/s of Ps 53 is present and begins at the right margin. (Method 1.) A blank space interrupts the s/s following the word mḥlt. Could this space indicate the scribe's recognition that the feminine-singular-construct form of mḥlt would require a *nomens rectum* which is omitted in MT? Or could this space arise from confusion with the similar s/s in Ps 88 . . . lmnṣḥ ʿl mḥlt lʿnwt mśkyl lhymn . . . (an erasure?). Except for this space, the s/s agrees with that of MT. Only the s/s remains extant of Ps 53.

4QPs^{d}

Col. I

Pss (?)-147:4

The hllwyh p/s is all that remains of the ps which precedes Ps 147. This hllwyh stands in the middle of the line immediately preceding the first line of 147. The hllwyh s/s of 147 is present and begins at the right margin. (Method 1.) The body of the ps continues immediately to the left.

Col. II

Pss 147:13-17, 20-104:5

Note the unusual ordering of these two pss contrary to MT 150. No blank intervenes. The p/s (hllwyh) of Ps 147 immediately follows the text of that ps and occurs in the middle of the line before that in which 104 begins. There is no s/s for Ps 104 in agreement with MT and the ps begins at the right margin. (Method 1.)

4QPs^{e}

fragment 1

Pss 76:10-77:1

An apparent blank line separates the remains of the two pss. However, it is possible that the last portion of 76:13 may have extended into the right part of this line. Only the fourth word of the s/s of Ps 77 (lʾsp) is preserved. The text is broken both to right and left. An exact reconstruction of the contents of the s/s and the position of the fragment in relation to the margins is impossible.

fragment 5

Col. I

Ps 88:1-5

The s/s of this ps is partially preserved. However, the context is too broken to reconstruct the dimensions of the column and to infer the length and contents of the s/s. It is not possible to determine whether the "double" s/s of MT (lbny qrḥ and lhymn) was known at Qumran as well. Only the latter is definitely supported by the evidence.

fragment 9

Pss 118(?):29b-104:3

The extant text of Ps 104 is preceded by the familiar phrase [hwdw lyhwh ky ṭ]wb ky lʿwlm ḥsdw which could be the final verse of a number of canonical pss. In private communication Skehan refers to the occurrence of Ps 104 in 11QPs[a], frag. e, where it is preceded by Ps 118 (also ending in this phrase). In 11QPs[a], Ps 104 has the s/s ldwyd preceding it. If we have the same combination of pss here, one might expect the s/s to have been written in the lacuna which precedes the first word of Ps 104. This would explain why 104 does not appear to begin at the right margin of the column as one would expect. The presence of such a s/s is contrary to the evidence of MT.

fragments 12, 16

Col. I

Ps 105:1-3

There is no evidence of any s/s preserved. However, the context is too broken to permit reconstruction of the extent of the text in relation to the margins, so conclusions regarding the s/s cannot be certain. Lack of a s/s would agree with the case in MT.

fragments 14-16

Pss 105:36-106(?):1

Ps 105:45 ends near the middle of line 6 of this column. Skehan's transcription suggests that the MT p/s hllwyh occurred in the lacuna to the left of the same line. If this is the case, the hllwyh preserved at the right margin of line 7 must represent the s/s of another ps. Since this is the only extant word of this ps, it is impossible to conclusively identify it, though Ps 106 may be the logical choice.

fragment 20

Ps 109(?):1

Only part of the s/s [ldw] d mzmw [r . . . remains. This is

insufficient to determine which ps it introduced. The existence of other fragments of Ps 109 might lend some support to the identification of this fragment with Ps 109. If this identification is correct, the s/s agrees with that of MT (lmnṣḥ ldwd mzmwr).

fragment 23

Pss 115:15-116:3

The p/s (hllwyh) of 115 is present in the MT position immediately following the last verse (only the initial hê of this p/s is preserved). There is no evidence of any s/s for Ps 116 (in agreement with MT), however, the context is very broken. No line separates the pss.

fragment 25

Col. I

Pss 125:2-126:5

No line separates these pss. 126:1 begins on the same line in which 125:5 ends, following a small space. (Method 5.) The s/s was omitted and has been added (by the same scribal hand) above the separating space.

Col. II

Pss 129:8-130:6

This is a very fragmentary column. Only the extreme right margin is extant. Ps 129 ends with one word (YHWH) at the right margin of line 2. Line 3 begins with the first word of 130:2 at the right margin. While there is no extant evidence of the MT s/s, perhaps it has been lost in the lacuna to the left of line 2 (following the end of 129:8). There is an interlinear insertion between lines 2 and 3 which consists of the letters ᶜwl and which does not correspond to anything in the s/s or body of Ps 130 as known from MT. Final interpretation of this and the preceding column is difficult at best.

4QPs^{f}

Cols. I-VII

Pss 107:2-5, 8-11, 13-16, 18-19, 22-30, 35-42; [108?]; 109:4-6, 24-28

This Ms extends over several fragmentary columns. The arrangement of columns I-VII seems to confirm the MT order of Pss 107-108-109. However, the fifth column is completely missing and there is not even fragmentary evidence of Ps 108, so the contents of this Ms must remain in question. These columns of canonical pss are followed by three apocryphal compositions. There is some reason to doubt that this Ms was intended to function as a "psalter" in the full sense of the word (see above, pp. 68-69).

4QPs^g and 4QPs^h

Both of these Mss contain only fragmentary copies of Ps 119. For this reason, they yield no evidence for the arrangement of the pss or for their explicit editorial comments.

4QPs^j

fragment 1

Ps 48:1-7

The s/s is present and begins at the right margin. Only the first two words of the s/s are extant. Apparently the body of the ps followed the s/s immediately to the left in the same line.

4QPs^k

Col. II

Ps 99(?):1

Skehan identifies this ps as possibly Ps 99 on the basis of the two words preserved (h^{c}mym and rwmmw) both of which *do* occur in MT 99 in this order. However, if the text of the Qumran ps approximates that of MT, a reconstruction of the text would necessitate lines of extraordinarily extended length. If this *is* Ps 99, it exhibits a s/s beginning at the right margin contrary to MT which lacks any such s/s.

4QPs^l, 4QPs^m and 4QPs^n

All these Mss are too fragmentary to provide any data regarding pss arrangement or explicit comments.

4QPs^o

fragment 1

Pss 114:7-115:1

No blank space separates these pss in the extant portion. There is no evidence of a s/s for Ps 115 (which agrees with MT). Tentative reconstruction indicates these pss may have been written together as one.

4QPs^{p}

There is no evidence regarding pss arrangement or explicit comments.

4QPs^{q}

Col. I

Pss 31:24-25 + 33:1-18 (Ps 32 omitted)

Note the omission of Ps 32 as in 4QPs^{a}. Ps 31 ends in a partial line. Then Ps 33 begins on the same line after a brief space. (Method 5.) Ps 33 exhibits a s/s contrary to MT. The s/s stands alone in the first line (following the end of Ps 31) while the body of Ps 33 begins at the right margin of the following line.

4QPs89

There is no evidence here for pss arrangement or explicit comments.

4QPs^{r}

fragments 1, 2, 3

Pss 26:7-27:1

The right margin is extant for part of this column and it is possible to reconstruct the text to some extent. Skehan's reconstruction would have Ps 26 end and Ps 27 begin on the same line. If the MT s/s was present, there would have been no space left between these two compositions, which would seem highly unusual. In any event a s/s is not extant and cannot be affirmed with any degree of certainty.

4QPs^{s}

fragment 1

Pss 5:8-6:1

No blank line separates the pss. As both margins are missing, it is not possible to reconstruct the extent of the column and the extent of the text. The s/s of Ps 6 is partially preserved (the first two words of the MT s/s) and evidence indicates the s/s did not stand at the right margin.

4QPs isolated fragment 2

Ps 99(?):1

Only two words are extant. It is impossible to determine the context. There is no evidence of any s/s which, if the identification is correct, agrees with the situation in MT.

11QPs[a]

fragments A, B, C

Pss 101:1-102:2

The s/s of Ps 101 is not extant. This line begins the top of a column and spacing indicates a s/s was probably present. The last line of Ps 101 extends into a partial line and then 102 begins at the right margin of the next line. (Method 1.) The s/s of Ps 102 is only partially preserved, but spacing indicates the whole was originally present.

fragment C

Pss 102:18-103:1

The right margin is extant throughout, permitting reasonably accuate reconstruction of the text. The last words of Ps 102 (dwr ldwr—an addition not found in MT) are written at the right margin of a partially filled line. Ps 103 then begins at the right margin of the following line. (Method 1.) No s/s is preserved, but the spacing suggests a minimal s/s (ldwyd?) may have been present originally.

fragment D

Ps 109:21-31

The first two words of the last verse of Ps 109 stand at the left margin of the last extant line of this fragment. Apparently the remainder of this verse extended into the next line. The next composition would begin at the right margin of the following line. Due to the fragmentary state of the text, reconstruction is not certain. My own analysis of fragments C, D and E of 11QPs[a] lead me to believe that the sequence of

Pss 102-103-109-118-104 represents the full extent of the first portion of the scroll. There are not, in my opinion, other compositions which have been lost in the lacunae.[4]

fragment E I

Pss 118:25-104:6

Note especially the unusual sequence of pss. The last line of Ps 118 extends into a partial line some 31 letter-spaces. Then the s/s and the first two words of Ps 104 begin on the following line after an indentation of approximately 30 spaces. The s/s of 104 (ldwyd) is contrary to the evidence of MT which has no s/s. (Cf. 4QPs^{e}, frag. 9.)

fragment E II

Pss 104:21-147:2

Again note the unusual sequence. Ps 104 concludes with the hllwyh p/s at the left margin of a completely filled line. A blank line separates this line from the initial line of Ps 147. There is no evidence of a s/s for Ps 147 such as appears in MT. The lacuna to the right of the initial line of 147 is too short to have contained a hllwyh s/s as well as the missing portion of the first stych which apparently began at the right margin. (Method 3.)

fragment E III

Pss 147:18-105:11

The last part of Ps 147 extends into a partial line. Then Ps 105 begins at the right margin of the following line. There is some confusion or assimilation in the first line with the hwdw-pss. The traditional hwdw phrases (hwdw lyhwh ky ṭwb ky l^{c}wlm ḥsdw) are added before the first verse begins. The hllwyh p/s of MT 147 is not extant here and it is not possible to determine whether or not it was originally present. There is no s/s for Ps 105 in agreement with MT.

---

[4]My decision is based on the MT consonantal text of the portions lost in the lacunae. Line length (in letter spaces) varies considerably (from 46 to 39 in fragments A, B, C and from 45 to 35 in fragment EI), so some caution must be exercised. However, the amount of text lost does seem compatible with the space represented in the various lacunae.

Col. I

Pss 105:25-45

Only the extreme left margin of the upper half of this column is preserved. Apparently the last of Ps 105 extended into a partial line in the lacuna at the bottom of the fragment. The hllwyh p/s, if it was written, would have been lost in this lacuna. It is impossible to know if it ever was written in fact.

Col. II

Pss 146:9-148:12

Note the variant sequence of pss. Ps 147 had already occurred in fragments E II-E III. The final portion of Ps 146 extends into a partial line after which Ps 148 begins at the right margin of the following line. There was no hllwyh s/s written for Ps 148, however, the hllwyh p/s of 146 is clearly present. The spacing of this column and those which follow indicates that the lacuna at the bottom of column II could have contained a composition the size of Ps 120 which has been completely lost. It would be reasonable to assume that the composition was indeed Ps 120.

Col. III

Pss 121:1-122-123:2

Ps 121:1 begins at the top of the column. The s/s is indented from the right margin. The last of Ps 121 apparently filled (or nearly filled) a line after which Ps 122 begins after an indentation from the right margin. (Method 2 or 4.) The s/s of 122 was present according the spacing considerations. The end of Ps 122 extends into a partial line after which the s/s of Ps 123 begins at the right margin of the following line. The s/s is only partially extant and does not correspond exactly with that of MT. The end of Ps 123 is lost in the lacuna at the bottom of the column.

Col. IV

Pss 124:7-125-126-127:1

Ps 124 extends into a partial line. Then Ps 125 begins at the right margin of the next line. (Method 1.) Only the first letter of the s/s of 129 is extant, but spacing indicates the whole was written. Ps 129 concludes with a completely filled line and Ps 130 then begins on the next line following an indentation. (Method 4.) The s/s of 130 is extant in full and agrees with MT. Ps 130 ends in a partial line and Ps 131 begins at the right margin of the next line. (Method 1.) While the s/s is not extant the spacing indicates it was probably written in full. The rest of Ps 131 and the beginning of Ps 132 are lost at the bottom of the column.

Col. VI

Pss 132:8-18 + 119:1-6

Ps 132 extends into a partial line and Ps 119 begins on the next line at the right margin. (Method 1.) There is no s/s written for Ps 119 in agreement with MT. Cols. VII-XIII are taken up completely with Ps 119. The end of this massive acrostic does not come until Col. XIV.

Col. XIV

Pss 119:171-135:9

Ps 119 ends with a completely filled line. Then Ps 135 begins at the right margin following a completely blank line separating the two pss. the hllwyh s/s of MT 135 is *not* written.

Col. XV

Pss 135:17-136:16

Ps 135 ends in a partial line. A p/s (hllwyh) is written in agreement with MT. Ps 136 then begins at the right margin of the next line. (Method 1.) No hllwyh s/s is written for Ps 136 in accordance with MT.

Col. XVI

Pss 136:26-Catena-145:7

Apparently the last three words of Ps 136 (ky lᶜwlm ḥsdw) began at the right margin of the first line of this column. Then a catena of verses (ostensibly from Ps 118) begins immediately to the left with no space between. It is attractive to consider this an independent ps,[5] but the lack of any separation suggests these two compositions were to be read as one. However, the catena also begins with the phrase hwdw lyhwh ky ṭwb ky lᶜwlm ḥsdw which seems highly redundant if these two are to be combined. It is worth noting in this regard that the phrase at the top of the column assumed to be part of Ps 136 also occurs in other compositions and no clearly identifiable part of Ps 136 appears in this column. It is at least possible that Ps 136 actually ended near the bottom of Col. XV and this line represents the beginning of a new ps. Admittedly this is questionable. Continuing the analysis, Ps 136, in agreement with MT, has no p/s. There is likewise no s/s for the Catena. Following the Catena, a hllwyh p/s is written completing a partial line. A blank line then separates this composition from the first line of Ps 145. The s/s of 145 is written and is extant in full. It begins near the right margin after a small indentation

---

[5]See below, pp. 126-27.

perhaps due to a flaw in the leather. Ps 145 is expanded throughout by the addition of a refrain brwk yhwh wbrwk šmw lᶜwlm wᶜd following each MT verse.

Col. XVII

Ps 145:13-21

Ps 145 continues and ends in this column. The only interesting feature preserved is the apparent p/s which occurs in the fragmentary portion of the column immediately following the conclusion of Ps 145.

. . . zwʾt lzkrwn . . . "this is for a memorial."

Due to the fragmentary state of the context, the significance of this statement is not fully clear.[6]

Col. XVIII

Ps 154:3-19

Note the variant sequence of the pss.

Col. XIX

Plea for Deliverance

This composition, the first of the "apocryphal" pss included in 11QPs[a], must have begun in the lacuna at the end of Col. XVIII and ends in the lacuna at the end of Col. XIX. Its relation to the pss which precede and follow it cannot be conclusively determined.

Col. XX

Pss 139:8 + 137:1

Ps 139 extends into a partial line. Then Ps 137 begins at the right margin of the next line. (Method 1.) There is no hllwyh p/s for Ps 139 and no s/s for 137, all in agreement with MT.

Col. XXI

Pss 137:9-138 + Sir. 51:13ff.

The last half verse of Ps 137 extends into a partial line. After a brief space, Ps 139:1 with s/s (ldwyd) begins to the left of center in the same line. (Method 5.) This line is the first of the column. The final verse of Ps 138 extends into a partial line after which Sir. 51:13ff. begins at the right margin of the next line. (Method 1.)

---

[6]See below, pp. 137-38.

Col. XXII

Sir. 51:30-Apostrophe to Zion-Ps 93:1-3

The last line of the Sirach composition extends into a partial line (about 10 spaces). After a brief space, the Apostrophe begins to the left of center on the same line. (Method 5.) The Apostrophe ends in a partial line and Ps 93, with hllwyh s/s, begins at the right margin of the next line. (Method 1.) MT 93 has no such hllwyh s/s.

Col. XXIII

Pss 141:5-133-144:7

After Ps 141 ends in a partial line (approximately 77 spaces), Ps 133 begins on the next line following an indentation (15 spaces). (Method 2.) The s/s of 133 is written in complete agreement with MT. The last line of Ps 133 extends into a partial line after which Ps 144 begins at the right margin of the next line. (Method 1.) Contrary to MT, there is no s/s for Ps 144.

Col. XXIV

Pss 144:15-155:9

Note the unusual sequence of pss. The last word of Ps 144 stands at the right margin of the second line of the column. Ps 155:1 begins at the right margin of the next line (line three). There are no p/ss or s/ss written.

Col. XXV

Pss 142:4-143:8

The last line of 142 extends into a partial line. Ps 143 then begins at the right margin of the next line. (Method 1.) The MT s/s of Ps 143 is written in full.

Col. XXVI

Pss 149:7-150:6 + Hymn to the Creator

The last line of 149 fills a complete line. The hllwyh p/s of MT is written. Ps 150:1 begins on the next line following an indentation. (Method 4.) No hllwyh s/s is written with Ps 150 (contrary to MT). The last line of 150 (with hllwyh p/s) extends into a partial line after which the "Hymn" begins at the right margin of the next line. (Method 1.)

Col. XXVII

2 Sam 23:7 + David's Compositions + Ps 140:1-5

The last part of 2 Sam 23:7 fils only a part of the first line of this column. Then David's Compositions begins on the next line. The first three lines of this composition are indented, followed by seven lines beginning at the right margin. The last line fills only a partial line (42 spaces) and Ps 140:1 begins on the next line after an indentation. (Method 2.) The s/s of MT 140 is written.

Col. XXVIII

Pss 134:1-3 + 151 A, B

The last line of Ps 134 fills a complete line. A completely blank line then intervenes, after which Ps 151 A begins at the right margin. (Method 3.) A hllwyh s/s is written for 151 A as well as the brief notation ldwyd bn yšy. This does not agree with the LXX s/s. The last word of 151 A is written at the right margin of an otherwise blank line. An historical s/s begins at the right margin of the next line which apparently introduced a further composition (Ps 151 B) which continued on immediately to the left in the same line. (Method 1.)

11QPs^{b}

As noted previously, this fragmentary Ms is of importance for its support of the variant content and arrangement of the major Qumran Psalms Scroll: 11QPs^{a}. 11QPs^{b} reduplicates that text in three of its major variations from the MT norm. (1) In fragments *a* and *b* it reproduces a large portion of the apocryphal composition "Plea for Deliverance" otherwise known only from 11QPs^{a}. (2) Fragments c, d and e preserve the variant arrangement of Pss 141-133-144 also found in 11QPs^{a}. (3) The "Catena" found in 11QPs^{a}, col. XVI is also exhibited in 11QPs^{b}, fragment f.

fragments c, d, e

Pss 141:10c + 133:1-3 + 144:1-2

These three fragments form a connected block of text containing parts of seven consecutive lines from a single column. While the margins have not been preserved, it is evident that Ps 141 ended in a partial line (only the last word is extant, followed by a blank space). Ps 133 then begins on the next line (according to van der Ploeg's reconstruction, this line was probably indented from the right margin). (Method 2?) After Ps 133 concludes with a very full line, Ps 144 begins in the following line after an indentation (again, according to van der Ploeg's reconstruction). The s/s of Ps 133 is only partially preserved: [šyr hmᶜl]wt ldwyd. The s/s of Ps 144 is not extant, having been lost in the lacuna to the right of fragment e.

11QPs^c

For my description of this fragmentary Ms, I am dependent, in part, on private communication from J. P. M. van der Ploeg who has most graciously assisted me. Van der Ploeg has previously published a brief catalogue of the contents of 11QPs^c, as well as the largest fragment containing Pss 17-18. There is apparently no evidence for apocryphal compositions among the fragments of the Ms and the arrangement, where extant, supports MT. As far as consecutive groupings of pss, there are fragments preserving the juncture of Pss 12-13 and others joining Pss 17-18.

Pss 12-13

Regarding this grouping, van der Ploeg indicates by letter that the s/s of Ps 13 is not extant, but was most probably included originally.

Pss 17-18

This fragment contains 17 lines of text with a blank line separating the two pss. The right margin is preserved for the first two lines, making it possible to reconstruct the limits of the text. Ps 17 apparently ended in a completely filled line (van der Ploeg suggests that the last word *may* have stood at the right margin of the blank line, but this seems improbable since, in that case, the s/s of Ps 18 could be expected to begin to the left in the same line after a suitable space). Ps 18 then began at the right margin following an entirely blank line left to separate the pss. The s/s of Ps 18 is partially extant: [ldwy] d ᵓšr dbr lyhwh [ᵓt d]bry hsyrh [. . .] ᵓwybyw wmyd šᵓw [l . . . .

11QPs^d

This unpublished Ms consists of several fragments which supply evidence of the juncture of only two pss: 39-40. Van der Ploeg informs me that the s/s of Ps 40 is partially preserved: lmnṣ[ḥ. . . . The rest of the fragments contain only parts of individual pss.

11QPs^e

This Ms consists of fragments documenting the juxtaposition of Pss

77-78 only. According to van der Ploeg, the s/s of Ps 78 is not extant, but may have been lost.

ANALYSIS OF THE DATA FROM THE QPSSMSS

The previous review of the individual Mss and fragments from Qumran yields considerable evidence regarding the arrangement of the pss which should now be brought together in a more organized and useful fashion.

1. Evidence Supporting the Canonical Arrangement of Consecutive Psalms

Psalms Joined Consecutively	Text Where Found
Pss 5-6	4QPs[a], frag. a
Pss 5-6	4QPs[s], frag. 1
Pss 12-13	11QPs[c]
Pss 15-16	5/6 ḤevPs
Pss 17-18	11QPs[c]
Pss 26-27	4QPs[r], frags. 1, 2, 3
Pss 27-28	4QPs[c], frags. e, f
Pss 33-[34]-35	4QPs[q], cols. I-II
Pss 33-34-35-36	4QPs[a], frags. c, d, e
Pss 39-40	11QPs[d]
Pss 49-50-51-52-53	4QPs[c], frags. l, m, n, o, p
Pss 53-54	4QPs[a], frag. i
Pss 62-63	4QPs[a], frags. k, l
Pss 66-67	4QPs[a], frags. k, m, n, o
Pss 76-77	4QPs[e], frag. 1
Pss 77-78	11QPs[e]
Pss 81-82-83-84-85	MasPs 1039-160
Pss 91-92-[93]-94	4QPs[b], cols. i-iv
Pss 95-96	1QPs[a], frag. 5
Pss 99-100	4QPs[b], cols. xv-xvi
Pss 101-102-103	11QPs[a], frags. A, B, C
Pss 102-103	4QPs[b], cols. xx-xxv
Pss 105-106(?)	4QPs[e], frags. 14, 15, 16
Pss 107-[108?]-109	4QPs[f], cols. i-vii
Pss 112-113 (?)	4QPs[b], cols. xxvi-xxvii
Pss 114-115	4QPs[o], frag. 1
Pss 115-116	4QPs[e], frag. 23
Pss 116-[117]-118	4QPs[b], cols. xxxiii-xxxvi
Pss [120]-121-122-123-124-125-126-127-128-129-130-131-132	11QPs[a], cols. II-VI
Pss 125-126	4QPs[e], frag. 25
Pss 129-130	4QPs[e], frag. 25

Pss Joined Consecutively	Text Where Found
Pss 135-136	11QPs[a], col. XV
Pss 137-138	11QPs[a], col. XXI
Pss 142-143	11QPs[a], col. XXV
Pss 149-150	11QPs[a], col. XXVI

2. Evidence Conflicting with the Canonical Arrangement of Consecutive Psalms

Pss Joined Consecutively	Text Where Found
Pss 31-33	4QPs[a], frags. c, d
Pss 31-33	4QPs[q], col. I
Pss 38-71	4QPs[a], frag. g
Apostrophe-Ps 93	11QPs[a], col. XXII
Pss 93-141	11QPs[a], cols. XXII-XXIII
Pss 103-112	4QPs[b], col. XXV
Pss 104-147	11QPs[a], frag. E, col. II
Pss 105-146	11QPs[a], cols. I-II
Pss 118-104	11QPs[a], frag. E, col. I
Pss 118(?)-104	4QPs[e], frag. 9
Pss 119-135	11QPs[a], col. XIV
Pss 132-119	11QPs[a], col. VI
Pss 141-133	11QPs[a], col. XXIII
Pss 141-133	11QPs[b], frags. c, d, e
Pss 133-144	11QPs[a], col. XXIII
Pss 133-144	11QPs[b], frags. c, d, e
Pss 134-151A	11QPs[a], col. XXVIII
Pss 136-Catena	11QPs[a], col. XVI
Pss 138-Sirach 51	11QPs[a], col. XXI
Plea-Ps 139	11QPs[a], cols. XVII-XX
Pss 139-137	11QPs[a], col. XX
David's Comp-Ps 140	11QPs[a], col. XXVII
Pss 140-134	11QPs[a], cols. XXVII-XXVIII
Pss 143-149	11QPs[a], cols. XXV-XXVI
Pss 144-155	11QPs[a], col. XXIV
Catena-Ps 145	11QPs[a], col. XVI
Pss 145-154	11QPs[a], cols. XVII-XVIII
Pss 146-148	11QPs[a], col. II
Pss 147-104	4QPs[d], cols. I-V
Pss 147-105	11QPs[a], frag. E, col. III
Pss 148-[120]	11QPs[a], cols. II-III
Pss 150-Hymn	11QPs[a], col. XXVI
Pss 154-Plea	11QPs[a], cols. XVIII-XX
Pss 155-142	11QPs[a], cols. XXIV-XXV

While the evidence thus displayed is quite impressive, it is most interesting to note that, when supportive data are arranged alongside conflicting data, instances of *overlap* involving the same groups of psalms are meager indeed.

3. Correlation of Supporting and Conflicting Data to Indicate Degree of Overlap

Psalms-Groups Supporting Canon	Psalms-Groups Conflicting
Pss 5-6	
Pss 12-13	
Pss 15-16	
Pss 17-18	
Pss 26-27	
Pss 27-28	
	Pss 31-33
Pss 33-[34]-35	
Pss 33-34-35-36	
	Pss 38-71
Pss 39-40	
Pss 49-50-51-52-53	
Pss 53-54	
Pss 62-63	
Pss 66-67	
	Pss 38-71
Pss 76-77	
Pss 77-78	
Pss 81-82-83-84-85	
Pss 91-92- [93] -94	Apostrophe-Ps 93
	Pss 93-141
Pss 95-96	
Pss 99-100	
Pss 101-102-103	
Pss 102-103	
	Pss 103-112
	Pss 118-104
	Pss 147-104
	Pss 104-147
Pss 105-106?	Pss 105-146
Pss 107-[108?]-109	
	Pss 103-112
Pss 112-113	
Pss 114-115	
Pss 115-116	
Pss 116-[117]-118	
	Pss 118-104
	Pss 132-119

Psalms-Groups Supporting Canon	Psalms-Groups Conflicting
	Pss 119-135
	Pss 148-[120]
Pss [120]-121-122-123-124-125-126-127-128-129-130-131-132	
	Pss 132-119
	Pss 141-133
	Pss 133-144
	Pss 140-134
	Pss 134-151A
	Pss 119-135
Pss 135-136	
	Pss 136-Catena
	Pss 139-137
Pss 137-138	
	Pss 138-Sirach 51
	Plea-Ps 139
	Pss 139-137
	David's Comp.-Ps 140
	Pss 140-134
	Pss 93-141
	Pss 141-133
Pss 142-143	
	Pss 143-149
	Pss 133-144
	Pss 144-155
	Catena-Ps 145
	Pss 145-154
	Pss 105-146
	Pss 146-148
	Pss 104-147
	Pss 147-104
	Pss 148-[120]
	Pss 143-149
Pss 149-150	
	Pss 150-Hymn

From this arrangement of the materials it becomes evident that, as far as the Qumran psalms manuscripts themselves are concerned, there are, in fact, only *three* instances of overlap between these two categories of evidence.

Conflicts with Canon	Supports Canon
1. Apostrophe-Ps 93 (11QPs[a]) 2. Pss 93-141 (11QPs[a])	4QPs[b] preserves the canonical order of Pss 91-92-[93]-94

3. Pss 105-146 (11QPs[a])	c. 4QPs[e] preserves possible canonical order of Pss 105-106(?)

It should be noted that all *three* instances of conflict occur in a single Ms (11QPs[a]) while supportive data are derived from two separate Mss (4QPs[b] and 4QPs[e]). The mutual support of these two Mss is somewhat diminished, however, when one observes that, of the two, 4QPs[e] is able to support the canonical arrangement only by hypothetical reconstruction of its fragmentary text. Further, since 4QPs[e] may also contain the non-canonical juxtaposition of Pss 118(?)-104, one should be careful not to make more of its supportive readings than the evidence allows.

If this questionable occurrence is omitted from consideration, we are left with only two instances of overlap from two Mss (11QPs[a] vs. 4QPs[b]). 4QPs[b], however, is not unambiguous in its support of the canonical arrangement of the psalms. It evidences its own major conflict with the canonical sequence when it *omits* the entire group of Pss 104-111 and juxtaposes the two bordering psalms 103 and 112. As a result one is left without a single example from a fully supportive manuscript in opposition to any of these instances of conflict.

The correlation of instances of support or contradiction of MT order with the segment of the Five Book Division in which they occur, while far from conclusive, does yield data consistent with the theory of gradual stabilization of the Psalter from beginning to end as proposed by Sanders.

1. Book One (Pss 1-42)

8 Mss yield 10 examples of confirmation of the MT arrangement of 29 pss from this division. This is to be compared with only two Mss exhibiting a total of three instances of variation involving three pss.

2. Book Two (Pss 43-72)

Here two Mss, in four instances confirm the MT arrangement of six pss from this book. By contrast, only a single Ms evidences an isolated example of variant juxtaposition affecting *one* ps (Ps 71).

3. Book Three (Pss 73-89)

The pinnacle of agreement with MT is reached in this book where three Mss, each exhibiting a single example of confirmation involving 6 pss, stand uncontested by any evidence of variation in this section.

4. Book Four (Pss 90-106)

A clear change is observable beginning with Book Four in the increased occurrence of examples of variation. MT is supported by three

Mss with a total of three instances of confirmation affecting 15 pss. In contrast, six instances of variant order from two Mss and involving six pss, indicate a marked increase over the first three sections.

5. Book Five (Pss 107-150)

This tendency continues to increase in the last division of the Psalter. Here 11 instances supporting MT arrangement of 28 pss are found in five Mss. Evidence of contradiction increases sharply with 20 examples of variation involving 25 pss taken from only four Mss.

The implications seem to be clear. While evidence in support of the MT arrangement of pss is fairly consistent throughout, examples of variation, practically non-existent in the first three books, increase markedly in Books Four and Five. While this evidence does not "prove" Sanders's thesis, it is certainly suggestive, especially when combined with an analysis of the information in relation to the relative age of the Mss in which it occurs. If one arranges all the significant Mss (those which either contradict MT or support it fully in all verifiable instances) according to date, a significant relationship emerges (see table 3, p. 122). There is a direct correlation between date and support or contradiction of the MT arrangement, with contradictory Mss occupying the earliest position and totally supportive Mss only appearing much later. Admittedly the evidence is fragmentary and not conclusive, but it is at least suggestive that there is *no* fully supportive Ms dated prior to the first half of the first century A.D. The impression gained from this analysis is of a certain looseness in pss arrangement which continued until ca. A.D. 50 and apparently died out soon thereafter.

EVIDENCE OF EXPLICIT EDITORIAL COMMENTS

In most instances where evidence is available, the Qumran texts support the MT 150 data regarding s/ss, p/ss, doxologies and hllwyh's. Out of 76 instances of comparison, the QMss agree with MT in 64. There are, on the other hand, twelve instances in which the Qumran texts contradict the evidence of MT by omitting or altering significantly those editorial statements found in MT or by adding such comments where MT lacks them. The following is a brief listing of these variations. For a full listing of the QPss data for the pss-headings compared with MT, see Appendix A.

MANUSCRIPT	DATE	RELATIONSHIP TO MT
4QPs^{a}	Mid 2nd c B.C.	Contradictory
4QPs^{f}	ca. 50 B.C.	Contradictory
4QPs^{d}	Mid 1st c B.C.	Contradictory
4QPs^{b}	2nd half 1st c B.C.	Contradictory
4QPs^{e}	1st half 1st c A.D.	Contradictory
11QPs^{a}	30-50 A.D.	Contradictory
11QPs^{b}	1st half 1st c A.D.	Contradictory
MasPs 1039-160	1st half 1st c A.D.	Supportive
4QPs^{q}	Mid 1st c A.D.	Contradictory
4QPs^{s}	50 A.D.	Supportive
4QPs^{c}	50-68 A.D.	Supportive
5/6 ḤevPs	2nd half 1st c A.D.	Supportive

INCONCLUSIVE MSS

DATE NOT ESTABLISHED	INSUFFICIENT CONTENTS	
11QPs^{c}—Supportive	4QPs^{g}	4QPs^{l}
11QPs^{d}—Supportive	4QPs^{h}	4QPs^{m}
11QPs^{e}—Supportive	4QPs^{j}	4QPs^{n}
4QPs^{r}—Supportive	4QPs^{k}	4QPs^{p}

Table 3. Qumran Mss Arranged by Date

Ps 33. In 4QPs[q], this ps bears the s/s ldwyd šyr mzmwr which is not present in MT. In 4QPs[a], however, it seems most likely that *no* s/s was written with this ps.

Ps 93. The 11QPs[a] version includes a hllwyh s/s contrary to MT.

Ps 100. 4Qps[b] omits the MT s/s mzmwr ltwdh.

Ps 103. While 4QPs[b] lacks the MT's ldwyd, 11QPs[a] apparently contained this s/s.

Ps 104. 11QPs[a] adds a ldwyd s/s while 4QPs[d] agrees with MT by omitting it.

Ps 116. 4QPs[e] probably lacked MT's hllwyh s/s.

Pss 121 and 123. Minor variations on the MT s/ss are noted in the 11QPs[a] version of these two pss. For Ps 121, 11QPs[a] reads šyr hmᶜlwt versus MT šyr lmᶜlwt. For 123, MT's šyr hmᶜlwt is replaced by šyr ldwyd lmᶜlwt.

Ps 144. 11QPs[a] omits MT's ldwyd s/s.

Ps 145. An additional p/s, contrary to MT, is found here in 11QPs[a]. The p/s reads: . . . zwʾt lzkrwn. . . . The context which immediately follows is broken and the purpose of the p/s is obscured.

Pss 148 and 150. For both these pss, 11QPs[a] omits MT's hllwyh s/s.

There is no apparent correlation between date of variant Mss and the evidence of explicit comments. Variations occur in Mss dating from the second half of the first century B.C. (4QPs[b]) to the middle of the first century A.D. (11QPs[a]). There also appears to be no simple correlation between agreement/variation and particular Ms. One Ms may agree and disagree with MT in different instances of comparison.

In addition to the canonical pss discussed above, certain of the "apocryphal" compositions have been provided with s/ss comparable to those found in the MT 150 collection. Van der Ploeg discusses one such composition in 11QPsAp[a] which bears the s/s ldwyd.[7] 11QPs[a] preserves two historical s/ss attached to the apocryphal pss 151 A and 151 B. Their s/s are:

151 A	hllwyh ldwyd bn yšy
151 B	tḥlt gbwrh ldwyd mšmšḥw nbyʾ ʾlwhym

The largest explicit editorial comment from the QMss does not occur in MT and, in fact has no comparison there. I refer to the extended

[7] J. P. M. van der Ploeg, "Petit rouleau," 128, 135-36.

prose composition in 11QPs[a], col. XXVII which is generally designated "David's Compositions." There is no comparable prose comment anywhere in the canonical Psalter. This addition is most important for our understanding of the structure and purpose of the Qumran Psalms Scroll (11QPs[a]) and will be discussed later.

11QPs[a]—Schematic Presentation of Contents

The fragmentary state of the QPssMss makes impossible (in most instances) the reconstruction of extended portions of their contents with sufficient precision to allow analysis of the use of explicit editorial statements in the grouping and arrangement of pss materials. The one exception in this regard is the Qumran Psalms Scroll (11QPs[a]) which is sufficiently well preserved to allow considerable analysis. The following is a schematic presentation of the contents of 11QPs[a] with the data for editorial comments displayed. Brackets [] contain restorations based on MT as well as space considerations. Parentheses () contain restoration on the basis of MT alone where space considerations could not be determined. Dots . . . . intervene between s/ss and p/ss.

Ps	Editorial Comment
101	[ldwyd mzmwr]
102	[tplh l]ᶜny ky yᶜṭw[p wlpny yhwh yšpwk śyḥw]
103	[ldwyd]
109	(lmnṣḥ ldwyd mzmwr?)
118	hwdw lyhwh ky ṭwb . . . . no p/s
104	ldwyd . . . . hllwyh
147	?] . . . . [hllwyh?]
105	hwdw lyhwh ky ṭwb . . . . (hllwyh?)
146	?] . . . . hllwyh
148	no s/s . . . . (hllwyh?)
[120]	(šyr hmᶜlwt?)
121	šyr hmᶜlwt
122	šyr hmᶜlwt ldwyd
123	šyr l]dwyd lmᶜlwt
124	(šyr hmᶜlwt ldwyd?)
125	[šyr hmᶜlwt]
126	šyr hmᶜlwt
127	[šyr hmᶜlwt] lšlwmh
128	(šyr hmᶜlwt?)
129	š[yr hmᶜlwt]
130	šyr hmᶜlwt

Ps	Editorial Comment
131	[šyr hm ᶜlwt ldwyd]
132	(šyr hm ᶜlwt?)
119	no s/s . . . . no p/s
135	(hllwyh?) . . . . hllwyh
136	hwdw lyhwh ky ṭwb . . . . no p/s
Catena	hwdw lyhwh ky ṭwb . . . . hllwyh
145	tplh ldwyd . . . . zwʾt lzkrwn
154	?
Plea	?
139	(lmnṣḥ ldwyd mzmwr?)
137	no s/s . . . . n p/s
138	ldwyd . . . . no p/s
Sir.	no s/s . . . . no p/s
Apos.	no s/s . . . . no p/s
93	hllwyh . . . . [?]
141	(mzmwr ldwyd?) . . . . no p/s
133	šyr hm ᶜlwt ldwyd . . . . no p/s
144	no s/s . . . . no p/s
155	no s/s . . . . [?]
142	(mśkyl ldwyd bhywt bmᶜrh tplh?) . . . . no p/s
143	mzmwr ldwyd . . . . [?]
149	[?] . . . . hllwyh
150	no s/s . . . . hllwyh
Hymn	no s/s . . . . [?]
2 Sam	[?] . . . . no p/s
David	no s/s . . . . no p/s
140	lmnṣḥ mzmwr ldwyd . . . . [?]
134	(šyr hmᶜlwt?) . . . . no p/s
151 A	hllwyh ldwyd bn yšy . . . . no p/s
151 B	tḥlt gbwrh ldwyd mšmšḥw nbyʾ ʾlwhym . . . . [?]

This schema reveals several interesting types of groupings highlighted by the juxtaposition of their s/ss and p/ss. The most obvious type brings together (on three occasions in this Ms) pss concluded with the familiar formula hllwyh. On two occasions these hllwyh groups are further connected with pss beginning with the characteristic phrases hwdw lyhwh ky ṭwb ky lᶜwlm ḥsdw.

a. Toward the end of the scroll (col. XXVI) the combination of Pss 149-150 is found.

149	[no s/s] . . . . hllwyh
150	no s/s . . . . hllwyh

This juxtaposition corresponds with the MT tradition and is not unexpected.

b. A more complex arrangement is found in cols. XIV-XVI.

135 no s/s . . . . hllwyh
136 hwdw lyhwh ky ṭwb. . . . . no p/s
Cat. hwdw lyhwh ky ṭwb. . . . . hllwyh

Regardless of whether the Catena which occurs here is a separate composition or is to be considered an expansion of Ps 136, the result is a grouping with a decidedly *chiastic* structure.

c. The last group of this type consists of the conjunction of six pss variously exhibiting hllwyh and hwdw elements.

118 hwdw lyhwh ky ṭwb. . . . . no p/s
104 ldwyd . . . . hllwyh
147 [no s/s] . . . . [hllwyh]
105 hwdw lyhwh ky ṭwb. . . . . [?]
146 [?]. . . . . hllwyh
148 no s/s . . . . [hllwyh]

The regularity of structure is striking as is the drastic variation from the MT arrangement. No two pss occur in their canonical order. The regular alternation between hwdw and hllwyh pss is made all the more obvious since the second hwdw phrase (Ps 105) is the result of an "addition" not to be found in the MT version of this ps. There 105 begins with the similar phrase hwdw lyhwh qrʾw bšmw. The effect of the Qumran version is to fill out the symmetry of the grouping. It is difficult to view this move as unintentional.

Similar groupings of hllwyh pss are incorporated in the fourth and fifth books of the MT Psalter (Pss 90-150)

a. Pss 104-106
104 . . . . hllwyh
105 . . . . hllwyh
106 hllwyh-hwdw . . . . doxology-hllwyh

b. Ps 111-117
111 hllwyh . . . .
112 hllwyh . . . .
113 hllwyh . . . .
114 ------ . . . . -----

115 ------ . . . . hllwyh
116 ------ . . . . hllwyh
117 ------ . . . . hllwyh

c. Ps 135 (stands alone)

135 hllwyh . . . . hllwyh

d. Pss 146-150

146 hllwyh . . . . hllwyh
147 hllwyh . . . . hllwyh
148 hllwyh . . . . hllwyh
149 hllwyh . . . . hllwyh
150 hllwyh . . . . hllwyh

A survey of these groupings and comparison with those of 11QPs[a] underlines a similarity of function in both texts. The first appearance of a group of hllwyh pss in the canonical Psalter (Pss 104-106) coincides precisely with the conclusion of the fourth book as indicated by the "doxology" at the end of Ps 106. The last grouping of such pss (146-150) occurs at the very end of the whole Psalter. This fact suggests that groups of hllwyh pss are used to mark the conclusion of segments of the Psalter—at least in the last two books.

Comparison with the 11QPs[a] data would seem to support this hypothesis. Following the pss grouping 101-102-103-109, which, except for 102, are all Davidic, the deliberately ornate combination of Pss 118-104-147-105-146-148 clearly indicates a transitional break before the series of hmᶜlwt pss which follows. At the conclusion of this second segment (which leads up to and includes Ps 119) a further hllwyh group (Pss 135-136-Catena) marks an additional break.

The remainder of the text is more obscure. There is a clear division/conclusion in col. XXVI with Pss 149-150 (and possibly including the "Hymn" if Skehan is correct) just prior to the "Last Words of David" (2 Sam 23:1-7) which apparently introduces the prose commentary on "David's Compositions." There may be an earlier division in col. XXII where the single Ps 93 is introduced by a hllwyh s/s (contrary to MT) analogous to canonical Ps 135 which also stands alone.

Here in 11QPs[a] then, hllwyh pss groupings stand at two rather clear points of disjunction: (1) just prior to the concluding discussion of David (2 Sam 23:1-7; "David's Compositions") and (2) just prior to the "Psalms of Ascent" (120-132). The indications are strong that the other occurrences of hllwyh pss groupings in both texts exercise the same "concluding" function.

This use in the Hebrew PssMss of "Praise" (hllwyh) pss to conclude segments of a collection is clearly related to the identical technique employed in the Sumerian Temple Hymns and their Abū Ṣalābīkh prototype (cf. chapter 2). There may also be some relation to the practice, in *CAT.* 10 of the hymnic incipits, of concluding each segment with an invocation of good health. There, however, the recipient of blessing is not the deity, but the commissioner of the catalogue. In any regard, this common technique of long standing should lead us to accept these groupings of hllwyh pss in the Hebrew Mss as editorial techniques to indicate the boundaries of discrete segments of the larger collection.

The juxtaposition of hwdw and hllwyh pss in 11QPs[a] calls for further comment. Here such juxtaposition seems to be part of the technique indicating closure of the preceding section. The juncture of hllwyh and hwdw is not without its representatives in MT. In fact, H. G. Williamson, in his book *Israel in the Books of Chronicles,*[8] cites Pss 106, 107, 118 and 136 as examples of hllwyh and hwdw combined in the same pss. He styles this connection "a standard expression in temple worship" and would like to trace its origins to Ps 100:4f.:

> bwʾ šʿryw *btwdh* ḥṣrtyw *bthlh*
> *hwdw* lw brkw šmw
> ky ṭwb yhwh lʿwlm ḥsdw

Williamson goes on to suggest that this combination of hllwyh and hwdw "is clearly a form of words that was familiar to the authors of Chr. and Ezr.-Neh."[9]

1 Chr 16:41	lhwdwt lyhwh ky lʿwlm ḥsdw
2 Chr 5:13	lhll wlhdwt lyhwh . . . wbhll lyhwh ky ṭwb ky lʿwlm ḥsdw
2 Chr 7:3	whwdwt lyhwh ky ṭwb ky lʿwlm ḥsdw
2 Chr 20:21	mhllym . . . hwdw lyhwh ky lʿwlm ḥsdw
Ezra 3:10f.	bhll wbhwdt lyhwh ky ṭwb ky lʿwlm ḥsdw

Williamson limits his discussion to single pss which combine both hllwyh and hwdw s/s. He must resort to limited textual traditions for

---

[8]H. G. Williamson, *Israel in the Books of Chronicles* (Cambridge: Cambridge University Press, 1977), pp. 47f.

[9]Williamson, *Israel in the Books of Chronicles,* 47.

most of his examples. For instance, in no Hebrew Mss does Ps 107 begin with hllwyh. Williamson must rely on LXX alone to maintain his case. The same is true for Pss 118 and 136. Only Ps 106 seems to fulfill his requirements without question. Only a few Mss and the Syriac omit the s/s for this ps. Regardless of the forced nature of his evidence, Williamson has made a significant observation, especially if his thesis is expanded beyond single pss to include groupings of consecutive pss such as are found in 11QPs[a]. One clear example in MT is the grouping of Pss 104-105-106 mentioned above.

A single qualification needs to be made *apropos* the evidence of MT. Taking Pss 104-105-106-107 as the point of departure, it becomes clear that MT makes a slightly different use of hllwyh and hwdw pss than would be expected from the discussion above. It is true that in the grouping 104-105-106 we have the combination of hllwyh and hwdw pss at the conclusion of a segment of the MT Psalter. With the addition of Ps 107, however, the picture changes considerably.

104	. . . . hllwyh
105	. . . . hllwyh
106	hllwyh-hwdw . . . . doxology-hllwyh
107	hwdw. . . . .

Here we have the addition of another ps beginning with the characteristic hwdw phrases. One would expect this ps to form part of the conclusion to the preceding segment. But the doxology at the end of Ps 106, marking the end of Book Four, clearly makes this impossible. Does this supply the key to understand the position of Pss 118 and 136 as well? Both immediately follow hllwyh groupings. The situation with Ps 107 would seem to indicate that these pss (118 and 136) do not form part of the conclusion, but *introduce* the segment which follows. This question will be considered more thoroughly at a later point.

Regardless of the ultimate solution of this issue all these factors confirm that the conjunctions of hllwyh and hwdw pss in these texts are not coincidental, but are the result of conscious arrangement according to accepted traditions and serve to mark the "seams" of the larger Psalter collection.

A second obvious group-type preserved in 11QPs[a], the šyr hmᶜlwt pss (MT Pss 120-134), occur here, for the most part, in an arrangement identical to that of MT. The following observations are significant. (1) While Ps 120 is not extant in 11QPs[a], it is almost certain that it has been lost in the lacuna preceding col. III. (2) The arrangement of consecutive pss is identical with MT for Pss [120]-132. (3) Pss 133 and 134, however, do not occur with the main collection. They appear separately (from the collection and from each other) in cols. XXIII and XXVIII respectively. Ps 133, even in isolation bears the s/s šyr hmᶜlwt ldwyd as in MT. Ps 134's s/s is not extant, but may well have been present. (4) The extant s/ss of the collection conform to MT with the exception of slight variations in Ps 121 (hmᶜlwt for MT's lmᶜlwt) and Ps 123 (šyr l]dwyd lmᶜlwt for MT's šyr hmᶜlwt).

This group of pss has been discussed in some detail in regards to Skehan's assertion that it indicates the dependence of 11QPsª on a prior, fixed MT 150 Psalter, with the conclusion advanced that Skehan's argument is not ultimately convincing. While the issues of priority and dependence may not be capable of final resolution, one fact is manifestly certain: 11QPsª has chosen (purposely) to separate pss 133 and 134 from MT 150's fuller collection. The key issue here is *purpose* which lies behind the opposing forms. This question will be taken up again in a discussion of the purposeful arrangement of 11QPsª as a whole.

The discussion of the s/s of Ps 123 with its non-MT attribution to David serves as a transition to the final pss-grouping noted here. I intend to refer, of course, to compositions which bear in their s/ss the common formula ldwyd. Several points will be raised concerning the occurrence of such compositions in 11QPsª. (1) In comparison to MT 150, there seems to be a *tendency* to multiply cases of Davidic attribution. Out of a total of fifty hymnic compositions included in 11QPsª (considering *Catena* as a separate composition and omitting "David's Compositions" as non-hymnic), 19 are attributed to David, compared with 17 Davidic pss in MT 101-150 (which is roughly equivalent to the Qumran text in content). Considering that 11QPsª completely omits MT's Davidic Pss 108 and 110 and that the Qumran version of Ps 144 omits any reference to David, this means that 11QPsª attributes five additional pss to David which are not so designated in MT 150. Of the five (2 Sam 23:1-7; Pss 151 A; 151 B; 104; 123), three are apocryphal works not contained in MT 150 while two are canonical works which here contain Davidic headings. While this might be compared to the similar tendency observed in LXX, there appears to be *no* firm correlation between the Greek text and 11QPsª in this regard. In the case of Ps 104, 11QPsª's addition agrees with LXX against MT, but for Ps 123, 11QPsª's ldwyd has no reflex in LXX.[10]

(2) Davidic pss are more consistently distributed throughout 11QPsª than in MT 101-150. The longest consecutive grouping of Davidic pss here

---

[10]For the expansive tendency of the LXX, see A. Pietersma, "David in the Greek Psalms,"" *VT* 30 (1980) 213-26.

is three (122-123-124). The rest are distributed in four pairs and eight single pss. By comparison, almost half (8 out of 17) of MT's Davidic pss in this section occur in a single grouping (138-145). There is a further group of three (108-110) and six single pss (101, 103, 122, 124, 131, 133). The effect of this broad distribution of Davidic pss in 11QPs[a] is to eliminate clear Davidic—non-Davidic oppositions and to give the whole text a decidedly "Davidic" tone. Coupled with the use of the prose piece "David's Compositions," it is difficult to escape the impression that the intent is to cast an aura of Davidic authority over the whole text, even those compositions not explicitly attributed to him.

This survey of the QPss evidence for the consecutive arrangement of pss would not be complete without a discussion of those occasions on which pss, included in MT 150 as distinct compositions, are joined as a single work at Qumran. There are several instances of such combination, some more certain than others.

1. Pss 38 and 71 (4QPs[a], frag. g)

As the analysis above shows, these two pss are clearly written together in this text. There is no blank line or blank space between the concluding words of Ps 38 and those beginning Ps 71. Since this transition takes place in the middle of a single line of text, it is impossible to escape the conclusion they were read as one.

This combination of Ps 71 with a preceding ps is most interesting in light of the Mss evidence cited in the critical apparatus of *BHS*. It seems that many ancient Mss of the Hebrew Psalter are known to combine Ps 71 and Ps 70. In MT (and related Mss), this combination is related to the lack of a s/s for Ps 71. For Pss 3-89 (omitting 1 and 2 as introductory) there are only four pss which do not bear a s/s of any kind (Pss 10, 33, 43, 71). For each of these there is strong Mss evidence for combination with the ps which precedes (10 with 9; 33 with 32; 43 with 42; 71 with 70). One is inclined to explain this phenomenon of combination as a secondary attempt to resolve the "problem" presented by the presence of such "untitled" pss in their MT context. A similar tendency can perhaps be discerned in the LXX treatment of Ps 33(32); 43(42); 71(70). LXX resolves this discrepancy by providing each offending ps with a s/s not known to MT. The Greek text also combines Pss 9 and 10 into a single composition.

This inclination is somewhat mitigated by the evidence of 4QPs[a] for the combination of Pss 38 and 71. Such a combination cannot be the result of the arrangement of pss in MT 3-89. It is certainly feasible to conclude that 4QPs[a] preserves a memory of a tradition in which Ps 71 did not stand alone, but was known to exist as part of a larger composition.

There are clear similarities of theme and actual wording in Pss 38 and 70 which are further paralleled in Ps 71.

a.	38:23	make haste to help me	hwšh lʿzrty
	70:2	O Lord, make haste to help me	YHWH lʿzrty hwšh
	70:6-7	O God, hasten to me, my help	ʾlwhym hwšh lyʿzry
	71:12	O my God, make haste to help me	ʾlwhym lʿzrty hwšh
b.	38:12	(those) who seek my life	mbqšy npšy
		(those) who seek my hurt	dršy rʿty
	70:3	(those) who seek my life	dršy npšy
		(those) who desire my hurt	ḥpṣy rʿty
	71:13	(those) who seek my hurt	mbqšy rʿty
	71:24	(those) who seek my hurt	mbqšy rʿty

It is also interesting to note that MT Pss 38 and 70 are the only two pss to bear in their titles the term lhzkyr.

Ps 38	mzmwr ldwd lhzkyr
Ps 70	lmnṣḥ ldwd lhzkyr

These parallels might explain the confusion (?) of Pss 38 and 70 at Qumran.

The matter is further complicated by the fact that Ps 70 is itself almost identical with Ps 40:14-18. The freedom with which pss and portions of pss are combined to create new compositions is well attested within MT itself. We should not be surprised then to find such methods at work at Qumran as well, especially in the case of Ps 71 with its strong Mss tradition of combination.

2. Pss 114 and 115 (4QPs^{o})

While the data for this combination is not completely unambiguous (being based on a severely limited fragment), my reconstruction of the text indicates these two pss were juxtaposed with no apparent indication of a separation. *BHS* also notes that Codex Leningradensis, many Mss of LXX, Theodotion, Syriac and Jerome combine Pss 114 and 115. Again, this might be related to the absence of either s/s or p/s for Ps 114 in most traditions. As the ps is preceded by Pss 111-113, all bearing hllwyh p/ss, it could not be combined with Ps 113. It has therefore, been connected with Ps 115 which bears a hllwyh p/s, but no s/s. This combination removes the "difficulty" of an "untitled" ps standing in the midst of a series of pss each bearing a hllwyh p/s (111-113; 115-117).

3. Pss 92 and 93 (4QPs^b, col. V)

4. Pss 94 and 95 (4QPs^b, col. VIII)

Less certain than the preceding are the combinations of Pss 92 and 93; 94 and 95 found in 4QPs^b. Uncertainty is due to the large amount of restoration necessary to reconstruct these columns. While *BHS* indicates no evidence to support these combinations, Kennicott's survey of Hebrew Mss[11] cites eight codices which combine pss 92 and 93 as well as six codices confirming the connection of Pss 94 and 95 (see table 4, pp. 134-35). The tendency to combine these pss may again be related to the paucity of explicit s/ss marking the boundaries between individual compositions. As previously mentioned, in the first three books of the Psalter (Pss 1-89) only six pss are included without some explicit comment attached (Pss 1, 2, 10, 33, 43, 71) and it is precisely these pss that appear subject to the combination tendency mentioned. For Book Four, however, 9 out of 17 pss occur with no s/s, while in Book Five a further nine (out of 44) occur. Whereas, in the first three books, untitled pss are isolated occurrences, in Books Four and Five they most frequently stand together in groups (91, 93-97, 99; 118-119; 136-137). The evidence of Kennicott indicates a clear tendency in many Ms traditions to combine such untitled pss. Indeed, where these pss occur in groups, some Mss combine all into a single extensive composition (see table 4, pp. 134-35).

Does this evidence of combination preserve an ancient tradition of intentional association of hymnic compositions or is it merely the result

---

[11]While the Mss evidence of Kennicott and de Rossi is admittedly very late, it may in certain instances (as in the combination of Pss 9 and 10) reflect very early tradition and cannot be dismissed out of hand. It certainly serves a purpose in confirming the tendency to combine certain pss as opposed to the total lack of such a tendency for the vast majority of pss.

CODICES	PSALMS COMBINED																						
	A	B	C	D	E	F	G	H	I	J	K	L	M	N	O	P	Q	R	S	T	U	V	W	X
17	X																							
36				X			X					X	X	X		X				X				
37	X									X		X					X			X				
67													X											
74			X						X	X	X	X		X	X	X	X			X		X	X	
82				X		X				X										X				
89				X						X								X						
93						X				X		X		X		X	X			X	X			
94																		X		X				
97			X		X	X		X	X	X	X	X		X	X	X	X			X		X	X	
99																						X		
131																		X		X				
133			X		X	X		X	X	X	X	X		X	X	X	X			X		X	X	
137			X																					
141														X							X			X
142	X																			X				
145														X										
150																				X	X			
155						X												X						
156				X		X											X				X			
164	X																							
173			X								X				X	X	X				X	X		
178				X																X				
206						X	X																	
210			X	X																				
216	X			X																X				
220																		X	X	X	X			
222		X																X		X				
239																					X			
245			X	X		X			X								X						X	
259							X																	
260				X		X			X															
326				X					X															
356				X															X		X			
409	X			X																	X			
499				X																	X			
505	X																							
541			X																		X			
590				X		X																		
681										X														
6 cc.																				X				
12cc.																					X			
13cc.																		X						
25cc.				X																				

Table 4. Kennicott: Data for the Combination of Psalms in Various Mss.

Explanation of Symbols for Pss Combined in Table 4

A - Pss	1/2	M - Pss	95/96
B - Pss	9/10	N - Pss	96/97
C - Pss	32/33	O - Pss	97/98
D - Pss	42/43	P - Pss	98/99
E - Pss	47/48	Q - Pss	103/104
F - Pss	70/71	R - Pss	114/115
G - Pss	71/72	S - Pss	115/116
H - Pss	73/74	T - Pss	116/117
I - Pss	90/91	U - Pss	117/118
J - Pss	92/93	V - Pss	118/119
K - Pss	93/94	W - Pss	134/135
L - Pss	94/95	X - Pss	144/145

of mistaken (secondary) combination of pss rising from their sequential juxtaposition in a fixed order without indication of boundaries? Were it not for the evidence of 4QPs[a] for the unification of Ps 38 and 71, I would be inclined to accept the secondary nature of these combinations. There, however, we have evidence of an independent tradition for the combination of Ps 71 which cannot be the result of its association with the sequential arrangement of pss in MT 150.

As a result, I suggest that the occurrence in MT of isolated pss without s/ss may indicate an editorial technique intended to preserve conflicting traditions as to the proper combination/division of the discrete units within the Psalter. While each ps is written separately, the lack of a s/s preserves the tradition of its combination with what precedes. Such a method might be compared with the k[e]tîv - q[e]rê system, which some think is intended to preserve alternate readings without judging the superiority of either.[12]

I would think this technique most likely to be in effect in cases of isolated, untitled pss. For those instances, preserved in Kennicott's Mss, of the connection of numerous consecutive pss, other considerations (largely positional) are more likely involved, and the combination is probably secondary. I will return to this topic in a discussion of its significance for the arrangement of MT 150.

In summary, the QPssMss yield evidence which illumines the question concerning the combination of certain pss in some Mss traditions. The Qumran material would seem to support the traditions for the

---

[12]Shemaryahu Talmon, "Double Readings in the Massoretic Text," *Textus* 1 (1960) 144-84; "Synonymous Readings in the Textual Traditions of the Old Testament," *Scripta Hierosolymitana* 8 (1961) 335-83.

combination of MT Pss 70-71 (indirectly) and 114-115. The Q support of these combinations suggests the existence in MT of an editorial technique intended to preserve alternate traditions of the combination/division of pss. By this method the disputed ps was included as a separate unit, but without any s/s, indicating that in some Mss traditions it was read as a part of the preceding ps.

A brief review of the primary findings regarding the use of explicit editorial comments at Qumran will serve to conclude this segment. The criteria which are operative in the juxtaposition of pss would seem to be of two major types: (1) Ps-types and (2) Functional concerns. The former are divided into two categories: (a) genre-groupings and (b) author-groupings. Genre groups isolated include: (1) hllwyh pss; (2) šyr hmʿlwt pss; (3) hwdw pss. Of these, the šyr hmʿlwt pss would appear to have been brought together largely for genre considerations, while the hllwyh and hwdw pss exhibit other important functional considerations involved in their grouping and position.

Author-groupings are rather limited in the QPssMss. Besides pss attributed to David there are only *four* cases of attribution to other authors, all of which correspond to the MT.

1. Ps 49 (4QPs^{c})	[lmnṣḥ] lbny qrḥ mzmwr
2. Ps 77 (4QPs^{e})	[lmnṣḥ]ʿl ydwtwn lʾs[p mzmwr
3. Ps 88 (4QPs^{e})	. . . . l]hymn hʾzr [ḥy . . . .
4. Ps 127 (11QPs^{a})	[šyr hmʿlwt] lšlwmh

In 11QPs^{a}, concerns of authorship seem to center around the exaltation of David as psalmist extraordinaire. As mentioned above, the explicit elevation of David in the prose epilogue, coupled with the tendency to multiply attributions of his authorship and the broad distribution of the Davidic pss throughout the scroll, all serve to increase the Davidic tone of the scroll and lend credence to the suggestion that the whole work (at least its contents) is considered Davidic.

The presence of the single non-Davidic attribution to Solomon in Ps 127 invites caution, nevertheless. This Solomonic s/s may owe its existence to being bound up as a part of the šyr hmʿlwt pss. The paucity of attribution to authors other than David is not a phenomenon limited to 11QPs^{a}, however, and cannot be considered conclusive evidence that the whole work is considered his work. Of the 61 pss included in Books Four and Five of MT 150, only two are attributed to persons other than David.

Ps 90	Moses
Ps 127	Solomon (as in 11QPs[a])

Yet, clearly the whole MT 150 Psalter recognizes a number of different authors for its compositions in the first books.

1. David—73 pss
2. Solomon—Pss 72, 127
3. Moses—Ps 90
4. Asaph—Pss 50, 73, 74, 75, 76, 77, 78, 79, 80, 81, 82, 83
5. Sons of Qoraḥ—Pss 44, 45, 46, 47, 48, 49, 84, 85, 87, 88
6. Heman—Ps 88
7. Ethan—Ps 89

Since 11QPs[a] by and large parallels Books Four and Five, the paucity of other authors is not surprising and does not give unique information of the character of 11QPs[a] itself.

Besides "type" considerations governing the grouping and arrangement exposed by the explicit comments appended to the QPss, certain compositions are marked by explicit statements indicating functional concerns. Some of these statements are unique to the QPss, while others are part of the MT tradition as well. In the category of unique functional comments, one must include the rather ambiguous p/s attached to Ps 145:21 in 11QPs[a], col. XVII.

. . . . zwʾt lzkrwn . . . . "this is for a memorial"

The fragmentary nature of the context prevents a final interpretation of the text but it certainly indicates the functional concern of the editor(s). That this phrase is appended to what amounts to the conclusion of the MT 150 Psalter (Pss 146-150 form the concluding *Hallel* and are liturgically dependent on Ps 145:21) is suggestive, though it must remain inconclusive. In the context of the 11QPs[a] arrangement its significance is unclear.

The prose "epilogue" "David's Compositions" must also be considered as functionally oriented. Its purpose is clearly to exalt David as the author of a myriad of pss for a variety of occasions. It may well intend to extend Davidic authorship and authority to all the works of the scroll.

One explicit comment, concerned with function is shared by MT 150 and 11QPs[a]. This is the s/s to Ps 102 preserved in 11QPs[a], frag. B. This s/s, while withholding comment on the genre-classification or authorship of the ps, concerns itself with its use.

> tplh l^{c}ny ky y^{c}ṭwp wlpny yhwh yšpwk śyḥw
> "Prayer of the afflicted, when he is faint and pours out before YHWH his complaint"

The comment is intended to provide guidelines for the proper use of this ps. Two implications are important. (1) The ps is viewed as properly accessible to the *individual* in his need. (2) There is no clear reference here to liturgical activity within the *cult*. If this ps owes its origin to a ritual act within the cult ceremonies, that origin is obscured in its present setting. The picture is of the needy individual who approaches his God, expressing his need in the words of this ps. This s/s in effect has loosed the ps from any cultic associations which may have spawned it and freed it to function on an individual, personal basis.

6

The Hebrew Psalter
I. Evidence of Editorial Shaping

From the previous study of the Mesopotamian and QPss texts, and the editorial/organizational technique and concern demonstrated there, one is almost prepared to find similar technique and concern at work in the organization of the canonical Hebrew Psalter. One expects the editor(s) to make use of explicit as well as tacit methods of organization. It is not surprising, therefore, to find so many of the MT 150 pss bearing s/ss purporting to record author, genre, manner of performance, instrumentation and the like. What *is* surprising, however, is the almost total absence of any explicit statements of organizational intent. Despite the existence of so may s/ss (and one p/s) of obvious secondary origin (i.e., they do not form an integral part of the compositions they accompany, but evidence various secondary concerns), only *one* of these explicit statements can be said to exercise any organizational function. The exceptional case is the p/s preserved in Ps 72:20.

kāllû t^e^pillôt dāwîd ben yišây

"Finished are the prayers of David son of Jesse"

This comment makes it clear that a collection of compositions (here styled "prayers" *t^e^pillôt*) attributed to a single author (*l^e^dāwîd ben yišây*) has come to its conclusion (*kāllû*).

No other *explicit* indicators of segmentation can be isolated in MT 150. The s/ss, regardless of their secondary nature, have no *explicit* concern with the larger question of structure or organization of the whole

Psalter. Each s/s refers only to the *single* composition it heads. Its purpose is "descriptive" and not "organizational."[1]

It is highly suggestive that the positional variation between s/s and p/s seems to be correlated with the functional distinction between "descriptive" and "organizational" concern. The correlation implied (that s/ss, in all cases, "describe" the single composition they precede, while p/ss, on the other hand, indicate the closure of larger blocks of material which precede them) receives support from the editorial positioning of the "doxologies" (which must be considered *tacit* elements)[2] at the *end* of the books they conclude. This use of the doxologies to conclude larger segments of the Psalter is, in addition, consistent with similar practice as observed in the Temple Hymns, the Catalogues of Incipits, and the QPssMss. The more ambiguous data of the hllwyh s/ss and p/ss are no

---

[1]The limited, descriptive concern of the pss-headings to characterize the individual pss which they introduce (in contrast to the broader, editorial concern to structure the Psalter) is confirmed by comparison with the Book of Proverbs, where the six s/ss which can be isolated (1:1; 10:1; 24:23; 25:1; 30:1; 31:1) each refer to a collection or segment containing numerous aphoristic units. This functional difference is accompanied by formal distinctions as well.

(1) While the pss-headings contain a large number of varied genre classifications (mzmwr, šyr, mśkyl, mktm, etc.), evidencing a concern to distinguish between units of different types, the proverbial s/ss employ the most general terms possible (mšly, dbry) to designate the broad spectrum of units included in each collection.

(2) The major concern of *Proverbs* is to separate the aphoristic units according to author (šlmh, gwr, lmwʾl). While authorship does play a part in the pss-headings, it is by no means the *major* concern, as authorship groups are nowhere consistently brought together.

[2]The doxologies are clearly not explicit statements of editorial purpose. Their editorial function becomes apparent only from the broader perspective of one who knows all the doxologies and their structural similarities. Only this comparison of all the examples allows the conclusion that any particular doxology is a "stereotyped formula" used by the editor(s) to indicate the larger divisions of the Psalter.

In fact, many would deny any original editorial purpose for the doxologies. They are instead integral parts of the compositions they accompany and only secondarily and/or accidentally come to be viewed as concluding segments of the Psalter. In this regard see: M. Dahood, *Psalms I* (Garden City, NY: Doubleday, 1965/6) xxx; N. H. Tur-Sinai, "The Literary Character of the Book of Psalms," *Oüdtestamentische Studien* 8 (1950) 264-65.

detraction, since it is best to view these hllwyh elements *not* as editorial comments appended for organizational purposes but as *liturgical* notes associated with their performance, which necessarily preceded the editorial concerns of arrangement. The restriction of p/s evidence to the single example in Ps 72:20 does advise caution, however.[3]

Summary: Anyone, then, who comes to the Psalter expecting to find explicit evidence of editorial organization comparable to the Sumerian and Babylonian tablets (with their summary lines totalling various types of compositions which have been enumerated) is bound to be disappointed. Outside of the single p/s of Ps 72:20, explicit organization of texts is not a feature of MT 150.

---

[3]Perhaps the enigmatic . . . . zwʾt lzkrwn . . . . in the fragmentary text following Ps 145 in 11QPs[a] should be included in the category of concluding p/ss. If so, this comment should indicate the conclusion of a preceding segment. Such a division is not inconsistent with the position in this text of Ps 145, as it immediately follows the hllwyh-hwdw-hllwyh complex of Pss 135-136-Catena, which have already been shown to exercise a similar concluding function.

On the other hand, there is evidence from outside the Psalter of at least one hymnic composition which exhibits a p/s which seems to refer only to that single composition. I refer to the hymn in Habakkuk 3 and its p/s in 3:19 lmnṣḥ bngynwty . The issue is further complicated by the presence in 3:1 of a perfectly acceptable s/s, which is itself quite in keeping with the form and terminology of the pss-headings.

tplh lḥbqwq hnbyʾ ʿl šgynwt

When viewed separately, either s/s or p/s finds analogies in the pss-headings. The attempt to combine the two, however, results in an awkward statement which violates on several accounts the patterns preserved in MT 150 (for more complete data, see Appendix B, pp. 237-38).

Explanations for the p/s vary. It may have been part of the original s/s which has been banished to its present position for editorial considerations (perhaps to smooth the transition from book to ps by removing the technical instructions and highlighting the authorship of Habakkuk). At least one author claims this p/s represents the s/s of a subsequent ps which was inappropriately included when this ps was copied here from its place in a larger collection of pss (Eberhard Nestle, "Miscellen: 3. Das Lied Habakkuks und der Psalter," *ZAW* 20 [1900] 167-68). H. M. I. Gevaryahu cites this comment as evidence that the present pss-headings were originally p/ss analogous to the colophons of clay tablets, and were only subsequently transferred to their current positions at the beginning of the pss (for a list of Gevaryahu's publications on this topic, see note 9 below).

The specific reference of the s/ss to the individual compositions they accompany eliminates them as evidence of *explicit* organizational concern. They refer *explicitly* only to single pss, not to the larger structure of the Psalter. Any organizational concern or purpose of the editor(s) must be inferred from the tacit arrangement of the pss. This does *not* mean that the s/ss are of no use in discerning the editorial organization of MT 150. It does, however, have certain implications for the manner in which I will approach the pss-headings.

The precise definition of the terms contained in the pss-headings has been a matter of concern ever since the early translation of these titles in the ancient versions. As many have noted before, the ancient translators of LXX and the *targumim* must have found many of these technical terms exceedingly obscure, as evidenced by the variety of their renderings.[4] While modern scholarship has brought greater precision to our understanding of these terms, in the final analysis, many still resist all attempts to drag them into the light of day.

In view of the "descriptive" reference of the s/ss to *single* pss rather than to larger structure, I am relieved of the necessity to follow the many masterful attempts to bring further precision to the meaning of these technical terms. Since the purpose of this study is to focus on the "editing of the Hebrew Psalter," it is no longer necessary to know the exact meaning of every term in order to perceive how the s/ss function in the organization of the whole collection. In support of my decision, I offer the following considerations.

1. I have already mentioned the long-standing nature of the problem of obscurity and the rather limited success of the numerous attempts to resolve it.

2. In the face of the general agreement on the cultic nature and origin of these terms, our lack of a clear, non-hypothetical understanding of that cult, especially in regard to its employment of the pss, would seem to present almost insurmountable difficulties in regaining the significance of these terms.

3. Alongside the lack of unambiguous information regarding the cultic setting of the pss-headings, there appears to be a purposeful

---

[4]The obscurity of these technical terms to the translators is a matter of general knowledge. See, for example the statements in W. Staerk, "Zur Kritik der Psalmenüberschriften," *ZAW* 12 (1892) 133; also Sigmund Mowinckel, *The Psalms in Israel's Worship*, vol. 2 (Nashville: Abingdon, 1962) 207.

obscuring of that original setting by the editor(s) which presents a further obstacle. I will expand on this idea.[5]

We find that in the final form of the Psalter the pss (regardless of their *original* setting) have been provided with a new context which influences their usage and function. This movement to provide a new context can be discerned in two instances rather clearly. First, the placement of Ps 1 as an introduction to the whole Psalter (see below) offers the *reader* a pair of "hermeneutical spectacles" through which to view the contents. As a result, those pss which originated in the communal liturgy of the cult are now seen in a new light. Ps 1 emphasizes individual meditation rather than communal recitation. The pss thus become the source of *each* man's search for the path of obedience to the "Torah of YHWH": the path which leads from death to life.

In a similar vein, the historical s/ss, with their references to events in the life of David, provide another avenue of private, individual access to these largely public communal hymns. The expansion of s/ss (which contain technical terms of obvious cultic origin) by the addition of historical/contextual statements relating the pss to particular events in the life of a single individual has the effect of obscuring the original cultic matrix of that ps and loosing it to function on a more personal level.[6] The implication is: If David responded to such events by expressing himself in a ps, then what better way for me to respond to similar conflicts in my own life than to appropriate the words of his classical utterance? Such a movement toward personalization would quickly extend to the remaining pss, regardless of their original function in the cult. This process of extension can be observed at work in the expansive pss-headings of LXX and the *targumim*.[7]

4. This development of a new context for the pss goes hand in hand with the apparent lack of concern on the part of the MT 150 editor(s) to group compositions solely on the basis of genre categories. This feature contrasts sharply with the Babylonian Catalogues of Hymnic Incipits whose strongest organizational criterion is genre. With the single exception of the hmᶜlwt pss (Pss 120-134), there is no one explicitly categorized ps-type which is brought entirely together in MT 150. The same is true of those ps-types isolated by modern Form Criticism. This is not to say

[5]B. S. Childs, *IOTS*, 504-25.

[6]Horst Dietrich Preuss, "Die Psalmenüberschriften in Targum und Midrasch," *ZAW* 71 n.s. 30 (1959) 144-45 (hereafter cited as "Targum").

[7]Preuss, "Targum," 53; B. S. Childs, "Psalm Titles," 143.

there is *no* indication of any grouping. There *are* groups of pss which share common genre categories (Davidic pss 3-41; mśkyl pss 52-55; mktm pss 56-60 and others). The point is: there is no clear effort in MT 150 to gather *all* pss of a single category into a complete collection. Indeed, there is clear evidence that earlier genre collections have been treated quite freely by the Psalter editor(s) who felt no compunction at breaking up such groupings and redistributing their contents according to different considerations (see for example the treatment of the Asaphite, Qorahite and Davidic pss in Pss 42-89).

In view of these considerations, it seems clear that the s/ss were not added editorially to aid in the definition of the *structure* of the Psalter. They are for the most part descriptive statements of cultic origin which refer to the ps to which they are attached. Certain indications suggest that, at the time of the editorial arrangement of the Psalter, these s/ss had already become fixed parts of their compositions with which the editor(s) could not freely tamper.

1. That the headings were translated by LXX and *targumim* in spite of their obvious obscurity, indicates they were fixed and could be neither altered nor omitted.

2. B. S. Childs's suggestion that the historical/contextual comments were late additions necessary to "overcome" the cultic connections of the technical terms and to provide linkage with certain narrative contexts again assumes that these terms were so firmly fixed that they could not be eliminated by the redactors.[8]

3. If at Qumran the scribes, to create an atmosphere of Davidic authority, were forced to resort to the distribution of accepted "Davidic" pss throughout the Psalms Scroll rather than simply by proliferating s/ss (as occurs in LXX and Syriac), it would seem the headings were fixed and immovable.

4. Further, in MT 150 what evidence of editorial activity does exist frequently makes use of "untitled" pss (as Pss 1 and 2; 90-106; 146-150), suggesting these were more adaptable for their editorial purposes than "titled" ones.

5. Finally, the way in which the later editor(s) make use of the s/ss to achieve their organizational purposes, indicates they had to "make do" with what they inherited from past tradition. While there is no evidence that the final editor(s) produced the s/ss to serve editorial ends in the organization of the Psalter, there are indications that they actively utilized these fixed s/ss in their purposeful arrangement of the pss.

---

[8]B. S. Childs, "Psalm Titles."

Summary. For these reasons, further attempts to shed light on the meaning of the various terms of the s/ss, while instructive for our understanding of their *original* use in the cult, would add little or nothing to our understanding of these pss' *secondary* function in the new context of the Psalter. It is this "secondary" function with which I am presently concerned and to which I will return below. There is, however, one further question regarding the nature and function of the pss-headings which must first be addressed: Were the pss-headings originally colophons?

THE HEBREW PSS-HEADINGS AND THE COLOPHONS

The attempt has been made in recent years to demonstrate a common origin for biblical s/ss (titles and headings) and the colophons at the end of cuneiform literary tablets. According to H. M. I. Gevaryahu, all biblical headings, titles, and s/ss were originally colophons written at the end of their respective compositions, which were "shifted" to initial position only at a later date. In their original state, the biblical colophons shared all the concerns expressed in their cuneiform counterparts. However, their peculiar interest in the *authors* of the compositions they accompanied led to the incorporation of biographical data about those authors which has no parallel in the cuneiform tablets. This concern with authorship resulted in a process of selective transmission of the colophonic materials which emphasized such biography and omitted "many technical details about the origin and nature of the text, and the names of the copyist-scribes," that comprised the bulk of the cuneiform colophons.[9] In this manner Gevaryahu attempts to draw together these two editorial phenomena and to explain away the distinctive characteristics which separate them.

---

[9]H. M. I. Gevaryahu has espoused his views in a number of articles, largely in Modern Hebrew. "Ṣrwr hᶜrwt ᶜl swprym wsprym bymy hmqrʾ," ["Notes on Authors and Books in the Days of the Bible"], *Beth Mikra* 43 (1970) 368-74; "ldrky qryʾt hšmwt lspry hmqrʾ," ["On the Method of Giving Names to Biblical Books"], *Beth Mikra* 45 (1971) 146-51; "lmwdym," ["Scribes Disciples in the Book of Isaiah"], *Beth Mikra* 47 (1971) 449-52; "brwk bn nryh hswpr," ["Baruch ben Neriah, the Scribe"], *Zer li-geburot* [Festschrift in honor of the late president Shazar] (Jerusalem: Kiryat-Sepher Ltd., 1973) 227-33; "Biblical Colophons: A Source for the 'Biography' of Authors, Texts and Books," *VTSup* 28 (1975) 42-59 (hereafter cited as "Biblical Colophons").

Gevaryahu is most concerned in his work to draw comparisons between the cuneiform colophons and the titles of the *prophetic* books. He lists the following "informative data included in biblical headings."

> 1. Name of the composition, e.g.: "An oracle concerning Nineveh" (Nahum), "The sayings of the wise" (Proverbs xxii 17; xxiv 23).
> 2. Name of the composition, including the name of the prophet: "The words of Amos" (without naming his father).
> 3. Name of the prophet as well as that of his father: "Isaiah the son of Amoz"; "Hosea the son of Be-eri."
> 4. The social or professional group to which the author belonged: "Amos who was among the shepherds"; "Jeremiah of the priests who were at Anathoth."
> 5. The title "prophet": "The oracle which Habakkuk the prophet saw."
> 6. The town from which the prophet came to Jerusalem: "Micah of Moresheth"; "Jeremiah of Anathoth"; "Nahum of Elkosh."
> 7. Concerning whom and to whom was the prophecy told: "Concerning Judah and Jerusalem," to Moab.
> 8. The date of the prophecy: "In the days of Josiah . . . King of Judah in the 13th year of his reign."
> 9. Chronology of the prophet's activity: "During the reign of the following Kings . . . "
> 10. Reference to historical events: "Two years before the earthquake." (Amos)
> 11 The specific nature of a given psalm: "A prayer of the one afflicted . . . who pours out his complaint before the Lord." (Psalm cii)[10]

Almost all these data (except numbers 5 and 9) have parallels in the colophons collected by Hunger, with the one *caveat* that there they are applied to the "copyist-scribe" and *not* to the purported author as in the biblical headings. This "authorship-gap" in the cuneiform materials leaves Gevaryahu without the necessary connection with the biblical headings. For this reason he cites the catalogues of texts and authors published by W. G. Lambert[11] as evidence the clay-tablet scribes were not totally

---

[10]Gevaryahu, "Biblical Colophons," 48-50.

[11]W. G. Lambert, "Ancestors, Authors, and Canonicity," *JCS* 11 (1957) 1-14; "A Catalogue of Texts and Authors," *JCS* 16 (1962) 59-77.

devoid of interest in authorship. He goes on to suggest that the biographical information included in biblical s/ss was incorporated there from similar catalogue of authors which must have existed in Israel as well.

Regardless of how one decides the issue of common origin, the cuneiform colophons yield very little data for comparison with the pss-headings. With very few exceptions, the cuneiform colophons are concerned with items which the biblical s/ss ignore. Hermann Hunger, in his *Babylonische und assyrische Kolophone* (*BAK*), lists the following statements which occur in cuneiform colophons:[12]

A. Bibliographical Statements
   - Catch phrase (tag-line, incipit)
   - Number of Tablet (in a Series)
   - Title of the Work (or Series)
   - Number of Lines (of the Tablet)

B. Scribal Procedure
   - Assurance of Care Taken in Copying
   - Inspection Process
   - Origin of the Prototype
   - Condition of the Prototype

C. Statements Concerning Persons
   - Credentials of the Scribe
   - The Owner
   - The One Commissioning the Copy
   - The Credentials of the Inspector

D. Other Statements
   - Purpose of the Copy
   - Wish of the Scribe
   - Curses
   - Blessings and Invocations
   - Date Copy was Made

The primary concern of practically all these statements is to assure (or insure) the accurate transmission of the original text in the present copy. The first group consists of scribal techniques employed to identify and fix the particular tablet in relation to other tablets in a series (catch phrase of the following tablet, sequence in the series, title of the series) and to provide a check on the accuracy of the copyist (number of lines). The next group is concerned to assure the reader (presumably the owner or patron) that utmost care has been taken to render an accurate copy of the

---

[12]Hunger, *BAK*, 1. Quotations from Hunger are my own translations of his original German.

original document. Section three describes the credentials of the Scribe and the Inspector and adds further assurances along with flattering phrases directed to the patron or owner. The final group contains the pious wishes of the scribe (again directed to his patron) along with curses and blessings which are called down on those who might respectively deface or protect the tablet in question.

The contents of the pss-headings overlap with the colophons only in a few instances. Besides their consistent interest in authorship, the s/ss evidence a varied concern with (1) genre classification, (2) instructions for cultic performance, (3) historical circumstance of the ps, and (4) function or purpose of the ps. While superficial comparison with colophonic materials is possible for all of these categories, actual correspondence is less than satisfactory.

Genre classification plays an exceedingly minor role in the colophons. A cursory examination of the 563 colophons in *BAK* produced the following *possible* classifications, many of which are probably *not* genre designations, but simply descriptions of contents.

1. dur-gar	Meaning uncertain. (Nr. 39)
2. šìr-nam-šub	"Incantation-song" (Beschwörungslied). Use of this term elsewhere indicates that it is an accepted genre designation. (Nr. 44)
3. šiptu	"Incantation" (Beschwörung). (Nrs. 175, 235, 257)
4. EN	"Incantation" (Beschwörung). (Nr. 425)
5. balag	"Harp(song)" (Harfe[nlied]); a true genre category. (Nr. 112)
6. niqû(SISKUR.SISKUR)	"Sacrifice" (Opfer). (Nr. 301)
7. <u>ṣa-a-tú u šu-ut pî</u>	"Commentary" (Kommentierte Wörter und Kommentar). (Nrs. 113, 168, 409, 410, 411)
8. pirištu(AD.ḪAL)	"Mystery" (Geheimnis). It is uncertain if this constitutes a category. It is always connected with the admonition to keep this tablet from the uninitiated. (Nrs. 206, 221)

The paucity of genre types represented is paralleled by the small number of examples of each. All these categories together yield but 14 (out of 563!) *possible* cases of genre classification in the colophons. It certainly does *not* seem that genre was of much concern to the scribes who wrote the individual colophons.

The second area of comparison yields as little satisfaction as the first. The closest prallels in *BAK* are classified by Hunger as statements of purpose (Zweck).

> Often rituals bear the comment ana ṣabāt epēši "for the performance of a (particular) ritual". . . . In Nr. 219 is written ana pišerti kišpi "for the dissolution [Auflösung] of magic". . . . In a similar manner there often stands under cultic songs ana zamāri "for the performance of song [das Singen]" . . . and ana šuzmur "to cause the Lamentation priests to sing."[13]

There is nothing here comparable to the complicated formulae of the biblical pss-headings. On the whole the terminology is extremely vague or general (the performance of song; the ritual performance). The type of ritual or song is designated only in Nr. 219, "to cause the Lamentation priests to sing." Even here there is no precise indication of melody, instrumentation, or any discussion of the manner of presentation.

It is also interesting that in those texts which indicate they are "for a ritual performance," this designation is consistently augmented by the phrase ḫa-an-tiš nasḫa[ḫa] "quickly excerpted." In light of the ongoing concern of the colophonic scribes to assure their readers of the accuracy of their tablets, this statement approximates a disclaimer for any errors which were the result of haste. By adding this comment the scribe prevents the reader from attributing any error to the scribe's lack of skill. Thus the references to cultic performance indicate no scribal interest in providing information about the text's use or function. In fact, in one instance, we are explicitly told that the specific ritual "has not been written down" (Nr. 200).

The historical information in the colophons most closely corresponds to the dating formulas of the prophetic s/ss. For the most part they merely date the completion of the tablet-copy and have nothing to say about its contents. Only in a very few cases do we find historical data which have bearing on the compositions they accompany.

---

[13] *BAK*, 12.

1. Nr. 290

In the time of Tiglath-pilesar the king of Assur, [a vision] was seen by Aḫassu-Šerū'a in the middle nightwatch. . . . (The context is unfortunately broken.)

2. Nr. 295

47 non-canonical predictions [Vorzeichen] which are related to the fall of the land of Akkad.

3. Nr. 533

Tested and controlled [Tried and True?] ointments and bandages which are suited for use, according to the word of the apkallu-sages from the time before the Flood, which Enlil-muballiṭ, the sage of Nippur left behind in Šuruppak in the second year of Enlil-bāni king of Isin.

Here the colophons begin to approach the concerns of their biblical parallels, since these historical statements are intended to indicate the context in which their compositions were produced.

Hunger feels the colophonic statements of *purpose* can be divided into two cases: (1) those related to the *use* of the tablet and (2) those related to the *compensation* which the scribe expects to receive from the gods. Of the former, I have already discussed those referring to cultic/ritual usage. The purpose or use of the remainder (with one exception)[14] is for "the reading" of some individual or group of individuals. The "reader" is usually the scribe himself but may be "scholars," the owner or patron. Again, these comments serve less to state the purpose or function of the composition than as a justification of the copying process.

In the second class mentioned in *BAK*, the copying process is viewed as an expression of worship of the gods.

ana palāḫ bēlūtī-šu išṭur	"for the reverent worship of the dominion [of the god] has he written" (Nr. 91 and 93)

[14]The exception occurs in Nr. 416 where the tablet is said to have been "hurriedly transcribed" (eilig übertragen) to be used in "dictation" (presumably for a school exercise).

This act of worship is expected to issue in benefit for the scribe from the gods.

ana balāṭ napšātī-šu . . . išṭur	"for the life of his soul . . . has he written" (Nrs. 126 and 129)

Expected benefits include (1) long life, (2) contentment and health, (3) absence of headaches, (4) establishment of position, (5) security of posterity, and others.[15] While these statements of worship and expected reward find many resonances in the *bodies* of the biblical pss, there are no such parallels in the s/ss.

This study of the colophons in *BAK* leads me to question the appropriateness of Gevaryahu's easy equation of biblical s/ss and cuneiform colophons. The colophons seem always to be concerned with the *process* of transmission rather than the actual composition itself. A brief glance at Ugaritic editorial comments confirms this impression of the colophons. I include below fourteen scribally introduced comments gleaned from the alphabetic cuneiform texts of Ugarit. I have arranged them in two groups which correspond to their position in the texts: colophons (A. 1-4) and other, internal scribal remarks (B. 1-10).

A. Colophons

1. CTCA 6, col. VI, 53-57
Gordon 62, rev. 53-57
Others IAB, col. VI, 53-57

spr ʾilmlk šbny
lmd. ʾatn. prln. rb
khnm rb. nqmd. mlk. ʾugr [t]
ʾadn. yrgb. b ʿl. ṯrmn

"Inscribed by Ilmlk, the Shabnite
Dictated by Atn prln, the Chief
Priest, Chief Shepherd
Donated (?) by Nqmd, King of Ugarit
Lord of Yrgb, Owner of Ṯrmn"

---

[15]*BAK*, 12.

2. CTCA 16, col. VI, left edge
Gordon 127, following line 58
Others IIK

spr ʾilmlk ṯʿy [. . .

"Inscribed by Ilmlk, Donated (?) by [. . . "

3. CTCA 4, col. VIII, edge
Gordon 51
Others IIAB

[spr. ʾilmlk. ṯʿ]y. nqmd. mlk. ʾugrt

"Inscribed by Ilmlk, Donated(?) by Nqmd, King of Ugarit"

4. CTCA 17, col. VI, edge
Gordon 2 Aqht, col. VI
Others IID

[spr. ʾilmlk. šbny. lmd. ʾatn] prln

"Inscribed by Ilmlk, the Shabnite, Dictated by Atn prln"

B. Scribal Comments

1. CTCA 6, above col. I
Gordon 49 + 62
Others IAB

lbʿl

"Concerning(?) Baal"

2. CTCA 14, above col. I
Gordon Krt
Others IK

[lk]rt

"Concerning(?) Krt"

3. CTCA 16, above col. I
Gordon 125-127
Others IIK

[l]krt

"Concerning(?) Krt"

4. CTCA 19, above col. I
Gordon I Aqht
Others ID

[l ʾa]q[h]t

"Concerning(?) Aqht"

5. CTCA 4, col. V, 104-105
Gordon 51, col. V
Others IIAB

[in the middle of the text, preceded by double dividing lines and followed by a single dividing line]

wṯb lmspr. ktlʾakn
ǵlmm

"Recite again [the account] where the two young men are sent"

6. CTCA 19, col. IV, edge
Gordon I Aqht
Others ID

whn bt. yṯb. lmspr

"And here let him recite again [the account] about the daughter"

7. CTCA 23, 12 [preceded and followed by a single dividing line]
Gordon 52

šbʿd. yrgm. ʿl. ʿd wʿrbm. tʿnyn

"Seven times he will speak on the dais and the entrants will reply"

8. CTCA 23, 28-29 [preceded and followed by a single dividing line]
Gordon 52

šd [ʾi]lm. šd. ʾaṯrt. wrḥmy
[mspr] . y [ṯ]b

"The field of the gods, the field of Athrt
the virgin, let him recite again"

9. CTCA 23, 56-57 [not marked off from its context]
Gordon 52

yṯb [n] yspr lḫmš

"Let him recite again five times"

10. PRU V, 19.39 [above the beginning of the text]

d šbʾil

"(Tablet) belonging to Šbil"

These groups show that the colophons are almost exclusively concerned with scribal credentials, while the s/ss and internal comments give information about the nature of the compositions and their recitation. This situation agrees with the data of the biblical pss-headings, which we have seen to be occupied primarily with information concerning authorship, historical motivation/setting, performance and function/usage of the particular composition. The results suggest that one ought to look not to the colophons (as Gevaryahu) but elsewhere for close correspondence to the concerns of biblical s/ss.

A more productive source of correspondence is the group of catalogues of hymnic incipits discussed in Chapter Three. While the colophons are appended to maintain the integrity of the textual transmission process, the catalogues give expression to classificatory and organizational concerns similar to those that mark the pss-headings. It will be of interest to compare these two sets of concerns as I discuss the editorial use of the pss-headings to group pss within the Hebrew Psalter.

THE EDITORIAL USE OF THE PSS-HEADINGS

When I first began to study the pss-headings, I was immediately aware of the frequent repetition of many of the terms throughout the s/ss. It was much more difficult, however, to visualize and isolate all the overlapping patterns and relationships which these repetitions presented, in order to discern any editorial purpose behind their distribution. To this end, I have analyzed the distribution of these terms in Appendix C, pp. 239-45. The numbers under the various terms for any one ps indicate the order of that element in the over-all sequence of terms in its s/s. It is thus possible using these numbers, to reconstruct the exact make-up of any given s/s while still permitting analysis into its individual elements.

A look at the chart reveals a number of interests at work in the grouping of pss. Some of the most obvious are old acquaintances: (1) author, (2) genre, (3) instructions, (4) historical/contextual statements. For Books One through Three of the Psalter (Pss 3-89) the primary organizational concern is apparently authorship. This is clearly demonstrated in Book One (3-41) where every Ps is attributed to David, either explicitly in its s/s or by implied combination with its predecessor (Pss 10, 33). This strong interest in authorship continues into Book Two where Pss 42/3-49 are attributed to the Qorahites and Pss 51-65 and 68-70/1 belong to David. The three exceptions (Pss 50, 66-67, 72) will be discussed later. Authorship remains an organizational factor through the end of Book Three. Here Pss 73-83 are attributed to Asaph while Pss 84-85, 87-88 (separated by Ps 86, the only Davidic ps in this book) are connected with the Qorahites.

Beyond Ps 89 the picture changes considerably. Of the remaining 61 pss, only 19 bear attributions of authorship. This is quite astounding in comparison with Pss 3-89 where only *six* pss have no author indicated (and four of these may well have been combined with preceding pss). Even so, authorship remains a factor for grouping in the last third of the Psalter. Of the 17 pss attributed to David, only six (101, 103, 122, 124, 131, 133) stand singly (of these, 122, 124, 131, 133 may participate in some internal organization of the šyr hmʿlwt pss). The other 11 form two groups (108-110 and 138-145), while only Pss 90 (to Moses) and 127 (to Solomon) are attributed to others.

Several observations can be made about this preoccupation with authorship. First, authorship cannot be considered the *primary* organizational concern of the final Hebrew Psalter. While there are a number of large groupings, in *no case* are all the pss of a particular author brought together into a single collection.

1. For the Asaphite pss, only number 50 stands isolated from the main collection (73-83).

2. The Qorahite pss are divided into three groups in Books Two (42/3-49) and Three (84-85 and 87-88).

3. The only two Solomonic pss (72 and 127) are clearly widely separated.

4. The Davidic pss, after forming two extensive collections in Books One and Two, are rather sparsely scattered through Books Three (only Ps 86), Four (only 101 and 103) and Five (108-110, 122, 124, 131, 133, 138-145). Some have claimed that this broad distribution of the Davidic pss throughout the Psalter was primarily intended to extend Davidic authorship to the whole.[16] This would seem to fly in the face of the *obvious* attribution of large numbers of pss to other authors. Even the rabbis, with their clear acceptance of the Davidic authorship of the Psalter, recognized this problem in their attempts to explain it away.[17]

Further, LXX, Syriac and the QPssMss all find it necessary to make this extension of Davidic authority more explicit by the multiplication of Davidic s/ss. The MT 150 arrangement is far from ambiguous in this regard. In comparison with 11QPs^{a}, the distribution of the Davidic pss in MT does not appear so broad. As I mentioned in my discussion of the Qumran Psalms Scroll (chapter 5), that document (1) seems to multiply cases of Davidic attribution beyond MT; (2) even more thoroughly distributes its Davidic compositions; (3) incorporates a prose epilogue with the rather obvious intent to boost the Davidic nature of the whole. These factors all call into question this motivation for the positioning of the Davidic pss in MT and raise the issue of other possible motivating factors: a matter to which I will return.

---

[16] As I suggested for the Qumran Psalms Scroll (11QPs^{a}) above.

[17] I. Epstein, ed., *The Babylonian Talmud* (London: Soncino, 1948); vol. 5, "Pesaḥim," p. 599; vol. 13, "Babba Batra," p. 71; W. G. Braude, *The Midrash on Psalms* (New Haven: Yale University Press, 1959), 1. 5, 10.

A third observation about these author-groupings is that they serve to mark strong disjunctions within the first three Books (3-89). This is most noticeable since these abrupt breaks correspond with the "seams" between the Books. The first Davidic collection (Pss 3-41) corresponds to Book One. With the opening of Book Two (42/3) we have an abrupt change of authorship to the "Sons of Qorah."[18] At the end of Book Two we observe another author-change. The second Davidic collection extends from Ps 51-70/1. Following this, Book Two is concluded by the single Solomonic Ps 72 and Book Three opens with the Asaphite collection (73-83). Finally, the transition from Book Three to Book Four is also marked by authorship change. Book Three closes with the Qorahite group 87-88 and Ps 89 which is bound to then by the similar s/s it shares with Ps 88.

Ps 88	. . . mśklyl lhymn hʾzrḥy
Ps 89	mśkyl lʾytn hʾzrḥy

Book Four then opens with the single Mosaic Ps 90.

This correspondence of authorship-change with the book divisions and the doxologies which serve to mark them is hardly fortuitous. It must represent conscious editorial activity either to introduce such author-changes in order to indicate disjuncture between such divisions or to make use of such existing points of disjuncture in the division of the Psalter. If the doxologies were not originally parts of the pss they now accompany, perhaps they have been added editorially at these points where authorship-changes indicated a division. I tend to accept the former premise as most likely.[19]

The use of author-groups to indicate disjuncture is conspicuous by its absence in Books Four and Five of the Psalter. As I have mentioned, the boundary between Books Three and Four are so indicated, but here the phenomenon ends. This is probably due to the paucity of non-Davidic

---

[18]It is interesting that when Book Two was combined with Book One, the second Davidic collection (51-70/1) was not combined with the first. Instead the Qorahite pss and the single Asaphite Ps 50 were allowed to intervene. This is further evidence that author-grouping is *not* the primary concern of the editor(s).

[19]There are other authorship-changes and breaks which occur *within* the book divisions (Pss 49-50-51; 65-66-67-68; 83-84; 85-86-87), but here other factors come into play which "soften" the abruptness of the transition. Since these factors involve the use of genre categories, I will complete this discussion when I take up that subject immediately below.

authors for Pss 90-150. Besides Ps 90 which opens the fourth Book, the only other author mentioned is Solomon for Ps 127, which has possibly become a fixed part of the hmᶜlwt collection. For obvious reasons, author-change can no longer serve as an effective indicator of disjuncture. In this segment, therefore, we find the hllwyh and hwdw pss performing the same function.

B. Genre Groupings

There are in the pss-headings a number of terms which are fairly clearly distinguished and generally accepted as genre categories. The major distinguishing characteristic of these terms is that they never occur together in the same s/s. The terms isolated in this fashion are:

1. šgywn (Ps 7)
2. mktm (6 pss)
3. tplh (5 pss)
4. mśkyl (13 pss)
5. thlh (Ps 145)
6. hllwyh (16 pss)

To these must be added two terms which frequently occur in combination with one another and occasionally with some other term.

7. mzmwr (57 pss)
8. šyr (30 pss)

It is clear that these last two are by far the most frequent and perhaps the most general of the genre designations included in the s/ss. This may explain their combination with other terms contrary to the general rule.[20]

---

[20]Besides the regular association of šyr and mzmwr, I note here four *possible* violations of the general rule, all but one of which seem to me highly questionable.

1. Ps 45 lmnṣḥ ᶜl-ššnym lbny qrḥ mśkyl šyr ydydt

This is the most probable example. Perhaps the explanation is to be found in the combination of the general term šyr with the term ydydt in order to bring more specificity to the designation.

2. Ps 60 lmnṣḥ ᶜl-šwšn ᶜdwt mktm ldwd llmd
3. Ps 80 lmnṣḥ ᶜl-ššnym ᶜdwt lʾsp mzmwr

The question here is whether ᶜdwt is a genre designation ("testimony"?) or

The chart analysing the distribution of the s/ss terminology highlights a number of groupings which are based on genre classifications.

1. mzmwr
   a. Pss 3-6
      3 mzmwr ldwd bbrḥw . . . .
      4 lmnṣḥ bngynwt mzmwr ldwd
      5 lmnṣḥ ʾl hnḥylwt mzmwr ldwd
      6 lmnṣḥ bngynwt ʿl hšmynyt mzmwr ldwd
   b. Pss 19-24
      19 lmnṣḥ mzmwr ldwd
      20 lmnṣḥ mzmwr ldwd
      21 lmnṣḥ mzmwr ldwd
      22 lmnṣḥ ʿl ʾylt hšḥr mzmwr ldwd
      23 mzmwr ldwd
      24 ldwd mzmwr
   c. Pss 29-31
      29 mzmwr ldwd
      30 mzmwr šyr ḥnkt hbyt ldwd
      31 lmnṣḥ mzmwr ldwd
   d. Pss 38-41
      38 mzmwr ldwd lhzkyr
      39 lmnṣḥ lydytwn mzmwr ldwd
      40 lmnṣḥ ldwd mzmwr
      41 lmnṣḥ mzmwr ldwd
   e. Pss 47-51
      47 lmnṣḥ lbny qrḥ mzmwr

---

serves to qualify šwšn/ššnym which precedes in both cases. While the data are ambiguous, I feel the latter is more likely.

4. Ps 88 šyr mzmwr lbny qrḥ
lmnṣḥ ʿl-mḥlt lʿnwt
mśkyl lhymn hʾzrḥy

This s/s appears to be the conflation of two originally separate headings which should be divided between lbny qrḥ and lmnṣḥ. The major violation of *three* genre terms in a single s/s is the result of this combination.

5. Ps 142 mśkyl ldwd bhywtw bmʿrh tplh

I am not altogether certain what to make of the term tplh at the end of this s/s. If it is the genre classification "prayer" (cf. Pss 17, 86, 90, 102) it stands in a highly irregular position. Never elsewhere does a genre designation *follow* the historical/contextual statement as here.

48 šyr mzmwr lbny qrḥ
49 lmnṣḥ lbny qrḥ mzmwr
50 mzmwr l'sp
51 lmnṣḥ mzmwr ldwd

f. Pss 62-68

62 lmnṣḥ ʿl ydwtwn mzmwr ldwd
63 mzmwr ldwd bhywtw . . . .
64 lmnṣḥ mzmwr ldwd
65 lmnṣḥ mzmwr ldwd šyr
66 lmnṣḥ šyr mzmwr
67 lmnṣḥ bngynwt mzmwr šyr
68 lmnṣḥ ldwd mzmwr šyr

g. Pss 75-77

75 lmnṣḥ l tšḥt mzmwr l'sp šyr
76 lmnṣḥ bngynwt mzmwr l'sp šyr
77 lmnṣḥ ʿl ydytwn l'sp mzmwr

h. Pss 82-85

82 mzmwr l'sp
83 šyr mzmwr l'sp
84 lmnṣḥ ʿl hgytyt lbny qrḥ mzmwr
85 lmnṣḥ lbny qrḥ mzmwr

i. Pss 108-110

108 šyr mzmwr ldwd
109 lmnṣḥ ldwd mzmwr
110 ldwd mzmwr

j. Pss 139-141

139 lmnṣḥ ldwd mzmwr
140 lmnṣḥ mzmwr ldwd
141 mzmwr ldwd

There are several instances of two consecutive s/ss with the term mzmwr (8-9; 12-13; 79-80; 87-88; 100-101) which I will not present fully here. In several of the groups given above it becomes evident that part or all of the pss included correspond in two or more elements of their s/s. See especially group (a) (Pss 3-6) where the effective phrase is mzmwr ldwd for all four pss. The same is true for group (b) (lmnṣḥ mzmwr ldwd for pss 19-22). Again in group (c) the phrase mzmwr ldwd is common to all three pss as well as the four included in group (d). The same phenomenon can be observed throughout the rest of these groups. This multiple correspondence over a number of consecutive s/ss certainly affirms the purposeful arrangement behind the juxtaposition.

2. mktm

Pss 56-60

56 lmnṣḥ ʿl ywnt rḥqym ldwd mktm bʾḥz . . . .
57 lmnṣḥ ʾl tšḥt ldwd mktm bbrḥw . . . .
58 lmnṣḥ ʾl tšḥt ldwd mktm
59 lmnṣḥ ʾl tšḥt ldwd mktm bšlḥ . . . .
60 lmnṣḥ ʿl šwšn ʿdwt mktm ldwd bḥṣtw . . . .

All these compositions share three terms: lmnṣḥ ldwd mktm. The three central s/ss correspond in the additional phrase ʾl tšḥt, while 56, 57, 59, and 60 all conclude with historical/contextual statements as well. All these correspondences eliminate any possibility of chance juxtaposition.

3. mśkyl

a. Pss 42/3-45

42/3 lmnṣḥ mśkyl lbny qrḥ
44 lmnṣḥ lbny qrḥ mśkyl
45 lmnṣḥ ʿl ššnym lbny qrḥ mśkyl šyr ydydt

b. Pss 52-55

52 lmnṣḥ mśkyl ldwd bbwʾ . . . .
53 lmnṣḥ ʿl mḥlt mśkyl ldwd
54 lmnṣḥ bngynt mśkyl ldwd bbwʾ . . . .
55 lmnṣḥ bngynt mśkyl ldwd

c. Pss 88-89

88 . . . mśkyl lhymn hʾzrḥy
89 mśkyl lʾytn hʾzrḥy

The tendency to juxtapose compositions whose s/ss have one, two, three or more terms in common is clearly established. As clear is the failure of the editor(s) to pull together *all* similar s/ss. Thus, outside the group of mktm pss (56-60) there is the isolated example in Ps 16 (mktm ldwd), and beside the two groups of Pss 42/3-45 and 52-55, we find individual occurrences of mśkyl in Pss 32, 74, 78, and 142. It is even more obvious from the chart that there is *no* attempt to group together all occurrences of any single term or of any identical combination of terms. Even if one abandons these genre designations in favor of the categories of the modern form-critics, the result is the same. Genre does not constitute a *primary* editorial principle for the organization of the Psalter. A glance at a few genre categories not covered above makes this plain.

1. *The "Pss of Ascents."* I will begin with the one apparently complete genre collection. The presence of this *one* group of pss (120-134)

emphasizes the lack of such concern in the rest of the Psalter. It is an anomaly, probably to be explained as a previously existing collection which has been incorporated as a whole into MT 150.

2. *The "Enthronement" Pss.* There is no agreement on the exact contents of this modern form-critical category. While there does seem to be a certain concentration of these pss between Pss 93 and 99, even there they are not consecutively arranged (93, 96-99) and even the most restrictive view of the corpus would include pss widely separated from this core group (certainly Ps 47 and probably Ps 149).[21]

3. *The "Royal" Pss.* This category includes compositions which are thought by some to have functioned in "ceremonies whose central figure was the King."[22] While there is relatively close agreement as to the number and identity of the pss in this category, they are widely distributed throughout the Psalter and show no editorial concern to group or otherwise mark them out. This is quite in contrast with the Mesopotamian catalogues which regularly juxtapose "royal" hymns in a larger list or "lump" them together in a summary line (cf. *CATS.* 1 and 3). In any case, the catalogues are careful to distinguish these hymns from those of other categories, a concern which is absent from the Hebrew Psalter in regards to these "Royal" pss.

4. *Hllwyh Pss.* While these pss are brought together in several groups, their actual position is not a matter of *genre*, but of *function*. They serve an editorial purpose to mark divisions within the last books of the Psalter. Here pss of the same genre are juxtaposed, not out of interest in *genre*, but to serve an additional purpose.

Summary: When one surveys the genre categories among the s/ss terms in view of their distribution as indicated in the chart, it is clear that, while there are clumps and clusters of pss in the same category, none (with the exception of the "Ascent" Pss) form a complete collection. Let me hasten to add, this does not mean there is *no* editorial concern expressed through their arrangement.

---

[21]J. D. W. Watts, "Yahweh Malak Psalms," *TZ* 21 (1965) 341-48; Gerhard von Rad, *OTT2*, p. 363, note.

[22]Quotation from G. von Rad, *Old Testament Theology* 1. 319 n. 1, where he also lists the contents of the category as Pss 2, 18, 20, 21, 45, 72, 89, 101, 110, 132. A Weiser, *The Psalms*, p. 45, includes Pss 2, 18, 20, 21, 72, 89, 101, 110. H. Gunkel's list (*The Psalms* [Philadelphia: Fortress, 1967]) 23, cites Pss 2, 18, 20, 21, 45, 72, 101, 110, 132 and 144:1-11.

THE USE OF S/SS AND P/SS TO MAKE TRANSITION BETWEEN PSS GROUPINGS

Just above I indicated how author-groupings are used to mark points of disjuncture in the Psalter, especially those which mark the boundaries between the first four books. The editorial use of genre categories in the s/ss is related to that phenomenon, but is different in that the genre designations are used to bind together, to "soften" transition between groups of pss. There are a number of instances of this "binding/softening" technique. I will begin with several clear examples.

1. *Pss 47-51.* In the middle of the second book, there occurs a rather abrupt transition from the first Qorahite collection (42/3-49) to the second Davidic collection (51-70/1). This transition involves two author-changes since a single Asaphite ps (50) intervenes. A look at the chart on pp. 239-45, however, indicates the use of genre categories in the s/ss of pss 47-51 bridges this disjuncture, softens the transition and binds the collections together.

47 lmnṣḥ lbny qrḥ *mzmwr*
48 syr *mzmwr* lbny qrḥ
49 lmnṣḥ lbny qrḥ *mzmwr*
50 *mzmwr* lʾsp
51 lmnṣḥ *mzmwr* ldwd

The effective term in this instance is mzmwr which is not used in the Qorahite collection prior to Ps 47 and is not used again after this group until Ps 62. Here, however, the term occurs in five consecutive s/ss, precisely spanning the point of transition.

2. *Pss 62-68.* Here again is an example of a point of disjuncture which is spanned and bound together by the use of genre categories. The second Davidic collection begins at Ps 51 and extends to Ps 70/1 with the single major break at Pss 66-67, which bear no attribution of authorship in their s/ss. This would seem to represent a serious breach in the Davidic collection, if it were not for the binding action of the genre categories in the s/ss of Pss 62-68.

62 lmnṣḥ ʿl ydwtwn mzmwr ldwd
63 mzmwr ldwd bhywtw . . . .
64 lmnṣḥ mzmwr ldwd
65 lmnṣḥ mzmwr ldwd šyr
66 lmnṣḥ šyr mzmwr

67 lmnṣḥ bngynwt mzmwr šyr
68 lmnṣḥ ldwd mzmwr šyr

Here the effective terminology is a combination of mzmwr and šyr which occur in pss 65-68 in various combinations. The non-Davidic Pss 66 and 67 are bound into this context by the consecutive usage of šyr and mzmwr as well as the repetition of the initial phrase lmnṣḥ which also bridges the gap. Once the transition is accomplished and Davidic attribution re-established in 68, neither mzmwr nor šyr occurs again in this collection. The effect is to bind these non-Davidic pss tightly into their context and to "soften" the transition across the disjuncture. In this instance the binding operation creates or preserves an apparent thematic unity which affirms the purposefulness of the juxtaposition. Pss 65-68 form a closely related unit of praise of YHWH which stands out in contrast to its surroundings (uniformly prayers for deliverance). This congruence of theme for these pss confirms the reality of the binding technique which is employed there.

3. *Pss 82-85*. In the Third Book of the Psalter, there is an abrupt transition from the Asaphite collection (73-83) to the second Qorahite collection (84-88). After several genre designations are applied in 73-80 (mzmwr—73, 77, 79, 80; mzmwr . . . šyr—75, 76; mśkyl—74, 78), there is no genre note for 81. Then, just at the point of transition, there are four consecutive pss (82-83 Asaphite; 84-85 Qorahite) which bear the term mzmwr in their s/ss.

82 mzmwr l'sp
83 šyr mzmwr l'sp
84 lmnṣḥ ʿl hgytyt lbny qrḥ mzmwr
85 lmnṣḥ lbny qrḥ mzmwr

The effect again is to soften the transition between these two author-groupings and to bind them together more closely.

4. *Pss 87-89*. At the very end of Book Three, there occurs a group of three pss which offers an intriguing example of this binding technique. Pss 87 and 88 are the last of the Qorahite pss and are so designated in their s/ss. Ps 89, just at the end of the third book is attributed to 'Etan the Ezrahite. This otherwise lonely s/s is brought into firm relation with Ps 88 which bears a *dual* s/s:

87 lbny qrḥ mzmwr
88 šyr mzmwr lbny qrḥ
lmnṣḥ ʿlmwt lʿnwt
mśkyl lhymn hʾzrḥy
89 mśkyl lʾytn hʾzrḥy

The dual s/s of 88 presents several problems. First, as it now stands, it contains *three* genre categories in a single s/s; a very questionable state of affairs. Second, it exhibits *two* author references (lbny qrḥ and lhymn hʾzrḥy). Finally, the term lmnṣḥ, which here stands in the middle of the s/s, occurs some 55 times in the pss-headings. This is the *only* instance in which it does not occupy *initial position*. Perhaps the present extended s/s is an attempt to preserve alternate traditions about this ps (as in the k^etîv/q^erê and the editorial juxtaposition of certain pss without s/s to indicate combination). Regardless of the origin, its effect is quite clear. The first half binds Ps 88 with what precedes (the Qorahite collection) while the second half, with its use of the terms mśkyl and hʾzrḥy, binds it to Ps 89 as well.

All these examples have been taken from *within* the book divisions of the Psalter. At each point of disjuncture, the occurrence of the same genre categories in consecutive pss-headings spans the gap, softens the harshness of transition and binds the whole more closely together. What, however, is the situation at the points of major disjuncture: at the boundaries between the books? The chart on pp. 240-46 again provides the needed perspective. The data of the chart indicate that at those points, genre designations *do not* come into play as a softening, binding technique. The move from Book One to Book Two offers an exception to which I will return at the last.

1. *Pss 70/1-73.* Here at the transition from the second to the third book, we encounter an abrupt transition through two author-changes.

70/1 lmnṣḥ ldwd lhzkyr
72 lšlmh
73 mzmwr lʾsp

There is no repetition or correlation of genre designations to bridge the gap. The disjuncture is allowed to stand without resolution. Coupled with the presence of the doxology in 72:18-19 and the p/s in 72:20:

72:18 brwk yhwh ʾlhym ʾlhy yśrʾl
ʿśh nplʾwt lbdw
:19 wbrwk šm kbwdw lʿwlm
wymlʾ kbwdw ʾt kl hʾrṣ
ʾmn wʾmn
:20 klw tplwt dwd bn yšy

this disjuncture indicates a clear, purposeful break between segments.

2. *Pss 87-90.* Book Three ends, as mentioned above, with the clear and purposeful binding together of Pss 87-89. Ps 90 follows, introducing another author-change.

87 lbny qrḥ mzmwr šyr
88 šyr mzmwr lbny qrḥ
lmnṣḥ ʿl mḥlt lʿnwt
mśkyl lhymn hʾzrḥy
89 mśkyl lʾytn hʾzrḥy
90 tplh lmšh ʾyš hʾlhym

Again there is no attempt to soften the abrupt transition and to bind these pss together. The unresolved disjuncture combines with the doxology of 89:53 to indicate a major new section.

3. *Pss 104-110.* For completeness I include the transition between Book Four and Book Five. Pss 104 and 105 bear hllwyh p/ss and 106 both s/s and p/s. Ps 107 bears no s/s or p/s while Ps 108 introduces a group of three consecutive Davidic pss, all bearing the term mzmwr in their headings.

104 .... hllwyh
105 .... hllwyh
106 hllwyh .... hllwyh
107 ....
108 šyr mzmwr ldwd
109 lmnṣḥ ldwd mzmwr
110 ldwd mzmwr

There is clear disjunction here and the disjunction is emphasized rather than softened by the headings.

4. *Pss 38-46.* I have left this group until last since it presents a slightly different phenomenon than the others previously cited. Here, at the generally accepted point of transition from Book One to Book Two, marked by a doxology in 41:14,

brwk yhwh ʾlhy yśrʾl
mhʿwlm wʿd hʿwlm
ʾmn wʾmn

one would expect to find no resolution of the disjuncture as in the previous cases. Indeed, the break is clearly indicated by author change and genre change. However, the consecutive repetition of the initial phrase lmnṣḥ in *eight* consecutive s/ss (Pss 39-47) does have a slight softening effect.

38 mzmwr ldwd lhzkyr
39 lmnṣḥ lydytwn mzmwr ldwd
40 lmnṣḥ ldwd mzmwr
41 lmnṣḥ mzmwr ldwd
42/3 lmnṣḥ mśkyl lbny qrḥ
44 lmnṣḥ lbny qrḥ
45 lmnṣḥ ʿl ššnym lbny qrḥ mśkyl šyr ydyt
46 lmnṣḥ lbny qrḥ ʿl ʿlmwt šyr
47 lmnṣḥ lbny qrḥ mzmwr

In short, while the analysis of the distribution of genre terms in the pss-headings reveals the existence of clusters of terms spread throughout the Psalter, there is no evidence of any consistent attempt to group all the pss by genre categories as in the Mesopotamian catalogues. There *is* evidence, however, of the editorial use of these genre terms and clusters to assist in the organization of the MT 150 collection. Basic divisions of the pss are indicated by the disjuncture (in the Pss-headings) of author attributions and genre designations. Such disjuncture is most noticeable at the "seams" of the Psalter: at the book divisions.

In contrast to this "divisive" function of the pss-headings, genre terms are used within these larger segments to bind together and to "soften" the transition between groups of pss. The widespread and consistent nature of this phenomenon militates against any chance distribution of the pss and supports the idea of purposeful, editorial activity behind the organization process.

S/SS CONCERNED WITH THE FUNCTION OF INDIVIDUAL PSS

Up to now I have shown primarily how the editor(s) of the Psalter used the pss-headings to assist their organization of the pss-corpus. There are, however, at least two groups of pss in which the s/ss tell us something about the use and/or function of particular pss as well as the pss as a whole. The two groups are very different in regards to the form and nature of their s/ss and the difference itself is instructive. The first group includes those pss which provide in their headings information about the cultic performance/function of the particular ps. The second is characterized by the addition of historical/contextual statements to the more technical elements of their s/ss.

A. The Cultic S/ss

J. F. A. Sawyer, in his article "An Analysis of the Context and Meaning of the Psalm-Headings," has achieved admirable results by his *consistent* approach to the "situational context" of the technical terms. On the basis of his analysis he concludes that certain terms, introduced by the preposition l^{e} (excluding lmnṣḥ and personal names) most probably refer to the "cultic purpose" of the ps. He cites six such terms.

1. lywm hšbt (Ps 92)
2. ltwdh (Ps 100)
3. lhzkyr (Pss 38, 70)
4. lʿnwt (Ps 88)
5. llmd (Ps 60)
6. lʿbd Yhwh (Pss 18, 36)

In each case, he feels these terms identify the specific "cultic occasion" or ritual with which this ps is to be connected. He is able to make some interesting suggestions about the cultic origin of some exceedingly obscure terms.[23]

Of these terms the most clear are the two which are generally accepted.

Ps 92	mzmwr šyr lywm hšbt
Ps 100	mzmwr ltwdh

The first requires no comment as the cultic occasion is clear (the "Sabbath"). For the second, twdh is generally taken to refer, not to "thanks-

---

[23] John F. A. Sawyer, "An Analysis of the Context and Meaning of the Psalm-Headings," *Transactions of the Glasgow University Oriental Society*, vol. 22 (1967/8) (Leiden: Brill, 1970) 26-38.

giving" in the general sense, but to *the* "twdh-offering" and attendant ritual.[24] While such an interpretation is clearly acceptable, the ambiguity of the term permits a broader understanding, so that the ps may increasingly be considered an example of individual praise rather than a ps composed for performance with a particular ritual. The same is true for all these terms where the terminology has been left sufficiently vague. The lack of specificity is the chief source of ambiguity which has, over the centuries, left these terms increasingly obscure as the cultic matrix from which they stemmed receded into the distant past.

Thus, if lᶜbd YHWH, lᶜnwt, lhzkyr did refer to a cultic ritual, it is no longer certain. There are other possible interpretations, some perhaps preferable. It is no longer necessary (or possible) to bind these pss to a communal, cultic rite. Their ambiguity (fostered by the obscurity of their origin) opens the possibility of individual appropriation. If Pss 38 and 70 can no longer be connected with the ʾazkara-ritual, might they not be private utterances to "cause YHWH to remember" one's plight and come to one's aid?

I would connect with this group of pss two others which, while they do not share the formulaic structure of the rest, also bear statements in their headings which may be construed as indicating the occasion for their use.

Ps 30	mzmwr šyr hnkt hbyt ldwd
Ps 102	tplh lᶜny ky yᶜṭwp
	wlpny yhwh yšpwk śyḥw

The occasion for Ps 30 is described as "the dedication of the house." The question that must be decided is: What house? Is this the Temple which David planned and Solomon built? Or does it refer to the palace of David the king? The preposition of ldwd adds to the confusion. Is this the standard "authorship" formula? Or does it modify hbyt "the house (of David)"? In view of the regular attribution to David in Pss 3-41, the

---

[24]E. Jacob, "Beigräge zu einer Einleitung in die Psalmen," *ZAW* 16 (1876) 273-77; Franz Delitzsch, *The Psalms*, vol. III (Grand Rapids, MI: Eerdmans, 1871) 104-5; H. Grimme, "Der Begriff von hebräischen *hwdh* und *twdh*," *ZAW* 58 (1940/1) 234-40; S. Mowinckel, *PIW2*, pp. 211-12; Sawyer, "Analysis," 34; M. Dahood, *Psalms II* (Garden City, NY: Doubleday, 1968) 371-2; A. E. Goodman, "*ḥsd/twdh* in the Linguistic Tradition of the Psalter," *Words and Meanings*, ed. Peter R. Ackroyd (Cambridge: University Press, 1968) 105-15.

former is most likely. Each view has its proponents and the question cannot ultimately be decided. The ambiguity does not permit absolute certainty.

As for Ps 102, the s/s is at once more specific and more general. While the occasion is more carefully delimited ("Prayer of an/the oppressed person when he is faint and pours out his burden before YHWH"), the agent is not clearly specified. Did this ps form part of a regular ritual in the cultus? There is no longer any way to know for certain. In its present state the s/s seems to suggest "If *you* are oppressed, lay your burden before YHWH in *this* manner." The ps becomes a model for personal piety.

The amazing fact in all these pss is that the cultic matrix has receded so far into the background as to become virtually irretrievable. Is this a hint as to one method and purpose of the Psalter editor(s)? Elsewhere I have suggested that in the final form of the Psalter there is a clear move to obscure the precise cultic origins of the individual pss and to build a new context for their interpretation: a context which emphasizes the private life of devotion and individual access to YHWH. The treatment of these obscure, cultic references in the pss-headings is further confirmation of that movement.

B. The Historical S/ss

Thirteen pss contain in their s/ss, in addition to the usual references to author, genre and method of performance, statements of historical/contextual significance.

Ps	3	mzmwr ldwd bbrḥw mpny ʾbšlwm bnw
Ps	7	šgywn ldwd ʾšr šr lyhwh ʿl dbry kwš bn ymyny
Ps	18	lmnṣḥ lʿbd yhwh ldwd ʾšr dbr lyhwh ʾt dbry hšyrh hzʾt bywm hṣyl yhwh ʾwtw mkp kl ʾybyw wmyd šʾwl
Ps	34	ldwd bšnwtw ʾt ṭʿmw lpny ʾbymlk wygršhw wylk
Ps	51	lmnṣḥ mzmwr ldwd bbwʾ ʾlyw ntn hnbyʾ kʾšr bʾ ʾl bt šbʿ
Ps	52	lmnṣḥ mśkyl ldwd bbwʾ dwʾg hʾdmy wygd lšʾwl wyʾmr lw bʾ dwd ʾl byt ʾbymlk
Ps	54	lmnṣḥ bngynt mśkyl ldwd bbwʾ hzypym wyʾmr lšʾwl hlʾ dwd msttr ʿmnw

Ps 56	lmnṣḥ ʿl ywnt ʾlm rhqym ldwd mktm bʾḥz ʾtw plštym bgt
Ps 57	lmnṣḥ ʾl tšḥt ldwd mktm bbrḥw mpny šʾwl bmʿrh
Ps 59	lmnṣḥ ʾl tšḥt ldwd mktm bšlḥ šʾwl wyšmrw ʾt hbyt lhmytw
Ps 60	lmnṣḥ ʿl šwšn ʿdwt mktm ldwd llmd bhṣwtw ʾt ʾrm nhrym wʾt ʾrm ṣwbh wyšb ywʾb wyk ʾt ʾdwm bgyʾ mlḥ šnym ʿšr ʾlp
Ps 63	mzmwr ldwd bhytw bmdbr yhwdh
Ps 142	mśkyl ldwd bhywtw bmʿrh tplh

I do not intend to discuss these pss and their headings in detail since a number of articles have already undertaken to do so.[25] Rather I propose to focus instead on the function of these historical/contextual statements in relation to their particular pss and to the Psalter as a whole. The following points, drawn from Brevard S. Childs's insightful study, "Psalm Titles and Midrashic Exegesis," will serve to develop the background needed for the discussion.

1. These historical/contextual statements developed as "connecting links" which provided transition between an historical narrative and a ps which was inserted into it. As an example of this literary technique, Childs cites especially the ps inserted at Isaiah 38:9-20, whose s/s exhibits remarkable formulaic parallels with the historical s/ss of the Psalter.

Is 38:9	mktb lḥzqyhw mlk yhwdh bḥltw wyhy mḥlyw

2. In comparison with other pss inserted in narrative contexts (2 Sam 22:1-7 = Ps 18; Jonah 2; Exod 15:1ff.; Judg 5:1ff.; Deut 31:30ff.; Deut 32:44ff.), those historical s/ss which exhibit the formulaic introduction ($\underline{b}^{e}$ + the construct infinitive) represent a late development subsequent to the fixation of the technical terms of the s/ss which made

[25]I mention here a few of the recent articles dealing with the subject. Brevard S. Childs, "Psalm Titles and Midrashic Exegesis," *JSS* 16 (1971) 137-50; Otto Eissfeldt, "Die Psalmen als Geschichtsquelle," *Near East Studies in Honor of W. F. Albright*, ed. H. Goedicke (Baltimore, MD: Johns Hopkins University Press, 1971) 97-112; N. H. Tur-Sinai, "The Literary Character of the Book of Psalms," *Oüdtestamentische Studien* 8 (1950) 263-81.

smooth incorporation within narrative more difficult. The additional historical/contextual material makes it clear to the reader that this obvious insertion is related to the incidents just narrated.[26]

3. The connection of ps and event has nothing to say about the actual historical continuity between the two. Continuity is solely literary.

4. The historical/contextual statements are the result of exegesis of the pss themselves and not the remains of ancient traditions. The purpose of the exegesis was to uncover "general parallels between the situation described in the Psalm and some incident in the life of David."[27]

5. These historical/contextual statements "stemmed from a pietistic circle of Jews" and were intended to open up the inner, spiritual life of David to the reader. In this way they provided models for individual response to the conflicts, crises and victories of life before YHWH.[28]

In reaction to Childs's study, I offer two, brief observations. (1) Childs is most certainly correct that the historical/contextual statements *adapt* previously existing pss to fit with a particular narrative context. If, as Tur-Sinai suggests, all the pss are "enlargements" of songs originally included in a narrative context, one would expect (a) much greater correspondence between ps and narrative events (b) no need to develop the historical context in the s/s in order to maintain the relation of narrative and ps. One would also wonder why so few of these 150 pss actually found a place within canonical narrative.

(2) That these statements were necessary to overcome the transition-inhibiting character of the technical terms, would seem to imply that the technical terms were already a fixed, immovable part of their compositions *prior* to the addition of the historical comments. Otherwise the redactor would simply have omitted them to provide a smooth transition.

The real focus of attention, however, should be on how these pss with their historical/contextual statements *function* within the Psalter. Here Childs is unquestionably right. As I have said before, the effect of these historical statements is to loosen these pss from their original cultic context by providing them a new context in particular events in the life of David. These pss, then, become individual responses to life situations (David's responses). This individual appropriation of cultic pss is affirmed and enhanced by the use of pss in the canonical narratives. The use in Isaiah, Habakkuk, Jonah, the Chronicler of originally cultic compositions

---

[26]Childs, "Psalm Titles," 142.

[27]Childs, "Psalm Titles," 147.

[28]Childs, "Psalm Titles," 148-49.

as the response of an *individual* to the crises of life, offers a clear stamp of approval to this means of access to the Psalter.

Perhaps these comments *were* originally intended to link these pss with various historical narratives. Perhaps the original purpose was to enhance the narrative by poetic expansion with a song. But the final effect within the Psalter has been to provide a hermeneutical approach to the use of the pss by the *individual*. As David, so every man!

THE FUNCTION OF "UNTITLED" PSS

Besides their use to group pss and to provide transition between groupings, the pss-headings provide further evidence of editorial concern in the juxtaposition of pss. I have suggested above in connection with the QPssMss that in some instances the s/s (or rather the *absence* of a s/s) may function as an intentional editorial method to indicate a tradition of the combination of the "untitled" ps with its immediate predecessor. This is not to say that *all* examples of pss without s/ss are to be so combined. However, there are a number of cases which suggest this conclusion. There are five rather clear examples of this phenomenon in the first three books of the Psalter (Pss 1 and 2; 9 and 10; 32 and 33; 42 and 43; 70 and 71). The evidence in the last two books is less clear since we are faced there with large groups of consecutive untitled pss which are variously combined or divided in the Mss traditions. Let us begin with the clearer examples and move to draw some conclusions which may apply to the less certain occurrences.

1. Pss 1 and 2. These pss present special problems since *both* are untitled and each possibly functions in an introductory capacity (Ps 1 to the whole Psalter and Ps 2 to the first Davidic collection). For this reason they will be considered separately at a later point.

2. Pss 9 and 10. Considerable evidence supports the tradition of the combination of these two pss. In MT there is no s/s for Ps 10 to defend its uniqueness over against Ps 9. Likewise the Targum of the Pss supports MT in this omission. Some LXX Mss combine these two pss into one. Kennicott cites 2 Hebrew Mss which read them together, while de Rossi notes an additional two.[29]

In support of the original combination of these two pss, many have pointed out the apparent remains of an acrostic pattern discernible in both pss and which is defective precisely at the point of juncture (see figure 5, below). The disruption of the acrostic pattern certainly

---

[29]See table 4, pp. 134-35.

Ps 9:2	א	4 stichoi
:4	ב	4 stichoi
:6	ג	4 stichoi
	[ד]	defective
:8	ה	4 stichoi
:10	ו	4 stichoi
:12	ז	4 stichoi
:14	ח	4 stichoi
:16	ט	4 stichoi
:18	י	Only 2 stichoi
:19	כ	6 stichoi
10:1	ל	14 stichoi
	[מ]	defective
	[נ]	defective
	[ס]	defective
:7	פ	disordered 4 stichoi
:8c	ע	disordered 8 stichoi
	[צ]	defective
:12	ק	4 stichoi
:14	ר	4 stichoi
:15	ש	4 stichoi
:17	ת	4 stichoi

Figure 5. Schematic Rendering of the Acrostic Pattern in Pss 9 and 10

indicates an early division of this unit into separate compositions and supports the idea of alternate traditions for the reading of these pss. If there were *not* a considerable history behind the separate reading of the pss, it is doubtful that the original alphabetic acrostic pattern would have been so severely disarranged. It appears in this context that the MT has preserved both alternate text traditions without rejecting one in favor of the other. This was accomplished by separating the two halves according to normal scribal convention but omitting any s/s for Ps 10 which would have emphasized its uniqueness and would have prevented any combination with Ps 9.

3. Pss 32 and 33. The lack of s/s for Pss 10 and 33 is particularly conspicuous since they are the only two pss in the First Book (Pss 3-41) which are not attributed to David. The obvious Davidic character of the collection heightens the peculiarity of the omission. The textual evidence indicates LXX supplies Ps 33 with a Davidic s/s, while the Targum supports MT with no s/s. Kennicott reports 8 Hebrew Mss which join these two pss and de Rossi adds two more.

The QPssMss offer interesting but ambiguous data. Two Mss (4QPs^a and 4QPs^q) omit Ps 32 entirely and juxtapose Pss 31 and 33. In 4QPs^a (mid second century B.C.) Ps 33 bears no s/s. 4QPs^q (mid first century A.D.), however, supplies a Davidic heading: ldwd šyr mzmwr. The dating of these Mss and the lack of agreement of the 4QPs^q s/s with that of LXX (tō dauid), suggest an original untitled pss with secondary attempts to resolve the peculiarity. It is interesting, nonetheless, that it is Ps 32 (with its s/s) which is here omitted, rather than the untitled Ps 33. This would seem to militate against the theory of late insertion of Ps 33 after 32.

Most authors have considered Pss 32-33 as originally independent. Certain internal considerations support this view. (1) In Ps 32, the first person singular "I" is employed frequently while in Ps 33, the only first person reference is plural (33:20-22). (2) The Psalmist addresses YHWH in the second person in Ps 32, while third person address is regular in Ps 33. (3) Ps 32 employs the liturgical formula selâ at three, regularly spaced intervals, while the word never occurs in the 22 verses of Ps 33.

There are however certain connections between these pss as well. As many have noted, Ps 33 begins as Ps 32 ends. In 32:11, two groups (ṣdyqym and yšry lb) are exhorted to be glad, rejoice and shout for joy (hrnynw) in YHWH. Ps 33 opens with similar encouragement.

rnnw ṣdyqym byhwh
lyšrym n'wh thlh

Dahood goes even so far as to suggest that this similarity "indicates that Ps xxxiii is not a later addition and at the same time explains its lack of superscription." Unfortunately Dahood does not clarify *how* the lack of s/s is explained.[30]

This similar phraseology at the end and beginning of consecutive pss is reminiscent of the Mesopotamian practice of providing successive tablets in a series with "tag-lines" in the colophon which consisted of the incipit (opening line) of the next tablet in sequence. While this phenomenon would not indicate an original unity for these two pss, it would suggest a close sequential relation and would stand against the "late insertion" theory.

There are other connections of a thematic or liturgical nature between these pss. First, the didactic section of Ps 32:8-11 begins with

---

[30]M. Dahood, *Psalms I*, xxxi.

the announcement of the Psalmist's intention to instruct his hearer(s) in "the way you should go" and ends with the exhortation to rejoice and shout for joy. In this context, Ps 33 could be viewed as a response to that command on the part of the hearers. Further, the concerns of 32:10 "steadfast love surrounds him who trusts in YHWH" are expanded in 33:16-19.

:16 A king is not saved by his great army
a warrior is not delivered by his great strength
:17 The warhorse is a vain hope for victory,
And by its great might it cannot save.
:18 Behold, the eye of YHWH is on those who fear him
On those who hope in his steadfast love,
:19 That he may deliver their soul from death
And keep them alive in famine.

Again, the speakers affirm their trust in YHWH in 33:20-22. Their willingness to "wait" for YHWH seems to contrast with the impatience of the "horse and mule" in 32:9 who must be restrained by "bit and bridle."

While this analysis does not affirm an original structural unity for these two compositions, these connections, along with the Mss evidence for combination, suggest the possibility of an early liturgical function of these pss which bound both together. In this case, the lack of s/s in MT would still serve to preserve the alternate traditions regarding the combination or division of these pss.

4. Pss 42 and 43. The affirmation of *BHS* that many Mss join these two pss "rightly," seems to reflect the consensus of scholars. Kennicott lists 39 Hebrew Mss joining 42 and 43; de Rossi an additional nine. Targum agrees with MT while LXX provides a Davidic heading (a few Hebrew texts also append a simple ldwd). The general agreement as to the original unity of these pss is based largely on agreement in vocabulary and style, bolstered by qînâ meter and a recurring refrain (42:5-6; 42:11; 43:5) which breaks the unified ps into three, balanced stanzas. Further grammatical connections are found in:

42:10 lāmâ š^{e}kaḥtānî lāmmâ qôdēr ʾēlēk b^{e}laḥaṣ ʾôyēb
43:2 lāmâ z^{e}naḥtānî lāmmâ qôdēr ʾethallēk b^{e}laḥaṣ ʾôyēb

Justification for division might be found in the change of mood and address which occurs at the beginning of 43:1. Up to this point the poet has been self-reflective, speaking of God in the third person (except for the quote included in 42:10). At 43:1 the psalmist addresses to God his plea for divine assistance (43:1-4). While this plea functions admirably in the context of the unified ps, it could as easily serve as an independent unit in its own right. It is not surprising, then, that MT has juxtaposed the two, signifying the tradition of unity by the omission of the s/s with Ps 43.

5. Pss 70 and 71. The combination of these pss has been discussed in some detail in relation to the QPssMss (above, pp. 131-32). Some comments regarding Mss evidence are in order. *BHS* confirms many Mss join 70 and 71 (Kennicott cites 10 Mss; de Rossi cites an additional Ms of Kennicott [532] as well as 14 more of his own). Targum agrees with MT, while LXX supplies a Davidic s/s. Clear grammatical relationships and strong Mss evidence for combination make it likely that here again MT preserves alternate traditions for combination/division.

This exhausts the data for isolated, untitled pss in Books One through Three. As I mentioned previously, the situation in Books Four and Five is far more ambiguous due to the large number of consecutive, untitled pss to be found there. A glance at the data from Kennicott and de Rossi (see table 4, pp. 134-35) shows a clear tendency toward combination of these untitled pss into larger compositions (several Mss group up to four MT pss together, while at least one joins five). This wholesale combination most frequently takes place in two groups of pss (90-99 and 114-119). Such large-scale unification of several consecutive pss results in extremely awkward constructions and probalby reflects a secondary development rather than original unity.

1. Pss 90-99. The bulk of these pss share a thematic focus on the kingship of YHWH and have been referred by some to the hypothetical Enthronement Ceremony at the supposed New Year celebration of Israel.[31] Regardless of one's evaluation of the social/cultic matrix of these pss, their commonality cannot be denied, since it so clearly expresses itself in shared formulaic expressions and other similarities. In fact, these many connections make it difficult to evaluate the evidence for division/combination of these pss. While I do not hope to resolve the issue finally a few suggestions can be made.

a. Pss 90-91. Kennicott cites six Hebrew Mss which join these pss. LXX supplies 91 with a Davidic s/s which firmly isolates it from 90. Targum follows MT with no s/s. Certain correspondences between the two may suggest a rationale for juxtaposition, if not for combination or unity. Ps 90 is attributed to Moses and praises YHWH in verse 1 as a "refuge in all generations." It then questions the reasons for God's

---

[31] See especially S. Mowinckel, *PIW 1*, 106-92.

distance from his people and pleads for his return. Ps 91 picks up on the refuge motif in 91:1 and suggests the protective presence of YHWH is still available to those who put their trust in him. Similarly, the suggestion in 91:1 that those who trust ʾElyôn "[God] Most High" and are protected by Šadday "The Almighty" (two pre-Mosaic epithets of the deity) will also trust in YHWH, is reminiscent of the revelation to Israel of the divine name in Exodus (Exod 3:1-22; 6:2-8), an event in which Moses played a most significant role. Again, while these connections suggest the reasons why Pss 90 and 91 came to occupy consecutive positions, it does not seem likely that they formed an original unity.

Data from the QPssMss indicates these hymns enjoyed an independent existence. Ps 91 figures prominently in 11QPsAp^{a} which contains the remains of several apocryphal compositions and concludes with Ps 91 (see above, p. 67). There is no evidence for a s/s, but it is clear that here Ps 91 is not connected with 90 in any way.[32]

b. Pss 92 and 93. While there is some evidence for combination in the Hebrew Mss (Kennicott cites 8 Mss, de Rossi 4), there is little else to commend the suggestion. LXX provides 93 with a title while Targum agrees with MT. While I have suggested *possible* evidence for combination in 4QPs^{b} (see above, pp. 99, 133-35), it is extremely tenuous being based on the restoration of an extensive lacuna. Further, the inclusion of Ps 93 alone in 11QPs^{a}, col. 22, would indicate the opposite conclusion. In light of Ps 93's clear thematic and formulaic connections with Pss 96-99, original unity with Ps 92 seems out of the question.[33]

c. Pss 93-99. With the onset of Ps 93, we are faced with a series of seven compositions of which six are completely untitled (Ps 98 bears the simple s/s mzmwr). The close thematic and formulaic agreements in this group renders certainty regarding its original division impossible. The presence of a s/s with Ps 98 and the existence of other compositions known to begin with the identical formula šyrw lyhwh šyr ḥdš (cf. Ps 149:1 and Isa 42:10-13), indicates that 96:1 and 98:1 probably correctly represent new starts (for a "new song"). The isolation of Ps 93 as an independent unit (separate from Ps 92), supports the conclusion that the formulaic introduction of that ps (YHWH mlk), which is repeated at 97:1 and

---

[32]See above, pp. 65, 67.

[33]The tendency to combine both Pss 90-91 and 92-93 offers clear support for the existence of a scribal technique indicating the possible combination of an "untitled" ps with a preceding "titled" one. Pss 90 and 92 both bear titles, while Pss 91 and 93 do not.

99:1, also represents the initiation of a new composition.[34] This affirms the integrity of the beginning of five of the seven pss indicated in MT. Beyond this it seems unwise to go, other than to suggest that Ps 93 is much more closely aligned grammatically and thematically with Pss 96-99 than are Pss 94-95 which intervene.

The analysis of this group of pss has demonstrated (1) a limited Mss tradition supporting various combinations of pss; (2) little evidence supportive of the original unity of those combinations. It should be emphasized that the editorial technique demonstrated above for Books One—Three is not ultimately concerned with the question of "original unity," but with possible alternative traditions for the combination/division of pss. In this regard, the data for Pss 90-99 do not disprove the thesis, but merely remain ambiguous in relation to it. The tendency to combine "untitled" pss indirectly supports such an editorical technique, as it certainly reflects an early scribal acceptance and transmission of legitimate arrangements of the pss.

2. Pss 114-119. These pss overlap partially with the so-called "Egyptian Hallel" (Pss 113-118) which formed a part of Jewish liturgy at the great festivals. According to tradition, at Passover Pss 113-114 were recited before the meal and Pss 115-118 were recited after. It would be most suggestive if the Mss tradition of combination corresponded closely to this liturgical grouping. Unfortunately it does not. In fact, the strongest evidence for combination comes precisely at the point of greatest liturgical disjunction: between Pss 114 and 115.

a. Pss 114 and 115. Kennicott cites 19 Hebrew Mss which combine Pss 114 and 115, while de Rossi mentions an amazing 52 corroborating Mss. Clearly this tradition is not constrained by the liturgical use which places 114 and 115 on opposite sides of the *seder*.

I have mentioned further evidence from 4QPs[o] that these two pss were possibly combined there. In addition, many mss of LXX as well as

---

[34]Notice also the similar phrases at the end of Pss 96 (v. 13) and 98 (v. 9) which serve to suggest the conclusion of these compositions.

96:13	98:9
lpny yhwh ky bʾ	lpny yhwh ky bʾ
ky bʾ lšpṭ hʾrṣ	lšpṭ hʾrṣ
yšpṭ tbl bṣdq	yšpṭ tbl bṣdq
wʿmym bʾmwntw	wʿmym bmyšrym

Similarly Pss 97 and 99 end on the same note of God's "holiness."

97:12	99:9
whwdw lzkr qdšw	ky qdwš yhwh ʾlhynw

the Syriac join these hymns. When one considers the arrangement of pss 111-118 in MT and Targum and the distribution of the hllwyh s/ss and p/ss among them, Ps 114 stands naked without either addition. LXX has rectified this anomaly by shifting the hllwyh p/s of Ps 113 (which also bears a hllwyh s/s) to the beginning of 114; combining 114 and 115; and shifting the p/ss of Pss 115, 116, and 117 to the beginnings of Pss 116, 117 and 118. The resulting completely balanced format of seven pss, each beginning with hllwyh, violates the scribal convention previously mentioned in which, following a series of hllwyh pss, a new section is introduced by a hwdw ps (Ps 118 in this case). In MT the tradition for the combination of Pss 114-115 is preserved without this loss. Ps 114 is left without s/s or p/s, signifying its possible connection with 115, since a hllwyh s/s would have emphasized independence and obscured any possibility of combination. MT, then, is not concerned to produce a balanced format (as LXX), but intends to preserve the alternate tradition of the combination of Pss 114 and 115, and does so without obscuring the function of Ps 118 to introduce the subsequent section.

b. Pss 116-117-118. Other than the combination of Pss 114 and 115, the largest amount of Mss evidence centers around the abbreviated text of Ps 117 (two verses; 16 words). According to *BHS*, many Mss combine 117 with either 116 or 118. Kennicott cites 21 Mss combining 116 and 117; 23 combining 117 and 118; and three Mss which combine all three. It seems most likely that this combination is a function of the size of Ps 117 which is by far the shortest composition in the Psalter. Its nearest competitors (Ps 134—3 verses; 32 words and Ps 131—3 verses; 30 words) contain almost twice as many words. This brevity and its general praise content would facilitate its connection as an epilogue or prologue to other compositions.

3. Pss 103 and 104. Here again the Mss testify to a tradition of combination for Ps 103 with its Davidic s/s (ldwd) and Ps 104 with no s/s but a hllwyh p/s. The effect of this combination is to extend Davidic authority to the second composition as well as the first. Kennicott cites eight Hebrew Mss which so combine, de Rossi another two. Targum, Syriac and LXX all divide these pss. LXX also provides Ps 104 with its own Davidic s/s. The presence of this s/s is supported by data from two QPssMss. In 11QPs[a], Ps 104 immediately follows Ps 118 and is preceded by the s/s ldwyd (the exact Hebrew reflex of LXX). Again, in 4QPs[e], Ps 104 occurs following what may be the remains of Ps 118. Although the context is broken, and no s/s is extant, the position of the opening lines of 104 suggest the possibility that such a s/s was originally present.

Along with this explicit support for the independence of Ps 104, several QPssMss juxtapose Pss 103 and 104 with other pss. In 4QPs[b] Pss 104-111 are omitted *en masse* and, as a result, Ps 103 is followed immediately by Ps 112. In 11QPs[a], both Pss 103 and 104 occur, but the MT sequence is disturbed since Ps 109 follows 103 and Ps 118 precedes Ps 104. Finally, in 4QPs[d], Ps 104 is preceded by Ps 147.

The clearest, single shared characteristic which binds Pss 103 and 104 together is the formulaic expression with which each opens and concludes.

brky npšy ʾt yhwh (103:1, 2, 22; 104:1, 35)

This verbatim repetition of phrases—especially at the end of 103 and the beginning of 104—again calls to mind the scribal technique employed in the colophons of clay tablets to maintain proper sequence of tablets. The incipit of the succeeding tablets was written in the colophon of the preceding to indicate the correct sequence. If the use here of repetitious formulae does not correspond exactly to this technical use of the incipit or tag-line, one is still reminded of the scribal tendency in the hymnic catalogues to group together compositions with the same or similar incipits (see above, pp. 55-58).

Briefly summarized, the study of the pss-headings reveals the anomalous occurrences of isolated "untitled" pss in Books 1-3 of the Psalter. This leads to the question of the reason or significance of the phenomenon, which is related to an impressive Mss tradition for the combination of these very pss with those which precede. Certain data suggest this is not a secondary resolution of the "problem" presented by the presence of untitled pss. (1) the original unity of Pss 9 and 10 as suggested by the disturbed acrostic pattern; (2) the apparent original unity of Pss 42 and 43; (3) the Qumran evidence supporting the combination of Ps 38 and 71 (and indirectly supporting the combination of 70 and 71) all suggest that the occurrence of untitled pss in these Books is directly related to a real tradition of combination.

The inference drawn is that the inclusion of these pss in their present contexts as separate compositions (indicated by scribal conventions of presentation) but *without* s/s, reflects an awareness on the part of the Psalter editor(s) of alternate traditions for the combination/division of these pss and represents a purposeful technique employed to preserve them. This inference can be extended to other examples of such pss in Books 4 and 5, with varying degrees of confidence.

THE "TACIT" ARRANGEMENT OF PSS

I have dealt just previously with the use of the explicit statements attached to the pss to assist in the organization of MT 150. By and large, I have found that, while explicit statements abound in the Psalter, explicit editorial concern and purpose are almost never voiced. With the exception of the p/s in Ps 72:20 (and even this has its difficulties), editorial purpose must be "divined" from internal considerations. I have shown how the explicit statements in the pss-headings were employed by the editor(s) to organize and to structure the Psalter. Are "non-explicit" elements (i.e., those found *outside* the s/ss) employed in the same fashion? If so, what are those elements and how do they function? These are the concerns to which I now turn.

Among the non-explicit elements which clearly function editorially in MT 150, I have already mentioned the "doxologies" which conclude Books One through Four. When I claim these "clearly function editorially," I do not intend to suggest there is unequivocal agreement in this regard. Both Mowinckel and Dahood are skeptical about the "conscious" use of these doxologies to divide the Psalter. Mowinckel is most direct in his criticism.

> The division into five, probably in imitation of "The Law," . . . only partially coincides with the divisions between the original smaller collections, but follows the liturgical doxologies, which happened to occur in the texts from the earlier collections. . . . These were taken to be intended divisions and concluding doxologies between "the books," and then Ps 150 might be looked upon as the concluding doxology of the whole Psalter. Originally . . . these doxologies had nothing to do with the collection, neither with the earlier . . . collections, nor with . . . the Psalter as a whole.[35]

Dahood is more cautious in his evaluation.

> Each of these five books ends with a doxology of benediction, and though these doxologies are found in the Greek translation of the 2nd Century B.C. this is not explicit evidence that

---

[35]Mowinckel, *PIW2*, 197 and note 3.

> the translators considered these benedictions as closing our Books of the Psalter.[36]

There are several questions involved in this issue. (1) Were the doxologies originally part of the pss to which they are now attached, or were they later editorial additions, inserted precisely for the purpose of indicating the ends of the first four books? (2) If the doxologies were original parts of their compositions, were these pss consciously utilized by the editor(s) at the ends of the books, or were the bounds of the books secondarily determined by the "accidental" position of these pss in the Psalter? I will pursue each of these questions in turn.

Against the late editorial insertion of the doxologies several criticisms have been advanced. First, there is the problem of the high degree of formal variation which exists among these doxologies. Comparison brings this out clearly.

41:14	72:19	89:53	106:48
brwk yhwh	brwk yhwh ʾlhym	brwk yhwh	brwk yhwh
ʾlhy yśrʾl	ʾlhy yśrʾl ʿśh nplʾwt lbdw wbrwk šm kbwdw		ʾlhy yśrʾl
mhʿwlm wʿd hʿwlm	lʿwlm	lʿwlm	mn hʿwlm wʿd hʿwlm
	wymlʾ kbwdw ʾt kl hʾrṣ		
			w ʾmr kl hʿm
ʾmn wʾmn	ʾmn wʾmn	ʾmn wʾmn	ʾmn

Only one phrase (brwk yhwh) is identically rendered in all four doxologies. The phrase ʾlhy yśrʾl is completely omitted in 89:53, and the other parallels are subject to variation throughout. 72:19 is very expansive, almost doubling the size of the benediction.

It is certainly questionable whether a single redactor (or group of redactors), dividing the Psalter into sections at one time, would have introduced such variety into the phrases which were intended to mark the conclusions of those sections. That this variety is not limited to the omission and/or addition of phrases, but extends to the formal makeup of

---

[36]Dahood, *Psalms I,* xxx.

those words and phrases (i.e., mhʿwlm vs. mn hʿwlm vs. lʿwlm; ʾmn wʾmn vs. wʾmr kl hʿm ʾmn) supports a diverse origin for these doxologies.

Aligned with the formal distinctions is the total lack of any concluding formula for the fifth and final book. This omission has been explained in two ways by the proponents of editorial insertion of the doxologies. (1) The Psalter originally concluded elsewhere than Ps 150, with a ps which also bore such a doxology. L. T. W. Riedel suggested Ps 135:19-21 as a doxology befitting the conclusion of the whole Psalter and viewed Pss 136-150 as a subsequent appendix.[37] (2) Others (as Mowinckel indicates above, p. 182) view Ps 150, with its all-consuming praise of YHWH, as the final doxology to the Psalter. This total deviation from the previous formal pattern seems somewhat dissatisfying, however.

Further, in two instances the "concluding" formula does not actually conclude, but is itself followed by an additional element which cannot have been part of the book division process. In Ps 106, the doxology is followed immediately by the liturgical element hllwyh, which is clearly to be connected with the individual ps, and not the Book or even the concluding formula (as the remaining occurrences of hllwyh show). Some have tried to remove the difficulty by shifting the p/s to the beginning of Ps 107 as its heading.[38] In view of my discussion above concerning the function of the hllwyh and subsequent hwdw pss (107 is a hwdw ps), this seems unlikely. Nowhere do we find hllwyh pss *beginning* a section.[39]

This positional difficulty is joined by the formal variant in the doxology of Ps 106, in which the otherwise consistently rendered ʾmn wʾmn receives a more narrative tone as wʾmr kl hʿm ʾmn. This variation has been connected with the parallel passage in 1 Chr 16:8-37, which utilizes phrases also found in Pss 96, 105 and 106:1, 47-48.

1 Chr 16:35-36	Ps 106:47-48
ʾmrw hwšyʿnw	hwšyʿnw
ʾlhy yšʿnw	yhwh ʾlhynw
wqbṣnw whṣylnw	wqbṣnw
mn hgwym	mn hgwym
lhwdwt lšm qdšk	lhwdwt lšm qdšk
lhštbḥ bthltk	lhštbḥ bthltk

[37] L. T. W. Riedel, "Zur Redaktion des Psalters," *ZAW* 19 (1899) 169-72 (hereafter cited as "Redaktion").

[38] Riedel, "Redaktion," 170.

[39] Mowinckel, *PIW2*, 196.

brwk yhwh
ʾlhy yśrʾl
mn hʿwlm wʿd hʿwlm
wʾmrw kl hʿm
ʾmn whll yhwh

brwk yhwh
ʾlhy yśrʾl
mn hʿwlm wʿd hʿwlm
wʾmr kl hʿm
ʾmn hllwyh

While some have tried to claim that the presence of these verses in the Chronicler presents proof of the five-fold division of the Psalter (and even the final closure of the whole MT 150) in the fourth century B.C., it seems much more obvious that the doxology of the ps is derived from the narrative of 1 Chr 16 rather than *vice versa.*[40] The perfect verb form (otherwise unparalleled in these doxologies) is clear evidence of the dependence of Ps 106 on 1 Chr 16. The situation is quite comparable to the relation between Ps 18 and 2 Sam 22:1-5 where again the Ps is an adaptation of the narrative.[41]

The second instance of an additional element following the concluding doxology occurs at the end of Ps 72 in verse 20. There we find an apparent p/s which marks the conclusion of a collection of "Prayers of David, the son of Jesse."

klw tplwt dwd bn yšy

"Finished are the prayers of David, the son of Jesse"

The p/s would seem to refer either to the immediately preceding group of pss (Book Two) or to the combined collection of pss up to that point (Books One and Two). Clearly there is no reason for it to stand *after* the doxology which indicates one of the structural divisions of a completed Psalter. Position implies the doxology is a part of the ps, which is itself a part of the collection concluded by the p/s in 72:20.[42]

As a result of these deliberations it is clear that the doxologies in 41:14; 72:19; 89:53 and 106:48 are not simply late editorial insertions for the purpose of dividing the Psalter into five "books." They are instead integral parts of the pss they accompany and have their origin in the

[40]See Brevard S. Child's discussion of the analogous relationship of Ps 18 and 2 Sam 22:1-7, "Psalm Titles," 138-39.

[41]Childs, "Psalm Titles," 138-39.

[42]See Herkenne's discussion, *Die Heilige Schrift des alten Testaments, Das Buch der Psalmen* (Bonn: Peter Hanstein, 1936) 3.

liturgical milieu of the cult.[43] If the doxologies are not to be separated from their pss, how then is one to explain the five-fold Psalter division? Are the five books an artificial division "imposed" on the Psalter text; a division which merely made use of doxologies which had assumed their positions as the result of random distribution? Or, on the other hand, have whole pss, with doxologies intact, been employed by the editor(s) to indicate the bounds of the five-fold division?[44]

My study of the distribution of the technical terms in the pss-headings has already shown that the five-fold division is a real and purposeful division which is indicated internally by the editorial use of author designations and genre categories to mark the points of division and to bind together disparate groups *within* these larger sections. This coincidence of internal breaks and the occurrence of the doxologies is certainly *not* fortuitous, but represent editorially induced methods of giving "shape" to the pss corpus.[45]

In the Mesopotamian hymns and catalogues, "praise" and "blessing" (Hallel and Doxology) frequently concluded documents or sections within documents. It is not surprising then to discover a similar technique in the Hebrew hymnic literature. The study of 11QPs^a has revealed the use of hllwyh pss to indicate internal divisions within that scroll. In an extended discussion at that point, I also traced this motif into MT 150 itself. There we find four groups of hllwyh pss, all of which mark the conclusion of Psalter segments.

---

[43]Mowinckel, *PIW2,* 193.

[44]Mowinckel, *PIW2,* is a bit confusing in his remarks on this subject. On p. 197 he seems to reject any editorial purpose behind the positioning of the doxologies when he claims they were (mistakenly) "taken to be intended divisions and concluding doxologies between the 'books' . . . ." But earlier he seemed to allow the possibility of the later editorial use of these pss. "The concluding doxologies . . . were not added by the collectors as 'concluding formulas' for the separate collections, it is the collectors who have used them as concluding doxologies for the psalm collections" (a rather confusing statement found on p. 193).

[45]It is most interesting that two of these four concluding pss are part of the most narrowly defined group of "Royal Psalms" (Ps 72 at the end of Book Two and Ps 89 at the end of Book Three). Coupled with (1) the positioning of Ps 2 (another "Royal Psalm") at the beginning of Book One and (2) the editorial move to soften the transition between Books One and Two (by the use of the lmnṣḥ terms), this all suggests a purposeful editorial arrangement; a suggestion which I will develop later.

a. Pss 104-106
b. Pss 111-117
c. Ps 135
d. Pss 146-150

In each of the first three instances, this concluding group of *hllwyh* pss is related to an immediately following ps beginning with the phrase: *hwdw lyhwh ky ṭwb ky l^{c}wlm ḥsdw.* I have presented evidence to suggest that these *hwdw* pss are not part of the concluding grouping, but serve to introduce the succeeding section. For this reason the *hwdw* Ps 107 begins the fifth book of the Psalter, regardless of any internal thematic similarities with Pss 104-106.[46] This also offers an explanation of the lack of any *hwdw* ps following Pss 146-150: there is no new section to be introduced.

Beginning with Pss 90 and 106, some interesting parallels develop when one compares the pss which would begin and end the later segments of the Psalter, as marked out by these *hllwyh-hwdw* pss groupings.

1. *Pss 90 and 106.* Ps 90 is the only ps in the Psalter attributed to Moses (cf. 90:1). In the light of the fact that it follows the doxology of Ps 89 and clearly begins a new section, it is interesting to note that there is a strong emphasis in Book Five on the person of Moses. Outside this group of pss the name of Moses is found only *once* in the Psalter (77:21). Yet here, in the space of only eight pss, his name is mentioned *seven* times (90:1; 99:6; 103:7; 105:26; 106:16; 106:23; 106:32). Even the distribution is illuminative. Other than the s/s of 90:1 and the single occurrence at 99:6, the instances are clustered near the end. Indeed, nearly half occur in the final ps (106) itself. A comparison of Pss 90 and 106 brings out certain thematic similarities which are not by themselves remarkable, but, in the context of the above, become suggestive.

Ps 90, after an opening expression of dependence on YHWH ("refuge in all generations"), considers the transient nature of mankind which finds itself "consumed" by God's anger because of its own iniquity and sin. Although there is no release in sight, the ps ends with a plea that YHWH show favor to his servants and remember his steadfast love. In a similar, but more complex vein, Ps 106 traces the rebellious history of Israel before God. "Both we and our fathers have sinned, we have committed iniquity, we have done wickedly" the poet claims (v. 6), resulting in the anger and wrath of YHWH (vv. 40-42). However, as YHWH has shown

---

[46]Riedel, "Redaktion," 170-71.

mercy in the past, there still is hope for mercy in the future (vv. 43-46). The hope is the basis of the poet's final plea that YHWH will "save us . . . and gather us from among the nations."

The coincidence of these thematic parallels with the presence of doxologies, hllwyh and hwdw pss-groupings lends strong support for purposeful editorial shaping of this segment.

2. *Pss 107 and 117.* The brevity of Ps 117 prohibits any sweeping comparisons and conclusions. There is, however, a certain "fitness" and balance between 107 at the beginning and 117 at the end of this group of pss. The constant refrain of Ps 107 repeatedly calls to mind that at times of great trouble, the people cried to YHWH and he delivered them (vv. 6, 13, 19, 28). Therefore the people are exhorted to praise YHWH for his steadfast love (vv. 8, 15, 21, 31, 39-43). Ps 117 stands as the communal response of the people to these repeated exhortations.

> Praise YHWH, all nations!
> Extol him, all peoples!
> For great is his steadfast love toward us
> And the faithfulness of YHWH endures forever!
> Halleluyah!

3. *Pss 118 and 135.* These two pss share several very clear thematic and verbal correspondences. In 118:2-4, the psalmist exhorts *three* groups to praise YHWH.

> Let Israel say,
> "His steadfast love endures forever."
> Let the house of Aaron say,
> "His steadfast love endures forever."
> Let those who fear YHWH say,
> "His steadfast love endures forever."

Ps 135 concludes with reference to these same three groups (with the addition of "the house of Levi").

> O house of Israel, bless YHWH!
> O house of Aaron, bless YHWH!
> O house of Levi, bless YHWH!
> O You that fear YHWH, bless YHWH!
> (135:19-20)

Both are pss of reliance on YHWH (118:8-9, 14 and 135:15-18). Ps 118 concludes with a procession into the "house of YHWH."

> Blessed be he who comes in the name of YHWH
> We bless you from the house of YHWH.
> (118:26)

Ps 135 begins with exhortation to those that stand "in the house of YHWH."

> Praise the name of YHWH
> give praise, O servants of YHWH
> You that stand in the house of YHWH
> in the courts of the house of our God!
> (135:1-2)

4. *Pss 136 and 145*. There must be some justification for the conclusion of this segment at Ps 145 and not Ps 150. It has long been observed that Ps 150 stands as a concluding doxology to the whole Psalter. In fact, the last five hllwyh pss (146-150) have been considered the concluding pronouncement of praise of YHWH. Joseph P. Brennan, in his recent article, "Psalms 1-8: Some Hidden Harmonies," tries to draw parallels between Pss 2 and 149 as the editorially affixed beginning and end of the final Psalter (omitting Pss 1 and 150 as introduction and conclusion).[47] I feel it is necessary to go a step farther and to realize that this whole group of hllwyh pss (146-150) is liturgically motivated and finds its motivating force in the final verse of Ps 145:21, where David calls forth this great paean of praise with his exhortation:

> My mouth will speak the praise of YHWH
> And let all flesh bless his holy name
> forever and ever!

I investigate this liturgical movement more fully below.

The comparison of Pss 135 and 145 again reveals numerous thematic parallels. Both are concerned to praise the "wonderful works" (nplʾwt) of YHWH (his creative works in both 136:4-9 and 145:4-7, 10-13). Both praise YHWH's enduring steadfast love (136 throughout; 145:8-9, 13-20).

---

[47] Joseph P. Brennan, "Psalms 1-8: Some Hidden Harmonies," *BTB* 10 (1980) 25-29.

In more explicit correspondences, both praise YHWH for the sustenance he provides to his creatures (136:25; 145:15-16) and both refer to "all flesh" (kl bśr) in their exhortations to praise (135:25-26; 145:21).

In summary, the survey of these pss reveals several facts about the editorial arrangement of the pss. First, the hllwyh pss conclude segments, both at the end of major divisions (as Pss 104-106) and within them (as Pss 111-117 and Ps 135). Second, rather than forming a related part of these concluding hllwyh groups, the hwdw pss which follow introduce the next segment of pss. This conclusion helps to understand better the relationship of such pss as 117 (hllwyh) and 118 (hwdw); 135 (hllwyh) and 136 (hwdw).[48] Finally, the results indicate that the positioning of the opening and closing pss of these segments reflects *purposeful* choice and arrangement of pss rather than chance juxtaposition.

THEMATIC GROUPING OF PSS

It has already become apparent through the previous discussions that pss-groupings do occur in MT 150 which are editorially induced and not accidental. I have shown groupings on the basis of author and genre. In the "Enthronement" pss, I have alluded to groupings according to "theme" or content. Thematic groupings are not surprising in such a hymnic collection. However, they are, perhaps, the most subject to individual interpretation and most resistant to convincing demonstration. I would be remiss, however, if I did not look at some examples of rather clear thematic juxtaposition of pss.

1. *Pss 65-68*. In the discussion of the use of genre designations to "bind together" disparate units, I mentioned in passing that this group of four consecutive pss shared a common concern of *praise*. This grouping stands out in its immediate context of consistent prayers of deliverance (cf. Pss 50-72). The one questionable entry in this unity of praise is Ps 68 which presents numerous interpretational problems and has been variously described as (1) a catalogue of hymnic incipits, (2) a festal liturgy, (3) two separate pss and (4) an anthology of short hymns. Regardless how one considers the unity of Ps 68, the praise motif and tone is sustained throughout by successive exclamations of praise.[49]

---

[48]It should be noted that there *are* correspondences between Pss 118 and 115 as well as between 136 and 135. These parallels tend to "soften" the breaks between these "internal" divisions more than the abrupt breaks between 106 and 107.

[49]Two basic references regarding this ps remain: W. F. Albright, "A Catalogue of Early Hebrew Lyric Poems (Psalm LXVIII)," *HUCA* 23 (1950-

Sing to God, sing praises to his name;
life up a song to him who rides upon the clouds;
his name is YHWH, exult before him!
(verse 4)
Blessed be YHWH, who daily bears us up;
God is our salvation.
(verse 19)

Bless God in the great congregation,
YHWH, O you who are of Israel's fountain!
(verse 26)

Sing to God, O kingdoms of the earth,
Sing praises to YHWH
to him who rides in the heavens.
(verses 32-33)

Blessed be God!
(verse 35)

While it does not seem feasible to suggest an over-arching editorial purpose behind the specifics of the arrangement, the thematic connection is unmistakable.[50]

2. *Pss 93, 96-99.* The "Enthronement" pss have already been the subject of discussion in relation to the use of genre groupings. As is obvious, this genre designation is nowhere explicitly set out in the pss, but is the result of the observation of internal verbal and thematic parallels which cluster in these pss. These thematic concerns have been clearly investigated and stated in the study of J. D. W. Watts, and I will but repeat his categories here.[51]

---

51) 1-39 and Samuel Iwry, "Notes on Psalm 68," *JBL* 71 (1952) 161-65. See also the discussions in the various commentaries.

The similarity of verses 4 and 32-33 as well as the parallel "blessing" in verses 19 and 26 offer support for the unity of this composition.

[50]The interesting alternation between "Praise" (Pss 65, 67) and "Blessing" (Pss 66:8, 20; 68:26, 35) are evidence of a larger editorial purpose at work in the arrangement.

[51]J. D. W. Watts, "Yahweh Malak Psalms," *TZ* 21 (1965) 341-48.

A. The characteristic and unique expectation of these Psalms that all the earth, all peoples, or the nations should be present.
B. References to other gods.
C. The signs of exaltation and kingship.
D. The words showing characteristic acts of Yahweh, including creating, making, establishing, sitting, doing wonders, judging, doing righteous acts, and saving.
E. All the words which indicated the attitude of praise before this heavenly king.

The verbal correspondences are striking. All five pss give voice to the kingship of YHWH (93:1; 96:10; 97:1—yhwh mlk; 98:6—hmlk yhwh). Pss 93, 97, and 99 all begin with the formulaic exclamation yhwh mlk "YHWH reigns!" and conclude with statements concerning YHWH's holiness.[52]

93:5

Thy decrees are very sure
holiness befits thy house
O YHWH, for evermore.

97:12

Rejoice in YHWH, O you righteous
and give thanks to his holy name!

99:9

Extol YHWH our God
and worship at his holy mountain
for YHWH our God is holy!

The šyrw pss 96 and 98 also exhibit parallel concern and phraseology at beginning and end.

96:1

Sing to YHWH a new song
Sing to YHWH all the earth

98:1

Sing to YHWH a new song
for he has done
marvelous things

---

[52]Edward Lipiński, "YÂHWEH MÂLÂK," *Bib* 44 (1963) 405-60 and Jarl H. Ulrichsen, "JHWH MĀLĀK: Einige sprachliche Beobachtungen," *VT* 27 (1977) 361-74.

96:12-13	98:8-9
Then shall all the trees of the wood sing for joy before YHWH for he comes for he comes to judge the earth	Let the hills sing for joy together before YHWH for he comes to judge the earth
He will judge the world with righteousness and the peoples with his truth	He will judge the world with righteousness and the peoples with equity.

Other parallels in these five pss include:

1. yrʿm hym wmlʾw
   "Let the sea roar and all that fills it."
   (96:11; 98:7; cf. 93:3-4)

2. ʾp tkwn tbl bl tmwṭ
   "Yea, the world is established, it shall never be moved."
   (93:1; 96:10)

3. *Pss 105-106.* These two songs have long been recognized for their similar concern with YHWH's acts in the history of Israel. Ps 105 consists of a recital of the formative contacts between Israel and her God from the patriarchs to the possession of the promised land. Emphasis throughout falls on the gracious activity of YHWH in Israel's behalf.

This ps is now connected by position with the more sober account in Ps 106. Again the relations of YHWH and Israel are recounted from Egypt until rather obscure references to the exile (vv. 40-46). Here, however, the emphasis is consistently on the rebellious attitude of Israel and the consequent chastisement. The ps concludes with the plea for salvation from exile based on YHWH's continued faithfulness to his covenant (vv. 43-45). In the exile, the loss of the land which serves as the logical conclusion of Ps 105:43-45, required reevaluation. Ps 106 advances the historical time-line of 105 and reinterprets the land experience in light of the exile.

4. *145-150.* I will note this final "hallel" only briefly here because I will return to it in more detail in the discussion of the final shape of the Psalter. It does stand (along with the other groups of hllwyh pss) as an example of a thematically related grouping. The "theme" is obviously the praise of YHWH throughout. I have no doubt that this grouping functions as an answer to the exhortation of David in Ps 145:21.

> My mouth will speak the praise of YHWH
> and let all flesh bless his holy name forever and ever.

In this context, Ps 146 (which is conveniently cast in the first person singular "I") represents the response of David himself to the first half of 145:21. In 147 Israel and Jerusalem join the chorus (cf. vv. 2, 12, 19-20). The infectious praise spreads ever further in Ps 148 where the angelic hosts and the creation break forth into song (vv. 2-3, 11-12). In 149, focus returns to the people of YHWH as Israel praises their God for the accomplishment of his purposes. In the final Ps 150, we hear the great hymnic answer to the second half of 145:21, toward which the whole hallel has been building.

> Let everything that breathes praise YHWH!
> PRAISE YHWH!

Surely this is the reflex of "all flesh" whom David adjures in 145:21. Apparently this final chorus of praise has been carefully affixed in its position. I will investigate later just what the significance of this arrangement is for our understanding and interpretation of the Psalter.

There are numerous examples of thematic groupings within the Psalter. Some (as 146-150) apparently play a significant role in the editorial organization and shaping of the final form of the book. I have not attempted to exhaust all possible thematic groupings, but have merely attempted to illustrate this category of editorial technique in the juxtaposition of the pss.

OTHER TECHNIQUES EMPLOYED

Some of the methods for grouping hymns observed in the Mesopotamian literature were (1) the juxtaposition of pss with identical or similar incipits; (2) the use of "catch phrases" or "tag lines" to indicate the sequence of tablets; and (3) the identification of the deity addressed (see chapter 3). All these techniques find few parallels in the Psalter.

1. *Juxtaposition by same or similar incipit.* I can offer but two instances of consecutive pss bearing the same or similar incipits. Interestingly enough, both groups are themselves immediately juxtaposed (103-104; 105-106-107). The first group consists of two pss (103 and 104), both of which begin and end with identical phrases.

brky npšy ʾt yhwh
"Bless YHWH, O my soul!"
(103:1 and 22; 104:1 and 35)

The three pss of the second group (105, 106, 107) share an identical initial term, while 106 and 107 have completely identical first lines.

105:1	hwdw lyhwh qrʾw bšmw
106:1	hwdw lyhwh ky ṭwb ky lʿwlm ḥsdw
107:1	hwdw lyhwh ky ṭwb ky lʿwlm ḥsdw

The juxtaposition of these three similar incipits is complicated by the separation of Books Four and Five between Pss 106 and 107. Whether these pss ever formed an original grouping which was secondarily divided (as some have suggested),[53] is questionable in light of the clear editorial technique utilising hwdw pss to begin sections of the Psalter.

2. *The use of "catch phrases" to indicate connection.* Because of the inscribing of the Hebrew pss on a continuous scroll, the use of "catch phrases" or "tag lines" cannot have assumed as much importance as in the Mesopotamian hymns where tablets often contained a single hymn devoid of any context. There may, however, be a very few remnants of tag lines in the Psalter. I tentatively suggest the following. Ps 7 concludes in verse 18 with the phrase ʾwdh yhwh kṣdqw wʾzmrh šm yhwh ʿlywn, "I will give YHWH thanks because of his righteousness and I will sing praise to the name of YHWH, the Most High." Ps 8 then follows, the beautiful hymn emphasizing the majesty of YHWH and the insignificance of Man, bracketed at beginning and end with the phrase: yhwh ʾdnynw mh ʾdyr šmk bkl hʾrṣ, "YHWH our Lord, how majestic is your name in all the earth!" Ps 9 then continues with phrases very close to 7:18.

ʾwdh yhwh bkl lby	I will praise YHWH with all my heart
ʾsprh kl nplʾwtyk	I will recount your wonderous works
ʾsmḥh wʾʿlṣh bk	I will rejoice and exult in you
ʾzmrh smk ʿlywn	I will sing (praise) to your name, Most High!

It is tempting despite the intervention of Ps 8 to view 7:18 as a "catch phrase" referring to these phrases in 9:2-3 by the "shorthand" method of mentioning only the first and last.

---

[53]Riedel, "Redaktion," 170-71.

The second possible instance of a "catch phrase" is less convincing since the verbal correspondence is not as exact as in the case above. It occurs in the final verses of Ps 32 as a reference to the initial phrases of Ps 33.

32:11 śmḥw byhwh wgylw ṣdyqym
whrnynw kl yšry lb

Rejoice in YHWH and exult, O you righteous
and shout for joy all you upright in heart!

33:1 rnnw sdyqym byhwh
lyšrym nʾwh thlh

Shout for joy, O you righteous in YHWH!
Praise is befitting to the upright.

Correspondence turns on the repetition of the terms ṣdyqym "righteous"; byhwh "in YHWH"; yšry lb/yšrym "upright in heart/upright"; hrnynw/rnnw "shout for joy."

These two pss are already bound together editorially by the lack of a s/s for Ps 33, which I have shown to be an indication of a tradition in which the two were combined as one ps. It may be that the rather loose correspondence between end and beginning is the result of the alternate tradition of separation and, rather than a strict "tag line" or "catch phrase," represents a memory of the connection (perhaps the same connecting phrase has developed in two different directions with the separate pss).

The paucity of clear examples of "catch phrases" in the Psalter emphasizes the lack of importance attached to this technique in the juxtaposition of the Hebrew pss. We must look elsewhere for indications of orderly, editorial arrangement of the pss.

3. *Juxtaposition by the name of the deity addressed.* In the Mesopotamian catalogues, the deity addressed in hymns is an important factor in the grouping of compositions. *CAT.* 11 is an especially clear example of arrangement by deity. On the Reverse of the tablet, col. III, lines 43-62 and col. IV, lines 1-29, 47 hymnic incipits are listed and grouped according to the deity to which they are addressed. All incipits to a particular deity (18 gods and goddesses in all are enumerated) are consecutively juxtaposed.

It is a matter of common knowledge that the name of the deity plays a role in the grouping of the pss in MT 150. The group of 42 pss from Ps

42 through Ps 83 has been designated the "Elohistic Psalter" because here the regular designation of the deity is ʾlhym "Elohīm" in contrast to the predominence of the name YHWH in the remaining 108 pss. The figures are quite impressive. In the 42 pss of the "Elohistic Psalter" ʾlhym occurs 197 times as the divine name. In the 108 pss outside this collection, the situation is far more than reversed. Here YHWH is the name of God more than 600 times, while ʾlhym occurs *as a name* on only 19 occasions.[54] Of these 19, nine occur in the speech of or in relation to unbelievers (and reflect the unbeliever's terminology); four occur in duplicate portions of two pss from the "Elohistic Psalter" (Ps 108 = Pss 57:8-12 + 60:7-14). This leaves only *six* occurrences in which ʾlhym appears to have a force equivalent to that of YHWH.

The really striking feature of these data is not so much the reduced occurrence of the name YHWH in the "Elohistic Psalter" as it is the *almost complete elimination* of ʾlhym as a designation for the God of Israel elsewhere. Could this be evidence of a concerted effort to eradicate the more ambiguous term in favor of the more particularistic YHWH?

Summary: Of the three techniques of juxtaposition mentioned here (similar incipits, catch phrases, deity addressed), only the last can claim any significant support in the arrangement of the Hebrew Psalter. The possible examples of juxtaposition by incipits and the use of catch phrases are all most tenuous and, as isolated examples, do not command a great degree of confidence. One is left to look elsewhere for indications of the editorial purpose behind the MT 150 arrangement.

[54]On four occasions ʾlhym occurs as the general term "gods" in reference to foreign deities (8:6; 135:5; 136:2; 138:1).

7

The Hebrew Psalter II. The Final "Shape" of the Canonical Collection

I have focused my attention thus far on demonstrating individual instances of editorial activity within the Hebrew Psalter. The results of the study have been considerable. I have been able to show (1) that the "book" divisions of the Psalter are real, editorially induced divisions and not accidentally introduced; (2) the "separating" and "binding" functions of author and genre groupings; (3) the lack of a s/s as an indication of a tradition of combination; (4) the use of hllwyh pss to indicate the conclusion of segments; (5) the use of hwdw pss to introduce segments; (6) the existence of thematic correspondences between the beginning and ending pss in some books. All of these findings demonstrate the presence of editorial activity at work in the arrangement of the pss.

A further question remains to be considered. Is there any evidence of an editorial plan and purpose behind the final arrangement of the *whole* Psalter? Or is MT 150 merely the result of a haphazard attempt to join together the remnants of ancient collections and individual pss into a loosely-knit whole? Without denying the existence of previous collections, I feel it is possible to show that the *final* form of MT 150 is the result of a purposeful, editorial activity which sought to impart a meaningful arrangement which encompassed the whole.

Most attempts to explain the structure of the Psalter have seized upon the more obvious organizing elements (the five-fold division; the placement of Ps 1 as an introduction; the final hallel) as keys to divine the editorial purpose behind the book. Other than the view that the five books were formed by the gradual inclusion of disparate ancient collections (Davidic, Qorahite, Asaphite, hm^{c}lwt, hllwyh, enthronement pss) in a rather loose arrangement, only one explanation has warranted continued reconsideration and has even spawned a recent revival with a slight new twist. I am referring to the ancient tradition which relates the five books of the Psalter to the Five Books of Moses, the Pentateuch.

We first learn explicitly of this tradition from the rabbis in the midrash on the psalms.

> As Moses gave five books of laws to Israel, so David gave five Books of Psalms to Israel, the Book of Psalms entitled *Blessed is the man* (Ps 1:1), the Book entitled *For the Leader: Maschil* (Ps 42:1), the Book, *A Psalm of Asaph* (Ps 73:1), the Book, *A Prayer of Moses* (Ps 90:1), and the Book, *Let the redeemed of the Lord say* (Ps 107:2).[1]

On the basis of this tradition, some of the older commentaries have attempted to uncover correspondences between the individual pss in the various books and their parallels in the *Torah*. The results are generally unsatisfactory and highly susceptible to subjective interpretation.[2]

In more recent years, this explanation has received renewed impetus from its connection with the related discussion of the lectionary cycle in the diaspora synagogue. According to opposing systems, the entire Pentateuch was read at public worship in consecutive sections over a period, on the one hand, of *one* year (Babylonian), or, on the other hand, *three* (Palestinian).[3] These weekly Pentateuchal readings were accompanied by appropriate selections (*not* a sequential reading) from the prophets. While

---

[1]William G. Braude, *The Midrash on Psalms* (New Haven: Yale University Press, 1954) 1. 5. M. Dahood, *Psalms I,* xxx and Anton Arens, *Die Psalmen in Gottesdienst des Alten Bundes* (Trier: Paulinus, 1968) 107 suggest that the rather vague statement in the fragmentary text 1Q30 (sprym ḥwmšym) may represent the earliest reference to the five-fold division of the Psalter. This fragment is dated in Dahood's terms "to the turn of the Christian era."

[2]See the comments of C. Th. Niemeyer, *Probleem,* pp. 137-39.

[3]Pertinent literature includes: E. G. King, "The Influence of the Triennial Cycle upon the Psalter," *JTS* 5 (1903) 203-13; Adolf Büchler, "The Reading of the Law and Prophets in a Triennial Cycle," *JQR* 5 (1893) 420-68, 6 (1894) 1-73; N. H. Snaith, "The Triennial Cycle and the Psalter," *ZAW* NF 10 (1933) 302-7; Aileen Guilding, "Some Obscured Rubrics and Lectionary Allusions in the Psalter," *JTS* NS 3 (1952) 41-55; L. Rabinowitz, "Does Midrash Tillim Reflect the Triennial Cycle of Psalms," *JQR* (1935/6) 349-68; Anton Arens, "Hat der Psalter seinen 'Sitz im Leben' in der synagogalen Lesung des Pentateuch?," *Les Psautiers, Orientalia et Biblica Lovaniensius IV* (Louvain: Publications Universitaires, 1961) 107-31; A. Arens, *Die Psalmen in Gottesdienst des Alten Bundes* (Trier: Paulinus, 1968) (hereafter cited as *Gottesdienst*).

there is no explicit tradition that the Psalms were included in the weekly liturgy, certain inferences from the rabbinic writings have led some to suggest that the number of pss (150); the five book division; and the sequential arrangement of the individual pss can best be explained on the basis of their incorporation in a *three*-year lectionary cycle.

The proponents of the triennial cycle generally cite close correspondence between the number of *sedarim* in the pentateuchal books and the number of pss in the parallel Psalter divisions. They further attempt to explain the position of certain pss in the Psalter as the result of their connection with certain pentateuchal pericopes. So Ps 1 came to its position, not so much as an introduction to the Psalter, but as an introduction or preface to the *Torah* lectionary cycle.[4]

One major difficulty confronted by all the advocates of this view is the large discrepancy in the number of pericopes in the pentateuchal books (especially Numbers and Deuteronomy) in comparison to the number of pss in the corresponding books of the Psalter. The *sedarim* for Genesis—Deuteronomy have been variously enumerated by these scholars themselves (see table 5 below).

	Büchler	Rabinowitz	Arens	Pss
Gn	42	43	44	41
Ex	30	29	31	31
Lv	17	23	25	17
Nu	27	32	30	17
Dt	28	27	31	44
Totals:	144	154	161	150

Table 5. Enumeration of Pentateuchal Sedarim Compared with the Pss in the Five Book Division

[4]Arens, *Gottesdienst*, p. 170 "Der [Ps 1] ist *per se* als Vorspruch der Toralesung hierher [to its present position] gekommen, *per accidens* hat er auch die Funktion des Eröffnungsliedes in der Sammlung des Psalters übernommen."

Even if one accepts the reconstruction of Büchler, which most nearly coincides with the MT 150 arrangement, there is an especially large discrepancy in the 4th and 5th books.

Num—27 pericopes	Book 4—17 pss (90-106)
Deut—28 pericopes	Book 5—44 pss (107-150)

The deletion of pss 146-150 as a final Hallel reduces Book Five to 39 pss, but does little to resolve the issue. Solution is generally sought by (1) denying that the doxology of 106 represents the original conclusion of Book Four and (2) positing a new point of conclusion more compatible with the pentateuchal pericopes. The method followed in determining the point of division is usually to accept Ps 119 with its emphasis on *Torah* as the appropriate ps to accompany the opening pericope of Deuteronomy. The "original" conclusion of Book Four, then, must have fallen after Ps 118. The resulting correspondences remain inexact, but fall more within an acceptable range.

Num—27 pericopes	Book 4—29 pss (90-118)
Deut—28 pericopes	Book 5—32 pss (119-150)

Other more minor deletions and adjustments attempt to achieve more exact correspondence in some instances.[5] In spite of the tempting nature of these suggestions, I find a number of difficulties with this attempt to explain the arrangement of the Psalter on the basis of the triennial synagogue lectionary.

1. There is no agreement, either among the Mss or among the scholars themselves, as to the exact number of pericopes for each of the five books of the *Torah*. Niemeyer criticizes Snaith and his predecessors for this very fact, and the same difficulty applies to Arens' more recent attempt. According to Niemeyer, the Mss cited by Büchler himself divide the *sedarim* variously into 154, 155, 161, 167, and 175 readings, and *none* approximate the 144 (Büchler, Hayes) or 148 (Snaith, Arens) which the reconstructions require.[6]

2. The necessity to alter the division between Books Four and Five is most damaging. First, the denial that the doxology of Ps 106 marks the proper division calls into question the similar function attributed to the preceding doxologies in 41, 72, 89. The attempts to suggest the movement

---

[5]Snaith (p. 304) finds it necessary to omit Pss 108 and 117.

[6]Niemeyer, *Probleem*, 79-81.

of this doxology from its "original" position are even more speculative and unconvincing. The attempt to divide after Ps 118 goes contrary to the evidence offered above that hwdw pss *introduce* rather than conclude their segments. Finally, if one is concerned to speak of the "final form" of the Psalter, it is apparent that a division after Ps 118 (if it *ever* existed) has not been preserved in the canonical "shape" which has all the earmarks of an intentional editorial arrangement.

3. The correspondences adduced in support of the connection of particular pss and parallel pentateuchal/prophetic readings are on the whole quite strained and not convincing. H.-J. Kraus is rather harsh in his evaluation.

> Whenever a contentual correspondence between the books of the Pentateuch and the books of the Psalter is constructed, the result is always a series of absurd combinations.[7]

Indeed, the correspondences cited by Arens are so tenuous, that they appear to me to be the results of an attempt to *find* links between passages which were originally unrelated, rather than natural correspondences.

4. Finally, if the pss *were* read in the three-year lectionary cycle (and this has *not* been established), this does *not* mean the Psalter was organized on that basis. The strained nature of the correspondences adduced would seem to confirm this. Certainly more appropriate selections could have been found within the Psalter itself to accompany many of the *Torah sedarim* discussed by Arens, had the editor been able to arrange or rearrange his collection freely!

Summary: It is not established that the pss were ever read in the three-year lectionary cycle. It is especially doubtful that the Psalter owes its final form to exigencies dictated by the pentateuchal *sedarim*. The widespread variation in enumeration of *sedarim*, the large discrepancy between *sedarim* and the distribution of pss in the five books, the large amount of "reconstruction" necessary to achieve agreement, and the strained nature of parallel readings adduced in the end fail to convince.

Where then is one to turn for an indication of the editorial purpose behind the arrangement of the pss? Nowhere else than to the pss themselves. The most likely starting points are those parts of the Psalter

---

[7]H.-J. Kraus, *Psalmen I* (Neukirchen-Vluyn: Neukirchener, 1972) xiv.

which most clearly exhibit evidence of editorial shaping and concern. Three which come readily to mind are (1) the "introductory" Ps 1; (2) the five-book division; and (3) the final Hallel (Pss 146-150).

1. *The Function of Ps 1 as an Introduction.* A number of factors have combined to indicate Ps 1 was intentionally set in its position as an introduction to the whole Psalter. (a) It bears no s/s or attribution of authorship, which in the first book is unusual. Elsewhere such "untitled" pss have been shown to be subject to editorial manipulation. (b) Certain "western" texts of Acts 13:33 cite a portion of Ps 2:7 as "in the first psalm." While this may be variously interpreted (as an error, a sign that Ps 1 was not at that point attached prior to Ps 2, a sign that Pss 1 and 2 were combined as one), the statement is not incompatible with a text form (actually demonstrated by several Mss cited by de Rossi) in which Ps 1, although present and initial, is unnumbered, with enumeration beginning with *our* Ps 2 (as Ps 1).[8]

---

[8]John T. Willis, in his recent article "Psalm 1—An Entity," *ZAW* 91 (1979) 381-401 (hereafter cited as "Psalm 1"), exhaustively considers the evidence and the literature concerning the relationship of Ps 1 to Ps 2 as well as to the rest of the Psalter. Extensive bibliographical information on the subject can be found there.

As for the data from Kennicott and de Rossi for the inclusion of Ps 1 before Ps 2 as an unnumbered "preface," I give below my translation from the original Latin of the pertinent portions.

A. From Benjamin Kennicott, ed., *Vetus Testamentum Hebraicum cum Variis Lectionibus,* Tomus Primus (Oxford: Clarendon, 1776).

> 1. Notes to Codex 157:
> Psalm 1 lacks a number, as if it is a preface; to the second is added a slightly larger א, as an indication of the first psalm: in the same manner also the third ב, fourth ג, etc. (cf. Acts 13:33).
>
> 2. Notes to Codex 168:
> Psalm 1 is considered a *quasi* Preface: because numeration by letters in the margin begins with א at the psalm [which] in our [Psalter] is the second, ב at the third, etc.

B. From Joh. Bern. de Rossi, *Variae Lectiones Veteris Testamenti ex immensa Mss. editorumq. codicum* (Parmae/ex Regio Typographeo, 1784-1798).

> 1. Volume 3, Notes to Psalm 1.
> Psalm 1 is not numbered, just as if a prologue, as in certain Greek codices, and moreover, number 1 begins at Psalm 2 in my codices 234, 879.

Although some (building on the rabbinic pronouncement that the first ps begins with "blessing" [ʾšry hʾyš—Ps 1:1] and ends with "blessing" [ʾšry kl ḥwsy bw—Ps 2:11]) have maintained that Pss 1 and 2 form a unified composition, the recent article by John T. Willis makes a conclusive case for their individual integrity.[9] Willis concludes on the basis of his study that:

1. The vast majority of Ms evidence supports separation of the two.

2. The church Fathers, while aware of Mss which combined 1 and 2, "almost unanimously" separated them in actual practice.

3. The verbal and thematic parallels adduced by the proponents of combination are strained and forced.

4. The two pss are of very different "types" (Ps 1 a "Wisdom" or "Torah" ps; Ps 2 a "Royal" ps).

5. Ps 1 evidences a clear, unmistakably unified internal structure which is complete in itself and independent of Ps 2.

6. "The subject matter, purpose, and setting of these two literary pieces are widely diverse."[10]

As Willis states, "the recurrence of certain words and phrases in Ps 1 and 2 may suggest one reason why these two psalms have been placed in juxtaposition, but it does not show that they should be interpreted together as one psalm."[11] He is certainly right in his assessment of these two pss.

> Ps 1 distinguishes two ways of life and two fates, that of the righteous and that of the wicked; it is timeless in its application, as far as its author is concerned; the author's purpose is didactic. Ps 2 is an address to hostile, rebellious nations, charging them to submit to Yahweh and his king, and warning

---

2. Volume 4, Appendix, p. 238.

Psalm 1 is not numbered and Psalm 2 is reckoned as number 1 also in Kenn. 157 and 168 [see above], as observed in their description. In the same manner Cod. Cantab. and other Greek and Latin codices in Paul's citation Acts 13:33. . . . Add after these codices Kenn. 164.

3. Volume 5, Supplements, p. 95.

Psalm 2 is marked as the first also in my codex 1117, in Erfurtensi 5, in the Haalens Bible, and in Ms. I Erfurtensi Jarchiani Commentarii according to Breithaupt in the notes to this book. So Paul, Acts 13:33 in the Greek, some Latin codices and fathers.

[9] John T. Willis, "Psalm 1," 381-401.

[10] Willis, "Psalm 1," 395.

[11] Willis, "Psalm 1," 393.

> them of the consequences of refusing to do so; it deals with a specific incident (historical and/or cultic in nature) and thus is bound to time and circumstance.[12]

The very qualities which Willis observes in Ps 1 enhance its appropriateness as an introduction. It *is* timeless and didactic. It holds up for the reader the two ways: the way of Life and the way of Death; the way of prosperity and the way of destruction. As Brevard S. Childs notes:

> Certainly in its final stage of development Ps. 1 has assumed a highly significant function as a preface to the psalms which are to be read, studied, and meditated upon. The Torah of God which is the living Word of God is mediated through its written form as sacred scripture. With the written word Israel is challenged to meditate day and night in seeking the will of God. Indeed, as a heading to the whole Psalter the blessing now includes the faithful meditation on the sacred writings which follow.[13]

The effect of the editorial fixation of the first ps as an introduction to the whole Psalter is subtly to alter how the reader views and appropriates the pss collected there. The emphasis is now on meditation rather than cultic performance; private, individual use over public, communal participation. In a strange transformation, Israel's words of response to her God have now become the Word of God to Israel.[14]

The Psalter has on occasion been styled "the Hymn Book of the Second Temple." This rather unfortunate designation has had the adverse effect of focusing a disproportionate amount of attention on the individual compositions contained within. A "hymn book" collects hymns so that they may be readily available for individual use in worship. Emphasis is placed on the secondary use of the individual members of the collection rather than the collection itself. While some hymn books evidence a limited attempt to group their contents by theme, interest or liturgical function, there is seldom any sustained, organizational purpose at work in consecutive arrangement.

It is this view of a "hymn book" which is normally applied to the Hebrew Psalter: a source book from which to extract individual pss which

---

[12]Willis, "Psalm 1," 396.
[13]B. S. Childs, *IOTS*, 513.
[14]Childs, *IOTS*, 513-14.

are then read in another context which is provided for our own purposes. It is this view also which I have termed "unfortunate," for it obscures the indications that in its "final form" the Psalter is a book to be *read* rather than to be *performed*; to be *meditated over* rather than to be *recited from*.

While Ps 1 as introduction sets the "tone" for an approach to the Psalter, it indicates this is a collection to be read rather than performed; it turns attention away from the individual cultic setting of single compositions to the larger *literary* context of the whole; it stresses the importance of the approach (it is a matter of Life or Death). While it provides hermeneutical principles for the correct approach to the pss, it does not provide a key to the nature of the *message* contained within. We know only that we are to find the "Word of God" there. The *content* of that Word is not specified. Hints as to the "message" which the editor(s) intended to convey through this collection begin to appear as one surveys the five-fold editorial division of the Psalter.

2. *The five-book division of the psalter.* A close survey of the five-book division reveals a number of distinctions which can be drawn between the earlier and the later books.

a. The first three books conclude with doxology formulae while Book Five concludes with a series of hllwyh pss. Book Four (90-106) combines the two methods with a series of hllwyh pss (104-106) as well as a doxology (106:48). The apparent variant quality of the doxology in 106:48 and its apparent dependence on 1 Chr 16 has been discussed previously.

b. The technique of concluding segments with hllwyh pss and introducing segments with hwdw pss is confined to Books Four and Five. It has no parallel in the first three books.

c. The separating/binding function of author/genre groupings is far more prominent in Books One-Three and is practically non-existent in the later books.

d. The marked concentration of "titled" pss in Books One through Three as compared with the relative paucity of such pss (28 out of 61 pss—considering hllwyh as a liturgical element and not a "title") in Books Four and Five as compared to only 6 "untitled" pss among the 89 pss of the first three books.

e. The appearance of "Royal" pss at the "seams" of the books is restricted to the first three divisions (Pss 2, 72, 89). These distinctions imply a separation between Books One-Three and Books Four and Five; a separation borne out by variations of content as well as editorial technique. Is there any explanation for this break?

The placement of the "Royal" pss mentioned above may provide an initial clue. Their occurrence at the "seams" has all the indications of intentional arrangement. They bracket the whole of Books One-Three at beginning and end (Pss 2 and 89) and mark the division between the second and third divisions (Ps 72). The omission of a recognized "Royal" ps at the juncture of Books One and Two may be related to the slight, editorial "binding" accomplished by the consecutive occurrence of lmnṣḥ in the s/ss of Pss 39-47 spanning the transition between these two books. Thematic connections between Pss 41 and 72, however, raise the possibility that Ps 41, while not included in the modern category "Royal" pss, may function here in a similar fashion to Ps 72.[15]

The presence in 72:20 of the p/s announcing the conclusion of "the prayers of David, son of Jesse" suggests Books One and Two may have combined to form an earlier collection introduced and concluded by "Royal" pss, a collection which because of its high Davidic content (60 of 70 pss) might well justify the description "prayers of David." With the inclusion of the Solomonic Ps 72, the collection takes on the character of a celebration of the faithfulness of YHWH to his covenant with David (introduced in 2:7-9), the benefits and responsibilities of which are the subject of Ps 72. The connection of the two great Davidic kings (David and his son Solomon), as well as the absence of a negative attitude toward YHWH's maintenance of the covenant promises (an attitude which is prevalent in Ps 89), makes it tempting to view this collection (2-72) as a celebration of YHWH's faithfulness to the covenant which found its fullest expression during the united monarchy under these two kings.

---

[15]As for the thematic similarities which may indicate Ps 41's use as a "Royal Psalm," it must first be remembered that the ps was supposed (as indicated in its s/s) to have been composed by David. The situation described, therefore, would be associated with his kingship. In this light, the opening blessing (v. 1)—"Blessed is the man who has concern for the helpless"—would be taken to refer to the *King's* responsibility to protect the poor, widows, orphans, etc., who cannot help themselves. The life-giving protection of YHWH which makes "the man" secure in the land from his enemies (v. 2) is also easily related to the troubles and concerns of kingship.

While the central portion of the ps (vv. 3-8) appears to be a plea for deliverance from *illness*, the closing verses revert to the theme of deliverance from one's *enemies* and the promise of eternal security (vv. 9-12). It seems quite plausible to me that here Ps 41 is viewed by the editor(s) as functioning quite on a par with the "Royal" pss 2, 72, 89.

BOOKS ONE—THREE

It has been suggested (by Arens for one) that to discover the editorial purpose behind the Psalter arrangement one must begin by looking at the pss which mark the seams between the books.[16] A brief glance at Pss 2, 41, 72, and 89 reveals an interesting progression in thought regarding kingship and the Davidic covenant.

Ps 2 introduces the idea of the Davidic covenant. While it does not mention it specifically, the focus of the ps is clearly the sovereignty of YHWH and the security which he extends to the king through the promise in 2:7-9.

> I will tell of the decree of YHWH
> He said to me, "You are my son,
>   to day I have begotten you
> Ask of me and I will make the nations
>   your heritage,
>   and the ends of the earth your
>   possession.
> You shall break them with a rod of iron
>   and dash them in pieces like a
>   potter's vessel."

While neither David nor the specific covenant are mentioned, the wording is clearly reminiscent of 2 Sam 7:14, where the Davidic covenant is promulgated. This promise of security in the face of the scheming of the rebellious "kings of the Earth" (2:1-8) finds echoes in the concerns of Ps 41, which concludes the first book. There David as the author, speaks of the assurance of YHWH's protection and security in the face of the malicious murmuring of his enemies.

> Blessed is he who considers the poor
> YHWH delivers him in the day of trouble;
> YHWH protects him and keeps him alive
>   he is called blessed in the land
> You do not give him up to the will of
>   his enemies.
>
> (41:1-2)

---

[16]A. Arens, *Gottesdienst*, 170.

Regardless of the evil intent of his detractors

> My enemies say of me in malice:
> "When will he die, and his name perish!"
> (41:5)

> All who hate me whisper together about me
> they imagine the worst for me.
> (41:7)

the king is sure of YHWH's protective action in his behalf.

> By this I know that you are pleased with me
> in that my enemy has not triumphed over me
> But you have upheld me because of my integrity
> and set me in your presence for ever.
> (41:11-12)

If Book One is viewed as an independent unit bounded by Pss 2 and 41, the resulting effect is a very Davidic group of pss in which the proclamation of YHWH's special covenant with his king in Ps 2 is matched by David's assurance of God's continued preservation in the presence of YHWH. The extension of the collection through Book Two and the insertion of the "Solomonic" Ps 72 at that point provides a different angle from which to view the special relationship between YHWH and king which was the concern of Book One at start and finish.

Ps 72, with its multiple petitions on behalf of "the king's son" could almost represent the prayer of David for his son Solomon in view of the latter's accession to the kingship. The petitions fall generally into three categories.

1. May he rule justly.

> Give the king your justice O God
> and your righteousness to the king's son
> May he judge your people with righteousness
> and your poor with justice.
> (72:1-2)

> May he defend the cause of the poor of the people
> give deliverance to the needy
> and crush the oppressor!
> (72:4)

2. May his dominion be secure from his enemies.

> May he have dominion from sea to sea
> and from the River to the ends of the earth!
> May his foes bow down before him
> and his enemies lick the dust!
> May the kings of Tarshish and of the isles render him tribute
> May all kings fall down before him
> all nations serve him.
> (72:8-11)

3. May he live long and be blessed.

> May he live while the sun endures
> and as long as the moon throughout all generations.
> (72:5)

> Long may he live, may gold of Sheba be given to him!
> May prayer be made for him continually
> and blessings invoked for him all the day!
> (72:15)

> May his name endure for ever
> his fame continue as long as the sun!
> May men bless themselves by him,
> all nations call him blessed!
> (72:17)

It seems important to note that these petitions for YHWH's blessing are not simply predicated on the basis of YHWH's covenant obligations. Rather the motivation behind the divine blessing is to be found in the king's proper action in behalf of his people. YHWH is to bless the king

> because he delivers the needy when he calls
> the poor and him who has no helper
> He has pity on the weak and the needy
> and saves the lives of the needy.
> From oppression and violence he redeems their life;
> and precious is their blood in his sight.
> (72:12-14)

So the covenant which YHWH made with David (Ps 2) and in whose promises David rested secure (Ps 41) is now passed on to his descendants in this series of petitions in behalf of "the king's son" (Ps 72).

With the addition of Book Three and its concluding Ps 89, a new perspective is achieved. Here (Ps 89) the concern with the Davidic covenant is made explicit.

> You have said, "I have made a covenant
> with my chosen one
> I have sworn to David my servant:
> 'I will establish your descendants for ever,
> and build your throne for all generations.'"
> (89:3-4)

> I have found David my servant
> with my holy oil I have anointed him
> So that my hand shall ever abide with him
> and my arm shall also strengthen him.
> (89:20-21)

> My steadfast love I will keep for him for ever
> and my covenant will stand firm for him.
> (89:28)

Several observations are pertinent here.

1. The covenant is viewed as established in the dim past.

> Of old you did speak in a vision
> to your faithful one and say,
> "I have set the crown upon one who
> is mighty,
> I have exalted one chosen from the
> people
> I have found David my servant. . . ."
> (89:19-20)

> YHWH, where is your steadfast love
> of old
> Which by thy faithfulness you did swear by David?
> (89:49)

2. The ps is concerned with the extension of the covenant to the descendants of David.

I will establish your descendants for ever
and build your throne for all generations.
(89:4)

I will establish his line for ever
and his throne as the days of the heavens.
(89:29)

His line will endure for ever
his throne as long as the sun before me.
(89:36)

3. The covenant is viewed as broken, failed.

But now you have cast off and rejected
you are full of wrath against your anointed.
You have renounced the covenant with your servant
you have defiled his crown in the dust.
(89:38-39)

You have removed the scepter from his hand
and cast his throne to the ground.
(89:44)

4. The hope expressed is that in his steadfast love YHWH will yet remember his covenant and uphold the descendants of David.

I will sing of your steadfast love,
YHWH for ever;
With my mouth I will proclaim
your faithfulness to all generations.
(89:1)

YHWH, where is your steadfast love of old,
Which by your faithfulness you did swear
to David?
Remember, YHWH, how your servant is scorned. . . .
(89:49-50)

At the conclusion of the third book, immediately preceding the break observed separating the earlier and later books, the impression left is one of a covenant remembered, but a covenant *failed*. The Davidic covenant introduced in Ps 2 has come to nothing and the combination of three books concludes with the anguished cry of the Davidic descendants.

> How long, YHWH? Will you hide yourself for ever?
> How long will your wrath burn like fire?
> (89:46)

The psalmist longs for the restoration of the Davidic line and even in exile prays for its return. Regardless of the guilt of the Davidic kings which brought on the punishment of exile, surely YHWH must honor his covenant and re-establish the Davidic kingdom. YHWH has said

> I will establish his line for ever
> and his throne as the days of the heavens.
> If his children forsake my law
> and do not walk according to my ordinances,
> if they violate my statutes
> and do not keep my commandments,
> then I will punish their transgression with the rod
> and their iniquity with scourges;
> but I will not remove from him my steadfast love
> or be false to my faithfulness.
> I will not violate my covenant,
> or alter the word that went forth from my lips.
> Once for all I have sworn by my holiness;
> I will not lie to David
> His line shall endure for ever,
> his throne as long as the sun before me.
> Like the moon it shall be established for ever;
> it shall stand firm while the skies endure."
> (89:29-37)

And yet YHWH delays. It is to this problem of the failure of YHWH to honor the Davidic covenant that Ps 89 directs its plea. How long? And it is with this plea that the first part of the Psalter ends.

BOOK FOUR

A number of elements have already been observed which indicate the distinctive character of the fourth book (Pss 90-106). Especially noticeable is the high proportion of "untitled" pss (13 out of 17 pss) in comparison with the rest of the books (Book Five is the closest competitor with 18 "untitled" pss out of 44). I have previously shown that such untitled pss are frequently subject to editorial manipulation. Though it is unlikely that (as some suggest) the lack of a title consistently indicates late composition (or late inclusion in the Psalter), it is quite possible that such "orphan" pss enjoyed relative freedom from the earlier collection processes characterized by the categorizing reflected in the s/ss. Such "loose" or unattached pss would provide a ready source for editorial use.

The curious conjunction of such a large number of "untitled" pss in Book Four, as well as its other distinctive features, lead me to suggest that this book is especially the product of purposeful editorial arrangement. This impression is heightened by the close interweaving of theme and verbal correspondences in these 17 pss which I will sketch briefly below. In my opinion, Pss 90-106 function as the editorial "center" of the final form of the Hebrew Psalter. As such this grouping stands as the "answer" to the problem posed in Ps 89 as to the apparent failure of the Davidic covenant with which Books One—Three are primarily concerned. Briefly summarized the answer given is: (1) YHWH is king; (2) He has been our "refuge" in the past, long before the monarchy existed (i.e., in the Mosaic period); (3) He will continue to be our refuge now that the monarchy is gone; (4) Blessed are they that trust in him!

The following is a brief sketch of the interrelationships between the 17 pss of Book Four.

Ps 90

This ps is attributed to Moses, the man of God, who led Israel before ever there was a monarchy. The Mosaic motif or context brackets this collection at beginning and end (see above, pp. 187-88).

1. The emphasis is placed upon YHWH as Israel's place of security "in all generations" (90:1) in contrast to the transient authority of the monarchy.

2. The frailty and transcience of human effort are contrasted with the eternality and endurance of YHWH (90:2-6, 9-10).

3. The iniquity of man is the cause for the outpouring of God's wrath (90:7-8). Is this the beginning of an answer to 89:46ff.?

4. Recognition of human frailty is the beginning of wisdom (90:11-12). One needs divine wisdom to achieve the necessary "new" perspective.

5. How long? (90:13ff.). This picks up the question in 89:46ff. which now stands in the new context of Israel's sin rather than YHWH's refusal to honor the Davidic covenant.

Ps 91

An "untitled" ps which some have combined with Ps 90. We have here a further response to the questions of Israel in 89:46ff. and 90:13.

1. Protection and security is offered to the one who relies on YHWH *alone* (91:1-2, 9-13).

2. God's own evaluation is concluded in the first person statement in 91:14-16.

> *Because* he cleaves to me in love,
> I will deliver him;
> I will protect him, *because* he knows
> my name
> *When* he calls to me, I will answer him. . . .
> (91:14-15, emphasis mine)

Ps 92

This ps forms a transition from the "Mosaic" theme of YHWH as refuge for those who trust in him to the central motif of the "Enthronement pss: "YHWH reigns!"

1. A two-fold insight is offered which is not available to the natural observation of the "dull man" (92:5-9). (a) Although the wicked flourish, they are already doomed; although the righteous suffer, they will surely prosper (92:6-9, 12-13). (b) Although Israel has been defeated militarily and carried into exile, YHWH is enthroned "on high for ever!" (92:15).

2. YHWH is not at fault for Israel's state, he is still her "rock" and refuge (92:15).

Ps 93

The first of the "Enthronement" pss celebrates throughout the kingship of YHWH as the whole of creation joins the cry YHWH mālāk, "YHWH reigns!"

Ps 94

The theme shifts once more to the current situational problem which prevents Israel from recognizing the kingship of YHWH.

1. The wicked continue to prosper. How long? (94:1-7).

2. The "dullest" of people needs a new perception informed by wisdom (94:8-11; cf. 92:5-9). Despite the present situation, YHWH is still in control.

3. Seek respite through observance of the Law. Be faithful until the wicked fall and justice returns to the righteous. "YHWH will not forsake his people . . ." (94:12-15).

4. Regardless of the precarious situation, YHWH remains the rock and refuge (94:22-23, picking up on the theme of Pss 90, 91, 92).

Ps 95

Here again the ps provides transition to the celebration of YHWH's kingship. It combines both the major themes of YHWH as "rock" (95:1) and YHWH as king (95:3).

1. YHWH is praised as the "rock of our salvation" (95:1 cf. 94:22 just preceding).

2. Transition is made to the kingship of YHWH and his power over all creation (95:3-7).

3. In a return to the current problem, Israel's failure to accept YHWH's kingship is compared to the rebelliousness of Israel before Moses in the Exodus (95:7-11). The result then (as now) was the loss of the rest promised by God. The contingent nature of God's promises is clearly emphasized.

Pss 96-99

We have in this cluster of alternating YHWH mālāk (97:1; 99:1) and šyrw lYHWH šyr ḥdš (96:1; 98:1) pss a litany of praise to the kingship of YHWH. The constant exhortation is for the reader to recognize and celebrate YHWH as king (96:7-10 and throughout the other pss). This consistent theme dominates through 99:5, after which the Mosaic theme reasserts itself in verses 6-8 as a transition back to the present situation.

1. When Moses, Aaron and Samuel cry to YHWH, he answers (99:6).

2. They kept the testimonies and statutes of God (99:7).

3. Israel's God answered those who called on him, he punished their iniquity, but stands ready to forgive in his mercy (99:8-9).

Ps 100

This "thank" ps, enjoining the people to serve and praise YHWH in his kingly courts, picks up on themes in 95:6-7 and serves as a fitting conclusion to the litany of praise expressed in Pss 96-99.

Ps 101

In this Davidic ps, the king gives a contrasting description of those who do and those who do not seek YHWH. This is the attitude which Israel must adopt, modelled by the "man after God's own heart."

Ps 102

Here, toward the end of Book Four, we discover a return to the themes set out in Ps 90.

1. The transient nature of man is emphasized (102:3, 11; cf. 90:5-6, 9-10).

2. In contrast, the psalmist sets the eternality of God (102:12, 24-27; cf. 90:1-2, 4).

3. God's wrath is poured out because of his indignation with man (102:9-10; cf. 90:7-8).

4. And yet the servants' children "will dwell secure" (102:28; cf. 90:16). YHWH will relieve the distress of his people.

The recurrence of so many of the themes and concerns of Ps 90 in such similar terms leaves a strong impression of intentional arrangement. It also forms an *inclusio* of the whole collection.

Ps 103

Once again David enters the picture as author of this ps. Here the king whose covenant is the subject of so much concern in Books One—Three, speaks out in praise of YHWH who *will* redeem the faithful (103:1-5) and forgives man's iniquities (103:3; cf. 90:7-8). Even more than Ps 102, this ps shares *multiple* correspondences with Ps 90 which I list briefly below.

1. YHWH forgives the iniquity of man (103:3, 10, 12; cf. 90:7-8).

2. YHWH responds to man with steadfast love and mercy (103:4, 8, 11, 17-18; cf. 90:14).

3. YHWH *satisfies* man with good as long as he lives (103:5; cf. 90:14).

4. Moses is mentioned as the mediator of the divine will (103:7; cf. 90:1).

5. YHWH pities those who fear him (103:13; cf. 90:13).

6. YHWH knows man is *dust* and therefore frail (103:14; cf. 90:3).

7. The transient nature of man is emphasized using comparison with "grass" which perishes (103:15; cf. 90:5-6).

These numerous correspondences can hardly be coincidental, but must represent purposeful arrangement. Ps 103 stands almost as an answer to the questions and problems raised in Ps 90; problems which received their impetus from the situation described in Ps 89. Ps 103's final answer has no correspondence in 90, but encapsulates the central themes of the fourth book.

> YHWH has established his *throne* in the heavens
> and his *kingdom* rules over all.
> (103:19, emphasis mine)

Therefore Israel can trust in him where human monarchs are doomed to fail.

Pss 104-106

While this group of hllwyh pss does function editorially to conclude this section, their selection was certainly not fortuitous. To the contrary, they clearly resonate with the major themes which thread their ways through these pss.

Ps 104, connected with Ps 103 by the identical *inclusio* brky npšy ᵓt YHWH, is a celebration of praise of the creative powers of YHWH and reintroduces themes common to the "Enthronement" pss.

Ps 105 reintroduces the Mosaic theme (which continues through Ps 106) with a rehearsal of YHWH's gracious act in delivering Israel from Egypt and bringing them to the land.

Ps 106 also depicts YHWH's historical acts in behalf of Israel. Here, however, the emphasis falls once again on the *rebellious response* of Israel to each of YHWH's merciful acts. Beginning with the confession in 106:6:

> Both we and our fathers have sinned
> We have committed iniquity, we have done wickedly

the ps chronicles Israel's rebellious acts against YHWH: the Red Sea (106:7-12), the wilderness (106:13-15), Dathan and Abiram (106:16-18), the "golden calf" (106:19-23), despising the land (106:24-27), Baal Pe or (106:28-31), Meribah (106:32-33), failure to destroy the inhabitants of the land (106:34-39). This chronicle concludes with a vague but certainly negative evaluation of the land and monarchy experience, which led to the exile (106:40-46). Yet YHWH's mercy still serves as the basis of future hope and the fourth book closes with a plea of its own: not a plea for YHWH to live up to his covenant obligations to David and his descendants, but a plea simply for restoration from exile.

> Save us, O YHWH our God
> and gather us from among the nations
> that we may give thanks to your holy name
> and glory in your praise.
> (106:47)

BOOK FIVE

Several factors combine to thwart a detailed analysis of the editorial organization of the fifth book. Its extent (44 pss) is considerably greater than that of the fourth book (17 pss); in addition, the presence in the book of several pss-groupings which exhibit evidence of a previous history of combination (Davidic 108-110, 138-145; hllwyh 111-118, 135, 146-150; hmᶜlwt 120-134) may have limited the amount of editorial manipulation possible in this section. Nevertheless, it is necessary to make a number of observations about the arrangement and structure of the book.

1. In the manner discussed previously, the hwdw ps 107 introduces this final section of the Psalter. It does so as a response to the plea of the exiles expressed in Ps 106:47.

> Save us, O YHWH our God
> and gather us (wᵉqabbᵉṣênū)
> from among the nations (min haggôyim)

Ps 107 views this act of "gathering" as an accomplished fact, which serves as the motivation for the praise of YHWH.

> O give thanks to YHWH for he is good
> for his steadfast love endures for ever
> Let the redeemed of YHWH say so
> whom he has redeemed from trouble
> and gathered in (qabbᵉṣām) from the lands (mēʾărāṣôt)
> from the east and from the west
> from the north and from the south.
> (107:1-3)

Even if this is an old "pilgrim" ps (as others suggest), it becomes in this connection a description of the ingathering of the exiles from the *diaspora*. The viewpoint of Ps 107 is essentially different from that expressed in 106 where the psalmist still looks forward in expectation of YHWH's deliverance. The perils here described are the "troubles" of the redeemed (107:2); the distress of the exiles (106) has been *overcome*. Close correspondence between the concluding summary in Ps 106:40-46 and the continuing refrain of 107:6-8, 13-15, 19-21, 28-31 leaves little doubt of the purposeful juxtaposition of these two pss.

2. There are two groups of Davidic pss preserved in this final book

(Pss 108-110, 138-145). Their placement at beginning and end implies purposeful editorial arrangement. While it is difficult to trace any clear strategy of editorial juxtaposition threading its way through the individual pss (the same may be said of the hm^{c}lwt pss), the groups as a whole seem to intend to set up David as model in response to the concerns of the pss which precede them. Thus, in Pss 108-110, David emerges as the "wise man" (107:43) who "gives heed" to the cautions of 107:39-42 and relies wholly on the steadfast love of YHWH. His willingness to sing the praise of YHWH "among the nations" (108:3) becomes a paradigm of action to be followed, whether by those yet in exile or among those vulnerable returnees surrounded by their foes. David knows that only reliance on YHWH is effective.

> . . . vain is the help of man!
> (108:12)

Faced by his foes, David does not despair, but continues to rely on the steadfast love of YHWH who "stands at the right hand of the needy, to save him from those who condemn him to death" (109:26-31), and who confirms David's trust with divine protection as he confronts his detractors (Ps 110).

Following this paradigmatic depiction of David in relation to his God, the hllwyh grouping of Pss 111-117 continues this theme of reliance on YHWH with its alternating descriptions of the powerful YHWH who is worthy of man's trust (111:2, 6-8; 112:5-9) and its repeated exhortations to "fear YHWH" and trust in him (111:5, 10; 112:1). The untitled Ps 114 stands at the central point of this *hallel*. Its subject is the graphic portrayal of the power of YHWH displayed in behalf of Israel in the Exodus event. As frequently elsewhere in scripture, so here YHWH's former acts of mercy and love serve as the basis for man's future trust. Pss 115-117 conclude this grouping (and the first segment of Book Five) with similar descriptions of YHWH's power (115:3-8 in contrast to the impotence of idols) and his intent and ability to save (116:1-2, 5-6, 8-11), as well as with further exhortations to fear and trust YHWH (115:9-11, 13).

In like fashion to the first group of Davidic pss, David serves as an example in Pss 138-144 following the plaintive cry of the exiles expressed in the words of Ps 137 which immediately precedes.

> How shall we sing YHWH's song
> in a foreign land?

As if in reply, David bursts forth in praise of YHWH in Ps 138.

> I give you thanks, O YHWH
>   with my whole heart,
> before the gods I sing your praise;
> I bow down toward your holy Temple
> And give thanks to your name for your
>   steadfast love and your faithfulness.
> (138:4-5)

The phrases "before the gods" and "toward your holy Temple" take on heightened significance in the broader context. They are reminiscent of the faithful piety of Daniel in exile, who, though in peril of his life, daily turned his face toward the Temple in Jerusalem and prayed to YHWH in a "foreign land" and "before the [foreign] gods." Clearly David's act (as Daniel's) is intended to serve both as *witness* to the nations and as *paradigm* to the exiles.

> All the kings of the earth shall
>   praise you, O YHWH,
> for they have heard the words of my
>   mouth;
> and they will sing of the ways
>   of YHWH
> for great is the glory of YHWH.
> (138:4-5)

The actual motivation of the nations' recognition and praise of YHWH is the testimony of David in his words of praise. Here is one who will sing YHWH's praise in *any* land.

David's example of confidence in YHWH's benevolent protection continues as the remaining pss (139-144) follow the lead of the first. All are classified as prayers for deliverance from distress and represent models of expression for the exiles who must continue to trust in YHWH in spite of their present situation of oppression. The last four pss (141-144) re-emphasize the theme of YHWH as "rock" or "refuge" which was introduced in the fourth book (Pss 90-91, 94-95; cf. 141:8; 142:5; 143:9; 144:1-2). In the same vein, Ps 144 further picks up on the frailty of man (144:3-4; cf. 90:5-6, 10; 102:11; 103:14-16); the singing of the "new song" (šyr ḥdš cf. 96:1; 98:1); and the prosperity of the "children" of the servants (144:12; cf. 90:16; 102:28).

3. The central section of the fifth book (Pss 118-135) is dominated

by the massive, acrostic *Torah* Ps 119. Ps 118 (a hwdw ps) serves as an introduction and is well suited as it combines a number of previous themes and shares a number of correspondences with Ps 135 which concludes this section. As an appropriate sequel to Ps 117 (which as complement to Ps 107 concludes the preceding section), Ps 118 picks up and develops the theme of YHWH's steadfast love (118:1-4, 14-16, 29); it reiterates the theme of YHWH as "refuge" (118:8-9, 14) so frequently emphasized in the "Mosaic" pss of Book Four (cf. 90, 91, 94); it encourages reliance on YHWH alone (118:6-9). The connections between Pss 118 and 135 have already been discussed above (pp. 188-89).

The massive presence of Ps 119, along with its clear relation to the introductory Ps 1 with its blessing on the student of *Torah* (1:1-2) and its emphasis on the contrasting "ways" of the righteous and wicked (1:3-6), make it difficult not to view this ps as the focus of this central section. The repeated emphasis in 119:1-9 on *Torah* as the guardian and guide to the *way* of righteousness makes the connection plain. The words of Ps 118:19-20

> Open to me the gates of righteousness
> that I may enter through them
> and give thanks to YHWH
> This is the gate of YHWH
> the righteous shall enter through it.

although referring originally to the Temple, here almost seem to take on reference to *Torah* as man's only true guide to the *way* of life.

> Blessed are those whose way is blameless
> who walk in the law [Torah] of YHWH
> (119:1)

> I will meditate on your precepts
> and fix my eyes on your ways
> (119:15)

Ps 119 emphasizes the primacy of the law in man's relationship to YHWH. This relationship is viewed as primarily one of *individual* approach and access through the appropriation of and obedience to *Torah*, a concept shared with Ps 1. The movement between Book Four and the first two segments of Book Five could be sketched as: Book Four—YHWH is king and refuge, relie only on him; Book Five, segment one—continued evidence of

YHWH's trustworthiness and the necessity to rely only on him, Book Five, segment two—How are those who fear YHWH to relate to him? They must enter "the gate of righteousness" by keeping his law and incorporating it into their very existence.

After this central *Torah* ps, Pss 120-134 (the hm^{c}lwt pss) join in an almost unbroken song of reliance on YHWH alone.

Ps 120 is an exile's prayer to YHWH for deliverance from his enemies

Ps 121:1

I lift up my eyes to the hills
From whence does my help come?
My help comes from YHWH
Who made heaven and earth.

Ps 123:1

To you I lift up my eyes
O You who are enthroned in the heavens.

Ps 124:1-3

If it had not been YHWH who was on our side
. . . then they would have swallowed
us up alive.

Ps 124:8

Our help is in the name of YHWH
Who made heaven and earth.

Ps 125:1

Those who trust in YHWH
are like Mount Zion
Which cannot be moved
but abides for ever.

Ps 126:1

Unless YHWH builds the house
Those who build it labor in vain.

Ps 128:1-2

Blessed is everyone who fears YHWH,
who walks in his ways. . . .
You shall be happy, and it shall
be well with you.

Ps 130:5, 7

I wait for YHWH. . . .
O Israel, hope in YHWH
For with YHWH there is
steadfast love.

Ps 131:3

O Israel, hope in YHWH
From this time and for evermore.

There is in the latter pss of the hm^{c}lwt collection a renewed reflection on the Davidic covenant and YHWH's faithfulness to it (Pss 132-134). It is impossible to determine whether this emphasis is part of the previous history of this collection which was not obliterated in its transference to the Psalter, or whether it represents the intent and purpose of the final editor(s). The emphasis here on the blessing of Zion (132:13-16; 133:3) does find parallels throughout the collection (122:3-9 Jerusalem; 125:1-2 Zion/Jerusalem; 126:1ff. Zion) which suggests these pss are integral parts of the collection which may have been difficult or impossible to delete.

The collection finds its conclusion in the brief Ps 134 which functions as a "hinge" to connect with the following hllwyh Ps 135. The connection is made more explicit by the strong verbal correspondences in 134 and 135.

134:1	135:1-2
brwk ᵓt Yhwh	hllw ᵓt šm Yhwh
kl ᶜbdy Yhwh	hllw ᶜbdy Yhwh
hᶜmdym bbyt Yhwh blylwt	šᶜmdym bbyt Yhwh
134:3	**135:21**
ybrkk Yhwh mṣywn	brwk Yhwh mṣywn
ᶜśh šmym wᵓrṣ	škn yrwšlm

4. Ps 145 stands as the "climax" of the fifth book of the Psalter, with the final *hallel* (Pss 146-150) drawing its impetus from 145:21. Set in the mouth of David (145:1), this ps draws together some of the major themes set forth by the editorial arrangement previously discussed. In so doing, connections are developed with (1) the introductory Ps 1 (the "two ways" of righteous and wicked—145:20; cf. 1:6 and 107:42); (2) the central pss of the fourth book (the kingship of YHWH—145:1, 11-13; cf. 93:1-3;

99:1-5; 102:12; the "mighty acts" of YHWH—145:4-7; cf. 92:5-9; 96:3-4; the "steadfast love" of YHWH—145:8-9, 13-20; cf. 103:6-13; 107:4-9, 12); and (3) Ps 107 which initiates the fifth book (see above, p. 188).

An interesting text from the QPssMss may affirm Ps 145's position as the "climax" of the Psalter. In 11QPs^{a}, Ps 145 occurs, not at or near the end, but toward the middle of the scroll. The text of the ps presents a rather peculiar variation from MT in that it expands the ps throughout by the addition after each *colon* of the refrain

brwk yhwh wbrwk šmw lʿwlm wʿd

Sanders has suggested that the presence in MT Ps 145:1 and 2 of the similar phrases

wʾbrkh šmk lʿwlm wʿd

and

wʾhllh šmk lʿwlm wʿd

may represent reminiscences of the ancient refrain preserved in 11QPs^{a}.[17] To this may be added the expanded version of this phrase in 145:21 (MT) wybrk kl bśr šm qdšw lʿwlm wʿd. If the 11QPs^{a} version of Ps 145 had occurred in MT, the similarity of its refrain to the other "concluding doxologies" would certainly not have gone unnoticed.

It is my opinion that, if such a "doxology" or "doxological refrain" ever had a place in MT 150, it has been purposely altered to its present form in 145:21 to provide the motivation for the final *hallel*. While I have already discussed the dependence of Pss 146-150 on 145:21 (see pp. 189-90, 193-94), it is now necessary to indicate the significance of this arrangement for the final shape of the Psalter.

Ps 146, as a response to the first half of 145:21 ("The praise of YHWH my mouth will speak" [spoken by David]) must in this context be viewed as the words of David himself in praise of YHWH. This makes the statements in Ps 146 even more suggestive as they are spoken by the recipient of the divine promises of the Davidic covenant.

---

[17] James A. Sanders, *Psalms Scroll*, 16.

Put not your trust in princes
    in a son of man, in whom there
    is no help.
When his breath departs, he returns
    to his earth
    on that very day his plans perish.
Happy is he whose help is the God
    of Jacob
    whose hope is in YHWH his God
Who made heaven and earth
    the sea, and all that is in them;
Who keeps faith for ever.

(146:3-6; cf. 121:1; 124:8)

David the king bows to the kingship of YHWH and denies the efficacy of temporary human rulers. He describes YHWH as fulfilling the responsibilities of kingship (6-9) and proclaims his eternal dominion.

YHWH will reign for ever (ymlk yhwh l^{c}wlm)
    Your God, O Zion, to all generations.

The following pss, which stand as the increasing response of "all flesh" to the second half of 145:21, praise the power of YHWH which renders him trustworthy (147:4-5, 15-18; 148:5-6). They praise his faithfulness to his exiled peoples (147:2-3; 148:14; 149:4). As more and more voices join the chorus until all creation harmonizes, the theme turns once more in Ps 149 to the kingship of YHWH (149:2) and his ultimate, victorious power over the nations who oppress and will continue to oppress Israel (149:6-9). With this dramatic panorama of the kingly YHWH in view, Ps 150 rings down the curtain while "everything that has breath" proclaims the praise of God.

Summary: Following the lead of Ps 107, it seems that in some sense the fifth book was intended to stand as an answer to the plea of the exiles to be gathered from the *diaspora*. The answer given is that deliverance and life thereafter is dependent on an attitude of dependence and trust in YHWH alone (107:12-13, 19, 28). David is seen modeling this attitude of reliance and dependence in Pss 108-110 and 138-145 and is rewarded with YHWH's protection. Throughout, emphasis falls on YHWH's power and former acts of mercy (especially in the Exodus, cf. Ps 114) as evidence of his trustworthiness. This attitude of dependence on YHWH will issue in obedience to his Law, as set forth in the central *Torah* Ps 119, which is to serve as man's guide on the "way" of righteousness and life.

Finally, David, in Pss 145-146, returns to the theme of YHWH's kingship that so dominates the formative Book Four and stands in tension with Pss 2-89. YHWH is *eternal* king, only *he* is ultimately worthy of trust. Human "princes" will wither and fade like the grass, but the steadfast love of YHWH endures for ever.

Praise YHWH!

Appendices

Appendix A

The Qumran Manuscript Data for the Psalm-Headings Compared with the Masoretic Text

Psalm 6	MT	- lmnṣḥ bngynwt ʿl hšmynyt mzmwr ldwd
	4QPs^{s}	- lm] nṣḥ bngywt [. . . .
Psalm 13	MT	- lmnṣḥ mzmwr ldwd
	11QPs^{b}	- [s/s not extant, but originally there]
Psalm 17	MT	- tplh ldwd
	4QPs^{c}	- tplh l[dwd
Psalm 18	MT	- lmnṣḥ lʿbd YHWH ldwd ʾšr dbr lYHWH ʾt dbry hšyrh hzʾt bywm hṣyl YHWH ʾwtw mkp kl ʾybyw wmyd šʾwl
	11QPs^{c}	- . . . ldwy]d ʾšr dbr lYHWH[. . . d]bry hšyrh [. . .]ʾwybyw wmyd šʾw[l]
Psalm 27	MT	- ldwd
	4QPs^{r}	- [ldwd] - (according to Skehan's reconstruction)
Psalm 28	MT	- ldwd
	4QPs^{c}	- [s/s not extant, but probably written]
Psalm 33	MT	-
	4QPs^{q}	- ldwyd šyr mzmwr
	4QPs^{a}	-
Psalm 35	MT	- ldwd
	4QPs^{a}	- [s/s not extant, but probably written]
Psalm 36	MT	- lmnṣḥ lʿbd YHWH ldwd
	4QPs^{a}	- lm]nṣḥ lʿbd YHWH ldwyd[. . .
Psalm 40	MT	- lmnṣḥ ldwd mzmwr
	11QPs^{d}	- lmnṣ[ḥ . . . .
Psalm 45	MT	- lmnṣḥ ʿl ššnym lbny qrḥ mśkyl šyr ydydt
	4QpPs37	- lmnṣḥ ʿl [ššn]ym[. . . .
Psalm 48	MT	- šyr mzmwr lbny qrḥ
	4QPs^{j}	- šyr m[zmwr . . . .
Psalm 49	MT	- lmnṣḥ lbny qrḥ mzmwr
	4QPs^{c}	- [lmnṣḥ] lbny qrḥ mzm[wr . . . .

Psalm	Source		Superscription		Postscript
Psalm 51	MT	-	lmnṣḥ mzmwr ldwd bbwʾ ʾlyw ntn hnbyʾ kʾšr bʾ ʾl bt šbʿ		
	4QPs^{c}	-	lmnṣḥ mzmwr ldwd bbwʾ ʾlyw ntn hnbyʾ kʾšr bʾ [ʾl] btšbʿ		
Psalm 53	MT	-	lmnṣḥ ʿl mhlt mśkyl ldwd		
	4QPs^{c}	-	lmnṣḥ ʿl mḥlt mśkyl ld[wyd		
Psalm 54	MT	-	lmnṣḥ bngynwt mśkyl ldwd bbwʾ hzypym wyʾmrw lšʾ wl hlʾ dwd msttr ʿmnw		
	4QPs^{a}	-	. . . . (spacing indicates whole s/s written) . . . . msttr ʿmnw		
Psalm 63	MT	-	mzmwr ldwd bhywtw bmdbr yhwdh		
	4QPs^{a}	-	[s/s not extant, but probably written]		
Psalm 67	MT	-	lmnṣḥ bngynwt mzmwr šyr		
	4QPs^{a}	-	lmnṣ[ḥ		
Psalm 69	MT	-	lmnṣḥ ʿl šwšnym ldwd		
	4QPs^{a}	-	[lmnṣḥ ʿ]l šwšnym ldwyd		
Psalm 71	MT	-			
	4QPs^{a}	-	[no s/s—joined directly to Ps 38]		
Psalm 77	MT	-	lmnṣḥ ʿl ydytwn lʾsp mzmwr		
	4QPs^{e}	-	. . . .]lʾs[p		
Psalm 78	MT	-	mśkyl lʾsp		
	11QPs^{e}	-	[s/s not extant]		
Psalm 88	MT	-	šyr mzmwr lbny qrḥ lmnṣḥ ʿl mḥlt lʿnwt mśkyl lhymn hʾzrḥy		
	4QPs^{e}	-	. . . . l]hymn hʾzr[ḥy		
Psalm 89:53	MT	-	(doxology) brwk yhwh lʿwlm ʾmn wʾmn		
	4QPs^{e}	-	brw[k		
Psalm 93	MT	-			
	11QPs^{a}	-	hllwyh (s/s)		
Psalm 94	MT	-			
	4QPs^{b}	-			
Psalm 99	MT	-			
	4QPs^{k}	-			
Psalm 100	MT	-	mzmwr ltwdh		
	4QPs^{b}	-			
Psalm 101	MT	-	ldwd mzmwr		
	11QPs^{a}	-	[s/s not extant, but probably written]		
Psalm 102	MT	-	tplh lʿny ky yʿtwp wlpny YHWH yšpwk śyhw		
	11QPs^{a}	-	. . .] lʿny ky yʿṭw[p		
Psalm 103	MT	-	ldwd		
	4QPs^{b}	-			
	11QPs^{a}	-	[s/s not extant, but probably written]		
Psalm 104	MT	-		-	hllwyh (p/s)
	4QPs^{d}	-		-	[p/s not extant]
	4QPs^{e}	-	[ldwyd?]	-	[p/s not extant]
	11QPs^{a}	-	ldwyd (s/s)	-	hllwyh (p/s)

Psalm 105	MT	-	- hllwyh
	4QPs^{e}	- [not extant]	- [not extant]
	11QPs^{a}	-	- [not extant]
Psalm 106	MT	- hllwyh (s/s)	- hllwyh (p/s)
	4QPs^{d}	- [not extant]	- hl] lwyh (identification of ps uncertain)
Psalm 109	MT	- lmnṣḥ ldwd mzmwr	
	4QPs^{e}	- . . . . ldwy] d mzmw [r	- (identification of ps uncertain)
	11QPs^{a}	- [not extant]	
Psalm 113	MT	- hllwyh (s/s)	- hllwyh (p/s)
	4QPs^{b}	- hll [w] yh	- [not extant]
Psalm 114	MT	-	
	4QPs^{o}	- [not extant]	- [not extant]
Psalm 115	MT	-	- hllwyh (p/s)
	4QPs^{e}	- [not extant]	- h [llwyh . . . .
	4QPs^{o}	- [not extant]	- [not extant]
Psalm 116	MT	-	- hllwyh (p/s)
	4QPs^{b}	- [not extant]	-
	4QPs^{e}	- [not extant]	- [not extant]
Psalm 118	MT	-	- hllwyh (p/s)
	4QPs^{b}	- [not extant]	-
	11QPs^{a}	- [not extant]	-
Psalm 119	MT	-	
	11QPs^{a}	-	
Psalm 120	MT	- šyr hm^{c}lwt	
	11QPs^{a}	- [not extant]	
Psalm 121	MT	- šyr lm^{c}lwt	
	11QPs^{a}	- šyr hm^{c}lwt	
Psalm 122	MT	- šyr hm^{c}lwt ldwd	
	11QPs^{a}	- šyr hm^{c}lwt ldwyd	
Psalm 123	MT	- šyr hm^{c}lwt	
	11QPs^{a}	- l] dwyd lm^{c}lwt	
Psalm 124	MT	- šyr hm^{c}lwt ldwd	
	11QPs^{a}	- [not extant]	
Psalm 125	MT	- šyr hm^{c}lwt	
	11QPs^{a}	- [not extant, but probably written]	
Psalm 126	MT	- šyr hm^{c}lwt	
	4QPs^{e}	- šyr hm^{c}lwt	
	11QPs^{a}	- šyr hm^{c}lwt	
Psalm 127	MT	- šyr hm^{c}lwt lšlwmh	
	11QPs^{a}	- . . . . .] lšlwmh	
Psalm 128	MT	- šyr hm^{c}lwt	
	11QPs^{a}	- [not extant]	

Psalm	Source		
Psalm 129	MT	- šyr hmᶜlwt	
	11QPsa	- š[yr . . . . . (whole s/s probably written)	
Psalm 130	MT	- šyr hmᶜlwt	
	11QPsa	- šyr hmᶜlwt	
Psalm 131	MT	- šyr hmᶜlwt ldwd	
	11QPsa	- [not extant, but probably written in full]	
Psalm 132	MT	- šyr hmᶜlwt	
	11QPsa	- [not extant]	
Psalm 133	MT	- šyr hmᶜlwt ldwd	
	11QPsa	- šyr hmᶜlwt ldwyd	
	11QPsb	- . . . .]wt ldwyd	
Psalm 134	MT	- šyr hmᶜlwt	
	11QPsa	- [not extant]	
Psalm 135	MT	- hllwyh (s/s)	- hllwyh (p/s)
	4QPsk	- [not extant]	- [not extant]
	4QPsn	- [not extant]	- [not extant]
	11QPsa	- [hllwyh?]	- hllwyh
Psalm 136	MT	-	
	11QPsa	-	
Psalm 137	MT	-	
	11QPsa	-	
Psalm 138	MT	- ldwd	
	11QPsa	- ldwyd	
Psalm 139	MT	- lmnṣḥ ldwd mzmwr	
	11QPsa	- [not extant]	
Psalm 140	MT	- lmnṣḥ mzmwr ldwd	
	11QPsa	- lmnṣḥ mzmwr ldwyd	
Psalm 141	MT	- mzmwr ldwd	
	11QPsa	- [not extant]	
Psalm 142	MT	- mśkyl ldwd bhywtw bmᶜrh tplh	
	11QPsa	- [not extant]	
Psalm 143	MT	- mzmwr ldwd	
	11QPsa	- mzmwr ldwyd	
Psalm 144	MT	- ldwd	
	11QPsa	-	
	11QPsb	- [not extant]	
Psalm 145	MT	- thlh ldwd	-
	11QPsa	- tplh ldwyd	- ....zwᵓt lzkrwn ....
Psalm 146	MT	- hllwyh (s/s)	- hllwyh (p/s)
	11QPsa	- [not extant]	- hllwyh
Psalm 147	MT	- hllwyh (s/s)	- hllwyh (p/s)
	4QPsd	- hllw yh	- hllwyh
	11QPsa	- [not extant]	- [not extant]

Psalm 148	MT	- hllwyh (s/s)	- hllwyh (p/s)
	11QPs[a]	-	- not extant
Psalm 149	MT	- hllwyh (s/s)	- hllwyh (p/s)
	11QPs[a]	- [not extant]	- hllwyh
Psalm 150	MT	- hllwyh (s/s)	- hllwyh (p/s)
	11QPs[a]	-	- hllwyh
Psalm 151 A	MT	- Not included	
	11QPs[a]	- hllwyh ldwyd bn yšy	
Psalm 151 B	MT	- Not included	
	11QPs[a]	- tḥlt gb [w] rh l [dw] yd mšmšḥw	

Appendix B

The Relationship of Habakkuk 3:1 + 19 to S/S Convention in MT 150

The study of the s/s and p/s of the hymn of Habakkuk 3 reveals that when the two elements are taken separately, correspondences with the normal s/s convention of MT 150 are easily demonstrated. The term tplh (with which the s/s of Hab 3:1 begins) occurs five times in the pss-headings as a genre classification.

Ps 17	tplh ldwd
Ps 86	tplh ldwd
Ps 90	tplh lmšh ʾyš hʾlwhym
Ps 102	tplh lʿny ky yʿṭwp . . . .
Ps 142	mśkyl ldwd bhywtw bmʿrh tplh

Ps 142 represents an unusual case since it includes *two* genre categories in a single s/s (mśkyl and tplh). Further, the term tplh follows the historical/contextual statement, a unique occurrence in the pss-headings. The other four occurrences appear highly regular. For all, tplh occupies initial position and is followed immediately by the author's name (or, in the case of Ps 102, the person expected to recite the ps—lʿny). In one s/s (Ps 90) the author's name is followed by an appositive (ʾyš hʾlwhym) much as in the case of Hab 3:1. It appears that, as far as can be determined, the s/s in Hab 3:1 conforms in all particulars to normal Psalter practice.

The same holds true for the p/s in 3:19. The lmnṣḥ and the bngynwt(y) occur together in six pss-headings (bngynwt never occurs without lmnṣḥ, cf. Lienhard Delekat, "Probleme der Psalmenüberschriften," *ZAW* 76 [1964] 284).

Ps 4	lmnṣḥ bngynwt mzmwr ldwd
Ps 6	lmnṣḥ bngynwt ʿl hšmynyt mzmwr ldwd
Ps 54	lmnṣḥ bngynwt mśkyl ldwd
Ps 55	lmnṣḥ bngynwt mśkyl ldwd
Ps 67	lmnṣḥ bngynwt mzmwr šyr
Ps 76	lmnṣḥ bngynwt mzmwr lʾsp šyr

In all cases lmnṣḥ occupies the initial position (as in 54 of its 55 occurrences in the pss-headings, the single exception being the conflated s/s of Ps 89); bngynwt follows immmediately. The p/s of Hab 3:19 conforms exactly.

Hab 3:19 lmnṣḥ bngynwt(y)

By contrast to the pss-headings, however, this p/s appears somewhat "truncated" since there is no mention of genre or author, these having been supplied in 3:1.

If one attempts to combine these two elements simply by juxtaposing the two halves, allowing 3:1 to precede 3:19, a further difficulty arises. Not only does tplh occur in an unusual position (i.e., not *initial*), but the ʿl šgywnwt phrase is also displaced.

lmnṣḥ bngynwt(y) tplh lhbqwq hnbyʾ ʿl šgywnwt

A study of the occurrence of ʿl phrases in the pss-headings reveals the following: (1) whenever an ʿl phrase occurs without an accompanying bngynwt, it always follows lmnṣḥ immediately; (2) on the one occasion that bngynwt is added, however, the situation is altered and bngynwt intervenes.

Ps 6 lmnṣḥ bngynwt ʿl hšmynyt mzmwr ldwd

Compared to these s/ss, the Habakkuk s/s as combined is conspicuous by placing the ʿl phrase at the end.

If, on the other hand, the two "halves" are combined with 3:19 preceding 3:1, the following results.

tplh lḥbqwq hnbyʾ ʿl šgywnwt lmnṣḥ bngynwt(y)

The closest comparison is the conflated s/s of Ps 89 which is itself an anomaly. Even here the ʿl phrase is out of place. If reconstruction was necessary, I would offer the following version of the Habakkuk s/s which conforms to the normal conventions observed in the pss-headings in all particulars.

lmnṣḥ bngynwt (y) ʿl šgywnwt tplh lḥbqwq hnbyʾ

The parallel with the s/s of Ps 6 is almost exact.

Appendix C

Distribution of Technical Terms in the Psalms Headings

					1												
PSALM	**1**	**2**	**3**	**4**	**5**	**6**	**7**	**8**	**9**	**0**	**1**	**2**	**3**	**4**	**5**	**6**	**7**
ldwd	/	/	2	4	4	5	2	4	4	/	2	4	3	2	2	2	2
mzmwr			1	3	3	4		3	3			3	2		1		
lmnṣḥ				1	1	1		1	1		1	1	1	1			
bngynwt				2		2											
ʾel hnḥylwt					2												
ʿl hšmynyt						3						2					
šgywn							1										
ʿl hgytyt								2									
ʿlmwt lbn									2								
mktm																1	
tplh																	1
lʿbd YHWH																	
ʿl ʾylt hšḥr																	
ḥnkt hbyt																	
mśkyl																	
lhzkyr																	
lydytwn																	
lbny qrḥ																	
ʿl ššnym																	
šyr																	
ydydt																	
ʿl lmwt																	
lʾsp																	
ʿl mḥlt																	
ʿl ywnt ʾlm rḥqym																	
ʾal tšḥt																	
ʿl šwšn																	
ʿdwt																	
llmd																	
ʿl ngynt																	
ʿl ydwtwn																	
lšlmh																	
ʿlʿnwt																	
lhymn																	
hʾzrhy																	
lʾytn																	
lmšh																	
lywm hsbt																	
ʾyš hʾlhym																	
lywm hšbt																	
ltwdh																	
lʿny																	
hllwyh																	
hmʿlwt																	
thlh																	
h/c statement			3					3									

/	=	no heading
S	=	s/s
P	=	p/s
B	=	s/s and p/s
h/c	=	historical/contextual

18	19	20	21	22	23	24	25	26	27	28	29	30	31	32	33	34	35	36	37	38	39	40	41	42	43	44
3	3	3	3	4	2	1	1	1	1	1	2	4	3	1	/	1	1	3	1	2	4	2	3		/	
	2	2	2	3	1	2					1	1	2							1	3	3	2			
1	1	1	1	1									1					1			1	1	1	1		1
2																		2								
				2																						
												3														
														2										2		3
																				3						
																					2					
																								3		2
												2														
4																2										

	4					5										6	
PSALM	**5**	**6**	**7**	**8**	**9**	**0**	**1**	**2**	**3**	**4**	**5**	**6**	**7**	**8**	**9**	**0**	**1**
ldwd							3	3	4	4	4	3	3	3	3	5	3
mzmwr			3	2	3	1	2										
lmnṣḥ	1	1	1		1		1	1	1	1	1	1	1	1	1	1	1
bngynwt										2	2						
ʾel hnḥylwt																	
ʿl hšmynyt																	
šgywn																	
ʿl hgytyt																	
ʿlmwt lbn																	
mktm												4	4	4	4	4	
tplh																	
lʿbd YHWH																	
ʿl ʾylt hšḥr																	
ḥnkt hbyt																	
mśkyl	4							2	3	3	3						
lhzkyr																	
lydytwn																	
lbny qrḥ	3	2	2	3	2												
ʿl ššnym	2																
šyr	5	4		1													
ydydt	6																
ʿl lmwt		3															
lʾsp						2											
ʿl mḥlt									2								
ʿl ywnt ʾlm rḥqym												2					
ʾal tšḥt													2	2	2		
ʿl šwšn																2	
ʿdwt																3	
llmd																6	
ʿl ngynt																	2
ʿl ydwtwn																	
lšlmh																	
ʿlʿnwt																	
lhymn																	
hʾzrhy																	
lʾytn																	
lmšh																	
ʾyš hʾlhym																	
lywm hšbt																	
ltwdh																	
lʿny																	
hllwyh																	
hmʿlwt																	
thlh																	
h/c statement							4	4		5		5	5		5	7	

6								**7**										**8**								
2	**3**	**4**	**5**	**6**	**7**	**8**	**9**	**0**	**1**	**2**	**3**	**4**	**5**	**6**	**7**	**8**	**9**	**0**	**1**	**2**	**3**	**4**	**5**	**6**	**7**	**8**
4	2	3	3			2	3	2	/															2		
3	1	2	2	3	3	3					1		3	3	4		1	5		1	2	4	3		2	2
1		1	1	1	1	1	1	1					1	1	1			1	1			1	1			4
					2									2												
																			2			2				
																								1		
												1				1										7
								3																		
																						3	2		1	3
							2											2								
			4	2	4	4							5	5							1				3	1
											2	2	4	4	3	2	2	4	3	2	3					
																										5
													2													
																		3								
2															2											
										1																
																										6
																										8
																										9
	3																									

PSALM	89	90	1	2	3	4	5	6	7	8	9	100	1	2	3	4	5
ldwd			/		/	/	/	/	/		/		1		1		
mzmwr				1						1		1	2				
lmnṣḥ																	
bngynwt																	
ʾel hnḥylwt																	
ʿl hšmynyt																	
šgywn																	
ʿl hgytyt																	
ʿlmwt lbn																	
mktm																	
tplh		1												1			
lʿbd YHWH																	
ʿl ʾylt hšḥr																	
ḥnkt hbyt																	
mśkyl	1																
lhzkyr																	
lydytwn																	
lbny qrḥ																	
ʿl ššnym																	
šyr				2													
ydydt																	
ʿl lmwt																	
lʾsp																	
ʿl mhlt																	
ʿl ywnt ʾlm rḥqym																	
ʾal tšḥt																	
ʿl šwšn																	
ʿdwt																	
llmd																	
ʿl ngynt																	
ʿl ydwtwn																	
lšlmh																	
ʿlʿnwt																	
lhymn																	
hʾzrhy	3																
lʾytn	2																
lmšh		2															
ʾyš hʾlhym		3															
lywm hšbt				3													
ltwdh												2					
lʿny														2			
hllwyh																P	P
hmʿlwt																	
thlh																	
h/c statement														3			

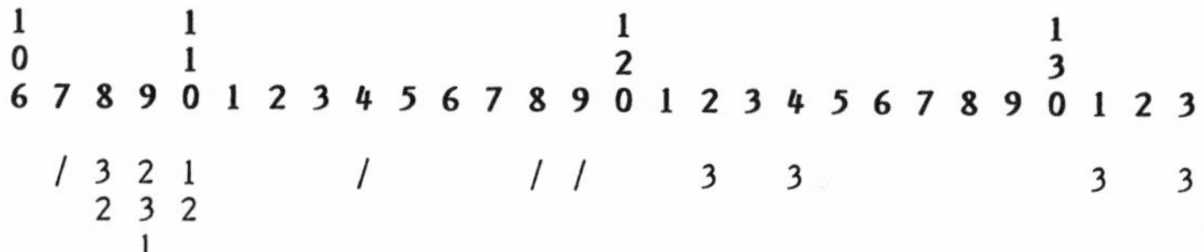

106	107	108	109	110	111	112	113	114	115	116	117	118	119	120	121	122	123	124	125	126	127	128	129	130	131	132	133
	/	3	2	1				/				/	/			3		3							3		3
		2	3	2																							
			1																								
		1												1	1	1	1	1	1	1	1	1	1	1	1	1	1
																					3						
B					S	S	B		P	P	P																
														2	2	2	2	2	2	2	2	2	2	2	2	2	2

PSALM	134	135	136	137	138	139	140	141	142	143	144	145	146	147	148	149	150
ldwd			/	/	1	2	3	2	2	2	1	2					
mzmwr						3	2	1		1							
lmnṣḥ						1	1										
bngynwt																	
ʾel hnḥylwt																	
ʿl hšmynyt																	
šgywn																	
ʿl hgytyt																	
ʿlmwt lbn																	
mktm																	
tplh									4								
lʿbd YHWH																	
ʿl ylt hšḥr																	
ḥnkt hbyt																	
mśkyl									1								
lhzkyr																	
lydytwn																	
lbny qrḥ																	
ʿl ššnym																	
šyr	1																
ydydt																	
ʿl lmwt																	
lʾsp																	
ʿl mhlt																	
ʿl ywnt ʾlm rḥqym																	
ʾal tšḥt																	
ʿl šwšn																	
ʿdwt																	
llmd																	
ʿl ngynt																	
ʿl ydwtwn																	
lšlmh																	
ʿlʿnwt																	
lhymn																	
hʾzrhy																	
lʾytn																	
lmšh																	
ʾyš hʾlhym																	
lywm hšbt																	
ltwdh																	
lʿny																	
hllwyh		B											B	B	B	B	B
hmʿlwt	2																
thlh												1					
h/c statement									3								

Selected Bibliography

I. GENERAL WORKS

Bruce, F. F., "The Earliest Old Testament Interpretation," *OTS* 17 (1972) 37-52.

Budge, E. A. Wallis, *The Book of the Dead*, 3 volumes in one, 2nd Edition Revised and Enlarged (New York: E. P. Dutton and Co., 1928).

Cassuto, Umberto, "The Arrangement of the Book of Ezekiel," *Biblical and Oriental Studies*, ed. U. Cassuto (Jerusalem: Magnes Press, 1973), Vol. 1, pp. 227-40.

__________, "The Sequence and Arrangement of the Biblical Sections," *Biblical and Oriental Studies*, ed. U. Cassuto (Jerusalem: Magnes Press, 1973), Vol. 1, pp. 1-6.

Chiera, Edward, *They Wrote on Clay* (Chicago, 1938).

Childs, Brevard S., *Introduction to the Old Testament as Scripture* (Philadelphia: Fortress, 1979).

Clements, R., *One Hundred Years of Old Testament Interpretation* (Philadelphia: Westminster, 1976).

Colwell, Ernest Cadman, *Studies in the Lectionary Text of the Greek New Testament* (Chicago: University of Chicago Press, 1933-44).

Delitzsch, Franz, *Biblical Commentary on the Psalms*, 3 vols. (Grand Rapids, MI: Eerdmans, 1871).

Driver, G. R., *Semitic Writing from Pictograph to Alphabet* (3rd ed.; London: Oxford University Press, 1976).

Eissfeldt, Otto, *The Old Testament* (New York: Harper and Row, 1965).

Gelb, I. J., *A Study of Writing, The Foundations of Grammatology* (Chicago: University of Chicago Press, 1952).

Gordis, Robert, "Quotations as a Literary Usage in Biblical, Oriental and Rabbinic Literature," *HUCA* 22 (1949) 157-219.

__________, "Quotations in Wisdom Literature," *JQR* 30 (1939-40) 123-47.

Gunkel, Hermann, *Einleitung in die Psalmen* (Göttingen: Vandenhoeck und Ruprecht, 1933).

__________, *What Remains of the Old Testament and Other Essays*, trans. A. K. Dallas (New York: Macmillan, 1928).

Holmes, Robert, and J. Parsons, *Vetus Testamentum Graecum cum variis lectionibus*, 5 vols. (Oxford: Clarendon Press, 1798-1827).

Hospers, J. H., ed., *Basic Bibliography for the Study of the Semitic Languages*, 2 vols. (Leiden: Brill, 1973, 1974).

Jacob, E., "Principe canonique et Formation de l'Ancien Testament," *SVT* 28 (1975) 101-22.

Jeremias, Gert, et al., eds., *Tradition und Glaube; das frühe Christentum in seiner Umwelt*. Festgabe für Karl Georg Kuhn zum 65. Geburtstag (Göttingen: Vandenhoeck und Ruprecht, 1971).

Kennicott, Benjamin, ed., *Vetus Testamentum Hebraicum cum Variis Lectionibus*, Vol. 1 (Oxford: Clarendon Press, 1776).

de Lagarde, Paule Anton, *Hagiographia Chaldaice* (Osnabrück: Otto Zeller, 1967)

Meyer, Rudolph, "Bemerkungen zum vorkanonischen Text des alten Testament," *Wort und Welt*, ed. Manfred Weise (Berlin: Evangelische Verlag, 1968), pp. 213-19.

Petersen, David L., *Late Israelite Prophecy: Studies in Deutero-Prophetic Literature and in Chronicles*, SBL Monograph Series Vol. 23 (Missoula: Scholars Press, 1977).

Sachs, Curt, *Altägyptische Musikinstrumente* (Leipzig: J. C. Hinrichs, 1920).

__________, *The History of Musical Instruments* (New York: W. W. Norton, 1940), pp. 105-27.

Sarna, Nahum M., "The Order of the Books," *Studies in Jewish Bibliography, History and Literature in honor of I. Edward Kiev*, ed. Charles Berlin (New York: KTAV, 1971).

Smith, Morton, *Palestinian Parties and Politics That Shaped the Old Testament* (New York: Columbia University Press, 1971).

Talmon, Shemaryahu, "Double Readings in the Massoretic Text," *Textus* 1 (1960) 144-84.

_________, "Synonymous Readings in the Textual Traditions of the Old Testament," *Scripta Hierosolymitana* (Jerusalem: Hebrew University, 1961), pp. 335-83.

Wagner, Siegfried, *Bibel und Qumran*. Beiträge zur Erforschung der Beziehungen zwischen Bibel- und Qumranwissenschaft. Hans Bardtke zum 22. 9. 1966 (Berlin: Evangelische Haupt-Bibelgesellschaft, 1968).

Weiser, Artur, *Einleitung in das Alte Testament*, 2nd ed. (Göttingen: Vandenhoeck und Ruprecht, 1949).

Wendel, C. T. E., *Die griechisch-römische Buchbeschreibung verlichen mit der des Vorderen Orients*, Hallische Monographien 3 (Halle: Max Niemeyer, 1949).

II. WORKS CONCERNING THE ANCIENT NEAR EAST

A. The Organization of Libraries and Archives

Budge, E. A. Wallis, *Babylonian Life and History*, 2nd ed. (London: Religious Tract Society, 1925).

_________, *The Book of the Dead: An English Translation of the Chapters, Hymns, etc.*, 2nd ed. (New York: E. P. Dutton, 1928).

Blau, Ludwig, *Studien zum althebräischen Buchwesen und zur biblischen Literatur und Textgeschichte* (Strassburg: K. J. Trübner, 1902).

Bushnell, George Herbert, *The World's Earliest Libraries* (London: Grafton, 1931).

Goossens, Godfrey, "Classement des Archives royales de Mari, I.," *RA* 46 (1952) 137-54.

_________, "Introduction a l'Archivéconomie de l'Asie Antérieure," *RA* 46 (1952) 98-107.

Harris, Rivkah, "The Archive of the Sin Temple in Khafajah," *JCS* 9 (1955) 35-37.

Jastrow, Morris, "Did the Babylonian Temples have Libraries?," *JAOS* 27 (1906) 147-82.

Kampman, A. A., "Archiven en bibliotheken in het Oude Nabije Oosten," *Handelingen van het zeed Weteschapplijk Vlaamsch Congres voor Boeken Bibliotheek wezen* (Schoten-Antwerpen: Lombaerts, 1942).

Mattiae, Paolo, "Ebla in the late Early Syrian Period: The Royal Palace and the State Archives," *BA* 39 (1976) 94-113.

Milkau, Fritz, *Geschichte der Bibliotheken im Alten Orient*, ed. Bruno Meissner (Leipzig: O. Harrassowitz, 1935).

Otten, Heinrich, "Bibliotheken in Alten Orient," *Das Altertum* 1 (1955) 67-89.

Papritz, J., "Archive in Altmesopotamien: Theorie und Tatsachen," *Archivalischen Zeitschrift* 55 (1959) 11-50.

Parsons, Edward Alexander, *The Alexandrian Library* (New York: Elsevier Press, 1952).

Pohl, A., "Bibliotheken und Archive in Alten Orient," *Orientalia* 25 (1956) 105-9.

_________, "Der Archivar und die Keilschriftforscher," *Orientalia* 29 (1960) 230-32.

Posner, Ernst, *Archives in the Ancient World* (Cambridge, MA: Harvard University Press, 1972).

Sasson, J. M., "Some Comments on Archive Keeping at Mari," *Iraq* 34 (1972) 55-67.

Schawe, Josef, "Der alten Vorderorient," *Handbuch der Bibliothekswissenschaft*, ed. Georg Leyh (Wiesbaden: O. Harrassowitz, 1955).

Soden, W. von, "Das Problem der zeitlichen Einordnung akkadischer Literaturwerke," *MDOG* 85 (1953) 22f.

Thompson, J. W., *Ancient Libraries* (Hamden, CT: Archon Books, 1940).

Weitemeyer, Morgens, "Archive and Library Technique in Ancient Mesopotamia," *Libri* 6 (1956) 217-38.

_________, *Babylonske og assyriske archiver og bibliotheker* (Copenhagen: Branner og Korch, 1955).

B. Cuneiform Texts of Mesopotamia

Abusch, Tzvi, "Mesopotamian Anti-witchcraft Literature: Texts and Studies, Part I The Nature of Maqlû: Its Character, Divisions, and Calendrical Setting," *JNES* 33 (1974) 251-62.

Bernhardt, Inez, and S. N. Kramer, "Götter-Hymnen und Kult-Gesänge der Sumerer auf zwei Keilschrift—'Katalogen' in der Hilprecht-Sammlung," *WZJ* 6 (1956/7) 389-95.

Bezold, C., *Catalogue of the Cuneiform Tablets in the Kounyunjik Collection of The British Museum*, vol. II (London: Harrisons and Sons, 1891).

Biggs, Robert D., "The Abū Salābīkh Tablets. A Preliminary Survey," *JCS* 20 (1966) 80-81.

_________, "An Archaic Sumerian Version of the Kesh Temple Hymn from Tell Abū Salābīkh," *ZA* 61 (1971) 193-207.

_________, *Inscriptions from Tell Abū Salābīkh* (Chicago: University of Chicago Oriental Institute Publications, 1974), pp. 45-56.

Borger, R., "Bemerkungen zu den akkadischen Kolophonen," *Die Welt des Orient* 5 (1970) 165-71.

Caplice, R., "Further Namburbi Notes," *Orientalia* 42 (1973) 514-16.

_________, "Namburbi Texts in the British Museum," *Orientalia* 34 (1965) 108-16; 36 (1967) 8-9.

Cumming, Charles Gordon, *The Assyrian and Hebrew Hymns of Praise* (New York: Columbia University Press, 1934).

Ebeling, Erich, *Die Akkadische Gebetsserie "Handerhebung"* (Berlin: Akademie Verlag, 1953).

_________, "Aus den Keilinschrifttexte aus Assur religiöse Inhalts," *MDOG* 58 (1917) 48-50.

_________, *Ein Hymnen Katalog aus Assur.* Berliner Beiträge zur Keilschriftforschung I, 3 (Berlin: E. Ebeling, 1923).

Falkenstein, Adam, "Das Betet in der sumerischen Ueberlieferung," *RLA* 3 (1959) 156-60.

_________, *Die Haupttypen der Sumerischen Beschwörung literarisch untersucht*, Leipziger Semitische Studien, 1 (Leipzig: J. C. Hinrichs'sche Buchhandlung, 1931), pp. 4-7.

_________, "Sumerische religiöse Texte," *ZA* 49 (1940) 87, 91, 103.

Galpin, Francis, W., *The Music of the Sumerians and their immediate Successors The Babylonians and Assyrians* (Cambridge: Cambridge University Press, 1937).

Gordon, Cyrus H., "The Aramaic Incantation in Cuneiform," *AFO* 12 (1937) 105-17.

Gragg, Gene B., *The Keš Temple Hymn*, Texts from Cuneiform Sources, No. 3 (Locust Valley, NY: J. J. Augustin, 1960), pp. 157-88.

Gurney, O. R., "An Old Babylonian Treatise on the Tuning of the Harp," *Iraq* 30 (1980-81) 229-33.

Güterbock, Hans G., "Appendix: Hittite Parallels," *JNES* 33 (1974) 323-27.

Halévy, Joseph, *Documents religieux de l'Assyrie à de la Babylonie* (Paris: Maisonneuve et Cie., 1882).

Hallo, William W., "Another Sumerian Literary Catalogue?" *Studia Orientalia* 46 (1976) 77-80.

_________, "The Cultic Setting of Sumerian Poetry," *CRRA* 17 (1969) 119-20.

_________, ed., *Essays in Honor of E. A. Speiser* (New Haven, CT: American Oriental Society, 1968).

_________, "Individual Prayer in Sumerian: The Continuity of a Tradition," *JAOS* 88 (1968) 71-89.

_________, "New Viewpoints on Cuneiform Literature," *IEJ* 12 (1962) 13-26.

_________, "On the Antiquity of Sumerian Literature," *JAOS* 83 (1963) 167-76.

_________, "Problems in Sumerian Hermeneutics," *Perspectives in Jewish Learning*, Vol. 5, ed. Byron L. Sherwin (Chicago: Spertus College of Judaica Press, 1973), pp. 1-12.

_________, "The Royal Correspondence of Larsa: I. A Sumerian Prototype for the Prayer of Hezekiah?," *AOAT* 25 (1976) 209-24.

_________, "Toward a History of Sumerian Literature," *Sumerological Studies in honor of Thorkild Jacobsen*, University of Chicago Assyriological Studies 20 (Chicago: University of Chicago Press, 1976), pp. 181-203.

_________, "Zāriqum," *JNES* 15 (1956) 220-25.

_________, and J. J. A. van Dijk, *The Exaltation of Inanna*, Yale Near Eastern Researches 3 (New Haven, CT: Yale University Press, 1968).

_________, and William Kelly Simpson, *The Ancient Near East. A History* (New York: Harcourt Brace Jovanovich, 1971).

Hartmann, Henrike, *Die Musik der Sumerischer Kultur* (Frankfurt am Main, 1960).

Hunger, Hermann, *Babylonische und assyrische Kolophone*, AOAT 2 (Neukirchen-Vluyn: Neukirchener Verlag, 1968).

Jacobsen, Thorkild, "Early Political Development in Mesopotamia," *ZA* 18 (1957) 91-140.

Jastrow, Morris, *The Religion of Babylonia and Assyria* (Boston: Ginn and Co., 1898).

Kramer, S. N., "The Death of Ur-Nammu and his Descent to the Netherworld," *JCS* 21 (1967) 104-22.

_________, "New Literary Catalogue from Ur," *RA* 55 (1961) 169ff.

_________, "The Oldest Literary Catalogue: A Sumerian List of Literary Compositions Compiled About 2000 B.C.," *BASOR* 88 (1942) 10-19.

_________, "Sumerian Literature, A General Survey," *The Bible and the Ancient Near East*, ed. G. Ernest Wright (Garden City, NY: Doubleday, 1961), pp. 249-66.

_________, "Sumerian Literature and the Bible," *Studia Biblica et Orientalia*. Analecta Biblica, vol. 12 (Rome: Pontifical Biblical Institute, 1959), pp. 185-204.

_________, "Two British Museum iršemma Catalogues," *Studia Orientalia* 46 (1975) 141-66.

Krecher, Joachim, *Sumerische Kultlyrik* (Wiesbaden: Harrassowitz, 1966).

Kunstmann, W. G., *Die babylonische Gebetsbeschwörung*. Leipziger semitische studien 2 (Leipzig: J. C. Hinrichs'sche Buchhandlung, 1968), pp. 3-6.

Kutscher, Raphael, *Oh Angry Sea: The History of a Sumerian Congregational Lament* (New Haven, CT: Yale University Press, 1975).

Laessoe, J., "Literacy and Oral Tradition in Ancient Mesopotamia," *Studia Orientalia Ioanni Pedersen* (Hauniae: E. Munksgaard, 1953).

Lambert, Maurice, "La littérature sumérienne . . . ," *RA* 55 (1961) 177-96; 56 (1962) 81-90, 214.

Lambert, William G., "Ancestors, Authors, and Canonicity," *JCS* 11 (1957) 1-14.

_________, *Babylonian Wisdom Literature* (Oxford: Clarendon Press, 1960).

_________, "A Catalogue of Texts and Authors," *JCS* 16 (1962) 59-77.

_________, "The Converse Tablet: A Litany with Musical Instructions," *Near Eastern Studies in honor of W. F. Albright*, ed. Hans Goedicke (Baltimore, MD: Johns Hopkins, 1971), pp. 337-39.

_________, "DINGIR.ŠÀ.DIB.BA Incantations," *JNES* 33 (1974) 267-327.

Landsberger, Benno, "Zu den aramäischen Beschwörungen in Keilschrift," *AfO* 12 (1937) 247-57.

Langdon, S., "The Assyrian Catalogue of Liturgical Texts: A Restoration of the Tablet," *RA* 18 (1921) 157-59.

_________, "Babylonian and Hebrew Musical Terms," *JRAS* (1921) 169-91.

_________, *Babylonian Liturgies. Sumerian Texts from the early Period and from the Library of Ashurbanipal, For the most part transliterated and translated, with introduction and Index* (Paris: Paul Geuthner, 1913).

_________, "A List of the Known Titles of Sumerian Penitential Psalms (ERŠAḪUNGA)," *RA* 22 (1925) 119-25.

_________, *Sumerian and Babylonian Psalms* (New York: G. E. Stechert, 1909).

_________, "Unidentified Duplicates of Part of the Sumerian Liturgy 'e-lum-gud-sun.' The Titular Litany," *Miscellanea Orientalia,* Dedicate Antonio Deimel (Rome: Pontifical Biblical Institute, 1935).

Leichty, Erle, "The Colophon," *Studies Presented to A. Leo Oppenheim* June 7, 1964 (Chicago: University of Chicago Oriental Institute, 1964).

Levy, S., and P. Artzi, "Sumerian and Akkadian Documents in Israel," *Atiqot* 4 (1965) no. 99.

Luckenbill, D. D., "A Neo-Babylonian Catalogue of Hymns," *AJSL* 26 (1909) 27-32.

Mayer, Werner, *Untersuchungen zur Formensprache der babylonische "Gebets beschwörungen,"* Studia Pohl: Series Major, Dissertationes Scientificae de Rebus Orientis Antiqui, 5 (Rome: Pontifical Biblical Institute, 1976).

Meek, Theophile James, "Babylonian Parallels to the Song of Songs," *JBL* 43 (1924) 245-52.

Meier, Gerhard, *Maqlû . . . Die assyrische beschwörungssamlung Maqlû* (Berlin: Gerhard Meier, 1937).

Oppenheim, A. Leo, *Ancient Mesopotamia* (Chicago: University of Chicago Press, 1964).

_________, "A Babylonian Diviner's Manual," *JNES* 33 (1974) 197-220.

_________, "A New Prayer to the Gods of Night," *Analecta Biblica* 12 (1959) 282-301.

Pohl, A., "Personalnachrichten," *Orientalia* 25 (1956) 105-9.

Pritchard, J. B., *The Ancient Near East*, vol. 2 (Princeton, NJ: Princeton University Press, 1975).

Rawlinson, H. C., *A Selection from the Miscellaneous Inscriptions of Assyria. The Cuneiform Inscriptions of Western Asia*, Vol. IV, 2nd ed. (London: Trustees of the British Museum, 1891), no. 53[60].

Reiner, Erica, "The Etiological Myth of the 'Seven Sages,'" *Orientalia* 30 (1961) 1-11.

Reisner, George Andrew, *Sumerisch-babylonische Hymnen nach Thontafeln griechischer Zeit* (Berlin: W. Spemann, 1896).

Sjöberg, Åke W., and E. Bergmann, *The Collection of the Sumerian Temple Hymns*, Texts from Cuneiform Sources, Vol. III (Locust Valley, NY: J. J. Augustin, 1969).

Thureau-Dangin, F., "Un Acte de Donation de Marduk-zâkir-šumi," *RA* 16 (1919) 121.

Ungnad, A., "The Babylonian Expedition of The University of Pennsylvania. Series A: Cuneiform Texts. Edited by H. V. Hilprecht. Volume XX, Part 1. Mathematical, Metrological and Chronological Tablets from the Temple Library of Nippur by H. V. Hilprecht," *ZMDG* 61 (1907) 705-7.

_________, "Sumerische Handerhebungsgebete," *OLZ* 21 (1918) cols. 116-19.

Widengren, Geo, *The Accadian and Hebrew Psalms of Lamentation as Religious Documents* (Stockholm: Thule, 1937).

Wilcke, Claus, "Der aktuelle Bezug der Sammlung der sumerischen Tempelhymnen und ein Fragment eines Klageliedes," *ZA* 62 (1972) 35-61.

_________, "Sumerische literarische Texte in Manchester und Liverpool," *AfO* 24 (1973) 1-18.

Wilson, Kinnier, "Two Medical Texts from Nimrud, I," *Iraq* 18 (1956) 136-40.

Wulstan, David, "The Tuning of the Babylonian Harp," *Iraq* 30 (1980-81) 215-28.

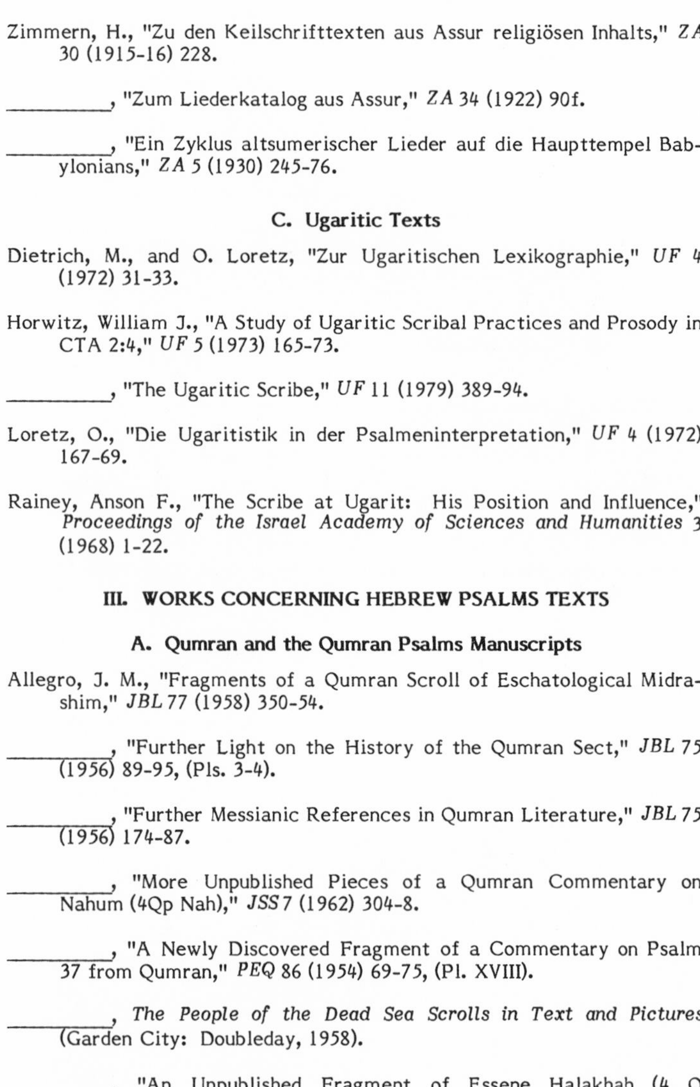

Zimmern, H., "Zu den Keilschrifttexten aus Assur religiösen Inhalts," *ZA* 30 (1915-16) 228.

__________, "Zum Liederkatalog aus Assur," *ZA* 34 (1922) 90f.

__________, "Ein Zyklus altsumerischer Lieder auf die Haupttempel Babylonians," *ZA* 5 (1930) 245-76.

C. Ugaritic Texts

Dietrich, M., and O. Loretz, "Zur Ugaritischen Lexikographie," *UF* 4 (1972) 31-33.

Horwitz, William J., "A Study of Ugaritic Scribal Practices and Prosody in CTA 2:4," *UF* 5 (1973) 165-73.

__________, "The Ugaritic Scribe," *UF* 11 (1979) 389-94.

Loretz, O., "Die Ugaritistik in der Psalmeninterpretation," *UF* 4 (1972) 167-69.

Rainey, Anson F., "The Scribe at Ugarit: His Position and Influence," *Proceedings of the Israel Academy of Sciences and Humanities* 3 (1968) 1-22.

III. WORKS CONCERNING HEBREW PSALMS TEXTS

A. Qumran and the Qumran Psalms Manuscripts

Allegro, J. M., "Fragments of a Qumran Scroll of Eschatological Midrashim," *JBL* 77 (1958) 350-54.

__________, "Further Light on the History of the Qumran Sect," *JBL* 75 (1956) 89-95, (Pls. 3-4).

__________, "Further Messianic References in Qumran Literature," *JBL* 75 (1956) 174-87.

__________, "More Unpublished Pieces of a Qumran Commentary on Nahum (4Qp Nah)," *JSS* 7 (1962) 304-8.

__________, "A Newly Discovered Fragment of a Commentary on Psalm 37 from Qumran," *PEQ* 86 (1954) 69-75, (Pl. XVIII).

__________, *The People of the Dead Sea Scrolls in Text and Pictures* (Garden City: Doubleday, 1958).

__________, "An Unpublished Fragment of Essene Halakhah (4 Q Ordinances)," *JSS* 6 (1961) 71-73.

Brownlee, W. H., "The 11Q Counterpart to Psalm 151, 1-5," *RevQ* 4 (1963-1964) 379-87.

_________, "The Significance of 'David's Compositions,'" *RevQ* 5 (1964-1966) 569-74.

Burchard, Christophe, *Bibliographie zu den Handschriften vom Toten Meer*, 2 vols. (Berlin: A. Töpelmann, 1957-65).

Carmignac, J., "La forme poétique du Psaume 151," *RevQ* 4 (1963-1964) 371-78.

_________, "Interpretation du Psaume 37 (4QpPs37)," Les textes de Qumran traduits et annotés, ed. J. Carmignac et al. (Paris: Letouzey et Ané), 1 (1961), pp. 119-26.

_________, "Notes sur les Peshârîm," *RevQ* 3 (1961-62) 505-38.

_________, "A propos d'une restitution dans le commentaire du Psaume 37," *RevQ* 1 (1958-59) 431.

_________, "Précisions sur la forme poetique du Ps 151," *RevQ* 5 (1965) 249-52.

_________, "Le Recueil de prières liturgiques de la grotte 1," *RevQ* 4 (1963-1964) 271-76.

Coote, R. B., "Another Sign of Scribal Copying in the Mythological Texts in Ugaritica V," *UF* 6 (1974) 447-48.

Cross, F. M., Jr., "The Development of the Jewish Scripts," *The Bible and the Ancient Near East*, ed. G. Ernest Wright (Garden City, NY: Doubleday, 1961), pp. 133-202.

_________, *Scrolls from the Wilderness of the Dead Sea* (Cambridge, MA: American Schools of Oriental Research, 1965).

_________, and Shemaryahu Talmon, eds., *Qumran and the History of the Biblical Text* (Cambridge, MA: Harvard University Press, 1975).

Delcor, M., "Cinq nouveaux psaumes esséniens?," *RevQ* 1 (1958) 85-102.

_________, "L'Hymne a Sion du rouleau des Psaumes de la grotte 11 de Qumrân (11 Q Ps[a])," *RevQ* 6 (1967) 71-88.

_________, *Le Hymnes de Qumran (Hodayot)* (Paris: Letouzey et Ané, 1962).

_________, "Zum Psalter von Qumran," *BZ* 10 (1966) 15-29.

Driver, G. R., *The Judean Scrolls* (New York: Schocken Books, 1965).

Dupont-Sommer, André, *The Essene Writings from Qumran*, trans. G. Vermes (Gloucester, MA: Peter Smith, 1973).

_________, "Explication de textes hébreux et araméens découverts a Qoumrân. II. Commentaire du psaume 37," *Annuaire du Collège de France* 64 (1964) 309-24.

_________, "Explication de textes hébreux découverts à Qoumrân," *Annuaire du Collège de France* 66 (1966) 347-72; 67 (1967) 355-70.

_________, "Explication de textes hébreux et araméens récemment découverts près de la mer Morte," *Annuaire du Collège de France* 69 (1969) 383-405.

_________, "Le Livre des Hymnes découvert près de la mer Morte (1QH)," *Sem* 7 (1957) 5-120.

_________, "Notes quomrâniennes. II. Sur 11 Q Ps[a], Col. XXII," *Sem* 15 (1965) 74-78.

_________, "Le Psaume CLI dans 11 Q Ps[a] et le problème de son origine essénienne," *Sem* 14 (1964) 25-62.

_________, Le psaume hébreu extra-canonique (11 Q Ps[a], Col. XXVIII)," *Annuaire du Collège de France* 64 (1964) 309-24.

Eissfeldt, Otto, "Eine Qumran-Textform des 91. Psalms," *Bibel und Qumran,* ed. Siegfried Wagner (Berlin: Evangelische Haupt-Bibelgesellschaft, 1968), pp. 82-85.

Fitzmyer, Joseph A., "A Bibliographical Aid to the Study of the Qumran Cave IV Texts 158-186," *CBQ* 31 (1969) 59-71.

_________, *The Dead Sea Scrolls. Major Publications and Tools for Study* (Missoula: Scholars Press, 1975/77).

_________, "The Use of Explicit Old Testament Quotations in Qumran Literature and in the New Testament," *NTS* 7 (1960-61) 297-333.

Goshen-Gottstein, M. H., "The Psalms Scroll (11 Q Ps[a]): A Problem of Canon and Text," *Textus* 5 (1966) 22-33.

Gurewicz, S. B., "Hebrew Apocryphal Psalms from Qumran," *Australian Biblical Review* 15 (1967) 13-20.

Habermann, A. M., "Mzmwrym hyswnyym mmdbr yhwdh," *Beth Miqra* 10 (1965) 3-9.

Hoenig, Sidney B., "The Dead Sea Psalms Scroll," *JQR* 58 (1967-1968) 162-63.

_________, "The Qumran Liturgic Psalms," *JQR* 57 (1966) 327-32.

Holm-Nielsen, Svend, *Hodayot: Psalms from Qumran* (Aarhus: Universitetsforlaget, 1960).

Hurwitz, Avi, "Observations on the Language of the Third Apocryphal Psalm from Qumran 11 Q Ps III ," *RevQ* 5 (1965) 225-32.

Jongeling, B., *A Classified Bibliography of the Finds in the Desert of Judah 1958-1969* (Leiden: Brill, 1971).

Kuhn, Karl Georg, *Konkordanz zu den Qumran Texten* (Göttingen: Vandenhoeck & Ruprecht, 1960).

_________, "Nachtrage zur Konkordanz zu den Qumran Texten," *RevQ* 14 (1963) 196-234.

Lane, William R., "A New Commentary Structure in 4Q Florilegium," *JBL* 78 (1959) 343-46.

Laperrousaz, É.-M., "Publication, en Israël, d'un fragment du 'Rouleau des Psaumes' provenant de la grotte 11 Q de Qumrân, et autre publications récentes de fragments de psaumes découverts dans les grottes 11 Q et 4 Q," *RHR* 169 (1966) 235-37.

_________, "Publication en Israël d'un fragment du 'Rouleau des Psaumes' provenant de la grotte 11 Q de Qumrân, et autre publications récentes de fragments de psaumes découverts dans les grottes 11 Q et 4 Q," *RHR* 171 (1967) 101-8.

_________, "Publication de fragments de psaumes apocryphes provenant de la grotte 4 de Qumrân," *RHR* 173 (1968) 108-10.

LaSor, William S., *Bibliography of the Dead Sea Scrolls 1948-1957* (Pasadena, CA: Fuller Theological Seminary Library, 1958).

L'Heureux, C. E., "The Biblical Sources of the 'Apostrophe to Zion' [11 Q Ps^a, Col. XXII]," *CBQ* 29 (1967) 60-67.

Lohse, Edward, *Die Texte aus Qumran: Hebräisch und Deutsch* (München: Kösel-Verlag, 1971).

Lührmann, Dieter, "Ein Weisheitspsalm aus Qumran (11 Q Ps^a xviii)," *ZAW* 80 (1968) 87-98.

Mackenzie, R. A. F., "Psalm 148:14b, c: Conclusion or Title?," *Biblica* 51 (1970) 221-24.

Magne, Jean, "Le Psaume 155," *RevQ* 9 (1977) 103-11.

Mansoor, Menahem, *The Thanksgiving Hymns* (Grand Rapids, MI: Eerdmans, 1961).

Martin, Malachi, *The Scribal Character of the Dead Sea Scrolls,* 2 vols. (Louvain: Publications Universitaires, 1958).

Milik, J. T., "Deux documents inédits du désert de Juda," *Biblica* 38 (1957) 245-55.

_________, "Fragment d'une source du Psautier (4 Q Ps 89)," *RB* 73 (1966) 94-104.

_________, "Le Travail d'Édition des manuscrits du désert du Juda," *SVT* 4 (1956) 17-26.

Morawe, Günter, "Vergleich des Aufbaus der Danklieder und hymnischen Bekenntnislieder (1QH) von Qumran mit dem Aufbau der Psalmen im alten Testament und in Spaetjudentum," *RevQ* 4 (1963) 323-56.

Moroder, R. J., "Ugaritic and Modern Translation of the Psalter. A Critical Examination of Die Psalmen-Ökumenische Übersetzung der Bibel," *UF* 6 (1974) 249-64.

Osswald, Eva, "Der gegenwärtige Stand der Erforschung der in Palästina neu gefundenen hebräischen Handschriften. 50) Die Psalmenrolle aus Höhle 11 (11 Q Ps^{a})," *TLZ* 91 (1966), cols. 729-34.

Ouellette, J., "Variantes qumrâniennes du Livre des Psaumes," *RevQ* 7 (1969-70) 105-24.

Paterson, John, *The Praises of Israel* (New York: Scribner's, 1950).

Philonenko, M., "L'Origine essénienne des cinq psaumes syriaques de David," *Sem* 9 (1959) 35-48.

Ploeg, J. P. M. van der, "L'edition des Manuscrits de la Grotte XI de Qumrân par L'académie Royale des Sciences des Pays-Bas," *Acta Orientalia Neerlandica:* Proceedings of the Congress of the Dutch Oriental Society. Held in Leiden 8-9 May, 1970, ed. P. W. Pestman (Leiden: Brill, 1971), pp.43-45.

_________, "Fragments d'un psautier de Qumrân," *Symbolae biblicae et mesopotamicae Francisco Mario Theodoro de Liagre Böhl dedicate,* ed. M. A. Beek et al. (Leiden: Brill, 1973), 208-9.

_________, "Fragments d'un manuscrit de psaumes de Qumran (11 Q Ps^{b})," *RB* 74 (1967) 408-12.

_________, "Un petit rouleau de psaumes apocryphes (11 Q Ps Ap^{a})," *Tradition und Glaube,* ed. Gert Jeremias et al. (Göttingen: Vandenhoeck und Ruprecht, 1971), pp. 128-39.

_________, "Le Psaume XCI dans une recension de Qumran," *RB* 72 (1965) 210-17.

Polzin, Robert, "Notes on the dating of the Non-Massoretic Psalms of 11 Q Ps[a]," *HTR* 60 (1967) 468-76.

Peuch, Émile, "Fragments du Psaume 122 dans un Manuscrit Hébreu de la Grotte IV," *RevQ* 9 (1977-78) 547-54.

Rabinowitz, Isaac, "The Alleged Orphism of 11 Q Pss 28 3-12," *ZAW* 76 (1964) 193-200.

Sanders, James A., "Cave 11 Surprises and the Question of Canon," *McCormick Quarterly Review* 21 (1968) 284-98. This article has been reprinted in the following volumes: *New Directions in Biblical Archaeology*, ed. D. N. Freedman and J. C Greenfield (New York: Doubleday, 1969), 101-16; *Nosaḥ hammiqra' be-qumran*, ed. R. Weis and I. Tov (Jerusalem: Hebrew University, 1972) 104-13; *The Canon and Masorah of the Hebrew Bible*, ed. Sid Z. Leiman (New York: KTAV, 1974) 37-51.

__________, *The Dead Sea Psalms Scroll* (Ithaca, NY: Cornell University Press, 1967).

__________, "The Dead Sea Scrolls—A Quarter Century of Study," *BA* 36 (1973) 110-48.

__________, "Palestinian Manuscripts 1947-67," *JBL* 86 (1967) 431-40.

__________, "Palestinian Manuscripts 1947-72," *Qumran and the History of the Biblical Text*, ed. F. M. Cross, Jr. and S. Talmon (Cambridge, MA: Harvard University Press, 1975).

__________, "Pre-Massoretic Psalter Texts," *CBQ* 27 (1965) 114-23.

__________, "Ps 151 in 11 Q Pss," *ZAW* 75 (1963) 73-86.

__________, *The Psalm Scroll of Qumran Cave 11*, DJD, vol. IV (London: Oxford University Press, 1965).

__________, "The Psalter at the Time of Christ," *The Bible Today* 22 (1966) 1462-69.

__________, "The Qumran Psalms Scroll (11 Q Ps[a]) Reviewed," *On Language, Culture, and Religion: In Honor of Eugene A. Nida* (The Hague: Mouton, 1974), pp. 79-99.

__________, "The Scroll of Psalms (11 Q Pss) from Cave 11: A Preliminary Report," *BASOR* 165 (1962) 11-15.

__________, "Two Non-Canonical Psalms in 11 Q Ps[a]," *ZAW* 76 (1964) 57-75.

_________, "Variorum in the Psalms Scroll (11 Q Ps[a])," *HTR* 59 (1966) 83-94.

Sauer, Georg, "Die Ugaritistik und die Psalmenforschung, II," *UF* 10 (1978) 357-86.

Siegel, Jonathan Paul, *Scribes of Qumran*, Brandeis University Doctoral Dissertation (Waltham, MA, 1972).

Skehan, Patrick W., "The Apocryphal Psalm 151," *CBQ* 25 (1963) 407-9.

_________, "The Biblical Scrolls from Qumran and the Text of the Old Testament," *BA* 28 (1965) 87-100.

_________, "A Broken Acrostic and Psalm 9," *CBQ* 27 (1965) 1-5.

_________, "Jubilees and the Qumran Psalter," *CBQ* 37 (1975) 343-47.

_________, "Liturgical Complex in 11 Q Ps[a]," *CBQ* 35 (1973) 195-205.

_________, "A Psalm Manuscript from Qumran (4 Q Ps[b])," *CBQ* 26 (1964) 313-22.

_________, "Qumran and Old Testament Criticism," *Qumrân: sa piéte, sa théologie et son milieu*, Bibliotheca ephemeridum theologicarum Lovaniensium 46 (Louvain: Duculot, University Press, 1978), pp. 163-82.

_________, "Qumran Manuscripts and Textual Criticism," *SVT* 4 (1957) 148-60.

_________, "Recent Developments in the Study of the Text of the Bible. Qumran and the Present State of Old Testament Text Studies: The Masoretic Text," *JBL* 78 (1959) 21-25.

_________, "The Scrolls and the Old Testament Text," *New Dimensions in Biblical Archaeology*, ed. D. N. Freedman and J. C. Greenfield (Garden City, NY: Doubleday, 1969), pp. 89-100.

Starcky, Jean, "Psaumes apocryphes de la grotte 4 de Qumran (4 Q Ps[f] vii-x)," *RB* 73 (1966) 353-71.

Stegemann, H., "Der pešer Psalm 37," *RevQ* 4 (1963-1964) 235-70.

_________, "Weitere Stücke von 4 Q Psalm 37, Von 4 Q Patriarchal Blessings und Hinweis auf eine unedierte Handschrift aus Höhle 4Q mit Exzerpten aus dem Deuteronomium," *RevQ* 4 (1961-1963) 193-227.

Strugnell, J., "The Angelic Liturgy at Qumran—4 Q Serek šîrôt 'ôlat haššabbāt," *SVT* 4 (1957) 318-45.

_________, "Notes on the Text and Transmission of the Apocryphal Psalms 151, 154 (= Syr II) and 155 (= Syr III)," *HTR* 59 (1966) 257-81.

_________, "More Psalms of 'David,'" *CBQ* 27 (1965) 207-16.

Talmon, Shemaryahu, "The Order of Prayers of the Sect from the Judean Desert," [modern Hebrew] *Tarbiz* 29 (1959-60) 1-20.

_________, "Pisqah beᶜemṣaʾ pasuq and 11 Q Ps^{a}," *Textus* 5 (1966) 11-21. This is a translation of an original article in modern Hebrew: "mzmwrym ḥyṣwnyym blšwn hᶜbryt mqwmrn," *Tarbiz* 35 (1965-66) 214-34.

_________, "The Psalms Scroll of Qumran," [modern Hebrew] *Tarbiz* 37 (1967-68) 99-104.

Thomas, D. Winton, "The Dead Sea Scrolls: What May We Believe?," *Annual of Leeds University Oriental Society* 6 (1968/69) 7-20.

Trever, J. C., "Completion of the Publication of Some Fragments from Qumran Cave l," *RevQ* 5 (1964-66) 323-44.

_________, "A Further Note About 1Q Prayers," *RevQ* 6 (1967-1969) 137-38.

Welch, J. W., "Chiasmus in Ugaritic," *UF* 6 (1974) 421-36.

Wernberg-Moller, P., "The Contribution of the Hodayot to Biblical Textual Criticism," *Textus* 4 (1964) 133-75.

Yadin, Yigael, "A Fragment of the Book of Psalms," *IEJ* 11 (1961) 40.

_________, "The Excavation of Masada—1963/4 Preliminary Report," *IEJ* 15 (1965) 103-4.

_________, *Masada: Herod's Fortress and the Zealots' Last Stand* (London: Weidenfeld and Nicolson, 1966).

_________, "Another Fragment (E) of the Psalms Scroll from Qumran Cave 11 (11 Q Ps^{a})," *Textus* 5 (1966) 1-10.

_________, "A Midrash on 2 Sam VII and Ps I-III," *IEJ* 9 (1959) 95-98.

_________, *The Temple Scroll* (Jerusalem: Israel Exploration Society, 1977).

Yizhar, M., *Bibliography of Hebrew Publications on the Dead Sea Scrolls (1948-1964)*, Bibliotheca Orientalis 30 (1973).

B. The Canonical Psalms and Psalter

Abbott, T. K., "On the Alphabetical Arrangement of Ps IX and X with some other Emendations," *ZAW* 16 (1896) 292-94.

Albright, W. F., "A Catalogue of Early Hebrew Lyric Poems (Psalm LXVIII)," *HUCA* 23 (1950) 1-39.

Anderson, G. W., "A Note on Ps 1:1," *VT* 24 (1974) 231-33.

Arens, Anton, "Hat der Psalter seinen 'Sitz im Leben' in der Synagogalen Leseordnung des Pentateuch?," *Le Psautier*, Orientalia et Biblica Lovaniensia 4 (Louvain: University Press, 1962).

_________, *Die Psalmen in Gottesdienst des Altes Bundes* (Trier: Paulinus-Verlag, 1968).

Auffret, Pierre, *The Literary Structure of Psalm 2, JSOTS* 3 (1977) 1-41.

_________, "Note Sur la Structure littéraire du Psaume CXXXVI," *VT* 27 (1977) 1-12.

Bardtke, Hans, "Erwägungen zu Psalm 1 und Psalm 2," *Symbolae Biblicae et Mesopotamicae Francisco Mario Theodoro de Liagre Böhl dedicatae*, ed. M. A. Beek et al. (Leiden: Brill, 1973), pp. 1-18.

Becker, J., *Israel deutet seine Psalmen*, Urform und Neuinterpretation in den Psalmen (Stuttgart: Katholisches Bibelwerk, 1966).

Bloemendaal, Willem, *The Headings of the Psalms in the East Syriac Church* (Leiden: Brill, 1960).

Braude, William G., *The Midrash on Psalms*, 2 vols. (New Haven, CT: Yale University Press, 1959).

Brennan, Joseph P., "Psalms 1-8: Some Hidden Harmonies," *Biblical Theology Bulletin* 10 (1980) 25-29.

Brownlee, W. H., "Psalms 1-2 as a Coronation Liturgy," *Biblica* 52 (1971) 321-36.

Bruce, F. F., "The Earliest O. T. Interpretation," *OTS* 17 (1972) 37-52.

Büchler, A., "Zur Geschichte der Tempelmusik und der Tempelpsalmen," *ZAW* 19 (1899) 96-133; 329-44; 29 (1900) 97-135.

de Buit, M., "Le David des Psaumes," *Le Monde de la Bible* 7 (1979) 6-7.

Buss, M. J., "The Psalms of Asaph and Korah," *JBL* 82 (1963) 382-92.

Butler, Trent C., "A Forgotten Passage from a Forgotten Era (1 Chr. XVI 8-36)," *VT* 28 (1978) 142-50.

Caquot, A., "Le Psaume LXXIII," *Sem* 21 (1971) 29-55.

_________, "Le psaume XCI," *Sem* 8 (1958) 21-37.

_________, "Remarques sur le Psaume CX," *Sem* 6 (1956) 33-52.

Cassuto, Umberto, "Psalm LXVIII," *Biblical and Oriental Studies*, ed. U. Cassuto (Jerusalem: Magnes, 1973), vol. 1, pp. 241-84.

Cheyne, Thomas Kelly, *The Origin and Religious Contents of the Psalter* (London: Kegan Paul, Trench, Trübner, 1891).

Childs, Brevard S., "Psalm Titles and Midrashic Exegesis," *JSS* 16 (1971) 137-50.

_________, "Reflections on the Modern Study of the Psalms," *Magnalia Dei*, ed. F. M. Cross (Garden City, NY: Doubleday, 1976), pp. 377-88.

Clifford, Richard J., "Style and Purpose in Psalm 105," *Biblica* 60 (1979) 420-27.

Clines, D. J. A., "Psalm Research Since 1955: I. The Psalms and the Cult," *Tyndale Bulletin* 18 (1967) 103-26.

_________, "Psalm Research Since 1955: II. The Literary Genres," *Tyndale Bulletin* 20 (1969) 105-25.

Coppens, J., "Les Études Récentes sur le Psautier," *Le Psautier*, ed. R. De Langhe (Louvain: Publications Universitaires, 1962), pp. 1-71.

Cornill, C. H., "Music in the Old Testament," *The Monist* 19 (1909) 240-64.

Cross, F. M., Jr., "The History of the Biblical Text in the Light of Discoveries in the Judean Desert," *HTR* 57 (1964) 281-99.

Dahood, Mitchell, *Psalms I; Psalms II; Psalms III* (Garden City, NY: Doubleday, 1965, 1968, 1970).

Dalglish, Edward Russell, *Psalm Fifty-one in the Light of Ancient Near Eastern Patternism* (Leiden: Brill, 1962).

Deissler, A., *Psalm 119(118) und seine Theologie. Ein Beitrag zu Erforschung der Anthologischen Stilgattung im Alten Testament* (Munich: Karl Zink, 1955).

Delekat, Lienhard, *Asylie und Schutzorakel am Zionheiligtum* (Leiden: Brill, 1967).

_________, "Probleme der Psalmenüberschriften," *ZAW* 76 (1964) 280-97.

Driver, G. R., "The Psalms in the Light of Babylonian Research," *The Psalmists*, ed. D. C. Simpson (London: Oxford University Press, 1926), pp. 109-75.

Eissfeldt, Otto, "Die Psalmen als Geschichtsquelle," *Near Eastern Studies in Honor of W. F. Albright*, ed. H. Goedicke (Baltimore, MD: Johns Hopkins, 1971), pp. 97-112.

Emerton, J. A., "Notes on Three Passages in Psalms Book IV," *JTS* 14 (1963) 374-81.

Encisco Viana, Jesús, "Como se formo la primera Parte del libro de los Salmos?," *Biblica* 44 (1963) 129-58.

__________, "Los titulos de los Salmos Y la historia de la formación del Salterio," *Estudios Biblicos* 13 (1954) 135-66.

Esterson, S. I., "The Commentary of Rabbi David Kimhi on Psalms 42-72," *HUCA* 10 (1935).

Finesinger, S. B., "Musical Instruments in the Old Testament," *HUCA* 3 (1926) 21-76.

Fretheim, Terence E., "Psalm 132: A Form-Critical Study," *JBL* 86 (1967) 289-300.

Gemser, B., "The Order and Arrangement of the Psalms," *Bibliotheca Orientalis* 9 (1952) 139-43.

Gese, Hartmut, "Die Entstehung der Büchereinteilung des Psalters," *Wort, Lied und Gottes-spruch, Festschrift für Joseph Ziegler* (Wurzburg: Echter Verlag, 1972).

Gevaryahu, H. M. I., "Baruch ben Neriah the Scribe," [modern Hebrew] *Zer li-gevurot*, Festschrift in honor of the late President Shazar, ed. B. Z. Luria (Jerusalem: Kiryat Sepher, 1973), pp. 227-32.

__________, "Biblical Colophons: A Source for the 'Biography' of Authors, Texts, and Books," *SVT* 28 (1975) 42-59.

__________, "Notes on Authors and Books in the Bible," *Beth Mikra* 43 (1970) 368.

__________, "On the Method of Giving Names to Biblical Books," *Beth Mikra* 45 (1971) 146-51.

__________, "Scribe's Disciples in the Book of Isaiah," *Beth Mikra* 47 (1971) 449-52.

Glueck, J. J., "Some Remarks on the Introductory Notes of the Psalms," *Die Ou-Testamentiese Werkgemeenskap in Suid-Afrika: Studies on the Psalms* (Potchefstroom: Pro-Rege Pers, 1963), pp. 30-39.

Gray, J., "A Cantata of the Autumn Festival: Psalm lxiii," *JSS* 22 (1977) 2-26.

Grimme, Hubert, "Der Begriff von hebräischen *hwdh* und *twdh*," *ZAW* 17 (1940/1) 234-40.

Guilding, Aileen, "Some Obscured Rubrics and Lectionary Allusions in the Psalter," *JTS* 3 (1952) 41-55.

Gunkel, Hermann, *Ausgewählte Psalmen übersetzt und erklärt* . . . (Göttingen: Vandenhoeck und Ruprecht, 1904).

__________, *The Psalms*, trans. Thomas M. Horner (Philadelphia: Fortress Press, 1967).

Gyllenberg, R., "Die Bedeutung des Wortes Sela," *ZAW* 17 (1940/1) 153-56.

Hallo, Rudolph, "The Psalter," *The Synagogue Review* 36 (1959) 38-43.

Haupt, P., "Die Psalmverse I Chr. 25:4," *ZAW* 34 (1914) 142-45.

__________, "Der acht und sechzigste Psalm," *AJSL* 23 (1907) 225.

Hayes, John H., "The Psalms and the Triennial Lectionary Cycle," unpublished paper.

Holm-Nielsen, Svend, "The Importance of Late Jewish Psalmody for the Understanding of Old Testament Psalmodic Tradition," *Studia Theologica* 14 (1960) 1-53.

Hunt, Ignatius, "Recent Psalm Study," *Worship* 41 (1967) 85-98; 47 (1973) 80-93; 49 (1975) 202-14; 283-94; 51 (1977) 127-44.

Hurvitz, Avi, *The Identification of Post-exilic Psalms by Means of Linguistic Criteria* [modern Hebrew] (Jerusalem: Magnes Press, 1966).

Illman, Karl-Johan, *Thema und Tradition in den Asaf Psalmen* (Åbo: Åbo Akademi Forsknings-institut, 1976).

Jacob, B., "Beiträge zu einer Einleitung in die Psalmen," *ZAW* 16 (1896) 129-81, 265-91; 17 (1897) 48-80, 263-79; 18 (1898) 99-119; 20 (1900) 49-80.

Jansen, Herman Ludin, *Die Spätjüdische Psalmendichtung. Ihr Entstehungskreis und ihr "Sitz im Leben,"* (Oslo: J. Dybwad, 1937).

Jirku, Anton, "Ajjelet haš-šaḥar (Ps 22_1)," *ZAW* 65 (1953) 85-86.

Keet, Cuthbert, C., *A Study of the Psalms of Ascents* (London: Mitre, 1969).

Kraus, Hans-Joachim, *Die Psalmen* (Neukirchen: Neukirchener Verlag, 1960).

Kugel, James L., "The Adverbial Use of Kî Ṭôb," *JBL* 99 (1980) 433-35.

Lack, R., "Le Psaume 1-une analyse structurale," *Biblica* 57 (1976) 154-67.

Lane, William R., "A New Commentary Structure in 4Q Florilegium," *JBL* 78 (1959) 343-46.

Langdon, S., "Babylonian and Hebrew Musical Terms," *JRAS* (1921) 169-91.

Lipiński, Edward, "La colombe du Ps 68, 14," *VT* 23 (1973) 365-68.

_________, "Les psaumes de la royauté de Yahwé dans l'exégèse moderne," *Le Psautier,* Orientalia et Biblical Lovaniensia 4 (Louvain: University Press, 1962), pp. 133-272.

_________, "YĀHWEH MÂLĀK," *Biblica* 44 (1963) 405-60.

Loretz, O., "Die Psalmen 8 and 67. Psalmenstudien V," *UF* 8 (1976) 117-21.

_________, "Psalmenstudien I," *UF* 3 (1971) 101.

_________, "Psalmenstudien II," *UF* 5 (1973) 213.

_________, "Psalmenstudien III," *UF* 6 (1974) 175-210.

_________, "Stichometrische und textologische Probleme in den Thronbesteigungs—psalmen: Psalmenstudien IV," *UF* 6 (1974) 211-40.

Magne, Jean, "Le texte Psaume XXII et sa restitution sur deux colonnes," *Sem* 11 (1961) 29-41.

May, Herbert Gordon, "'Al. . . .' in the Superscriptions of the Psalms," *AJSL* 58 (1941) 70-83.

Meyer, Rudolf, "Die Septuaginta-Fassung von Ps. 151, 1-5 als Ergebnis einer dogmatischen Korrektur," *Das Ferne und Nahe Wort,* ed. F. Maass (Berlin: Töpelmann, 1967), pp. 164-72.

Michel, D., "Studien zu den sogenannten Thronbesteigungspsalmen," *VT* 6 (1956) 40-68.

Miller, J. M., "The Korahites of Southern Judah," *CBQ* 32 (1970) 58-68.

Mowinckel, Sigmund, *Psalmenstudien IV. Die technischen Termini in den Psalmenüberschriften* (Oslo: Skrifter utgitt av Det Norske Videnskaps-Akademie, 1923).

_________, *The Psalms in Israel's Worship,* 2 vols., trans. D. R. Ap-Thomas (Nashville, TN: Abingdon, 1962).

Murphy, Roland E., "A Consideration of the Classification 'Wisdom Psalms,'" *SVT* 9 (1962) 156-67.

Nestle, Eberhard, "Das Lied Habakkuks und der Psalter," *ZAW* 20 (1900) 167-68.

Niemeyer, Th. C., *Het Probleem van de rangschikking der Psalmen* (Leiden: Luctor et Emergo, 1950).

Noldeke, Th., "*tplwt dwd* Ps 72, 30," *ZAW* 18 (1898) 256.

Pietersma, A., "David in the Greek Psalms," *VT* 30 (1980) 213-26.

Pinto, Basil de, "The Torah and the Psalms," *JBL* 86 (1967) 154-74.

Ploeg, J. P. M. van der, "Réflexions sur les genres littéraires des Psaumes," *Studia Biblica et Semitica*, ed. W. C. Van Unnik and A. S. van der Woude (Wageningen: H. Veenman, 1966), pp. 265-77.

Preuss, Horst Dietrich, "Die Psalmenüberschriften in Targum und Midrasch," *ZAW* 30 (1959) 44-54.

Rabbinowitz, L., "Does Midrash Tillim Reflect the Triennial Cycle of Psalms?," *JQR* 26 (1935-36) 349-68.

Rad, Gerhard von, "Erwägungen zu den Königpsalmen," *ZAW* 17 (1940/1) 216-22.

Riedel, Lic. Th. W., "Zur Redaktion des Psalters," *ZAW* 19 (1899) 169-72.

Robert, A., "Le Psaume CXIX et des Sapientaux," *RB* 48 (1939) 5-20.

Rosenthal, L. A., "Sonderbare Psalmenakrostica," *ZAW* 16 (1896) 40.

Rossi, Johannes Bernardus de, *Variae Lectiones Veteris Testamenti ex immensa Mss. editorumq. codicum* (Parmae: ex Regio Typographeo, 1784-98).

Rowley, H. H., "The Text and Structure of Psalm II," *JTS* 42 (1941) 143-54.

Sabourin, Léopold, *Un Classement littéraire des Psaumes* (Brussels: Desclée De Brouwer, 1964).

__________, *The Psalms: Their Origin and Meaning*, 2 vols. (Staten Island, NY: Alba House, 1969).

Sarna, Nahum M., "Prolegomenon," Moses Buttenwieser, *The Psalms, Chronologically Treated with a New Translation* (New York: KTAV, 1969), pp. XIII-XXXVIII.

__________, "Psalm XIX and the Near Eastern Sun-God Literature," *Papers of the Fourth World Congress of Jewish Studies* (Jerusalem: World Union of Jewish Studies, 1967), pp. 171-75.

__________, "Psalm 89: A Study in Inner Biblical Exegesis," ed. A. Altmann, *Biblical and Other Studies* (Cambridge, MA: Harvard University Press, 1963), pp. 29-46.

Sawyer, John F. A., "An Analysis of the Context and Meaning of the Psalm-Headings," *Transactions of the Glasgow University Oriental Society* 22 (1967-68) 26-38.

Scott, R. B. Y., "The Meaning and Use of *Selah* in the Psalter," *Bulletin of the Canadian Society of Biblical Studies* 5 (1939) 23-24.

Simpson, D. C., ed., *The Psalmists* (London: Oxford University Press, 1926).

Slotki, Israel W., "Antiphony in Ancient Hebrew Poetry," *JQR* 26 (1935-36) 199-219.

Smend, R., "Über das Ich der Psalmen," *ZAW* 8 (1888) 49-147.

Smith, Morton, "The Present State of Old Testament Studies," *JBL* 88 (1969) 19-35.

Snaith, N. H., "The Triennial Cycle and the Psalter," *ZAW* 10 (1933) 302-7.

__________, "Selah," *VT* 2 (1952) 43-56.

Soggin, J. Alberto, Review of Joachim Becker, *Wege der Psalmenexegese* (Stuttgart: Verlag Katholisches Bibelwerk, 1975), *Biblica* 58 (1977) 112-13.

Staerk, W., "Zur Kritik der Psalmenüberschriften," *ZAW* 12 (1892) 91-151.

Stieb, Robert, "Die Versdubletten des Psalters," *ZAW* 16 (1939) 102-10.

Tournay, R., "Note sur le Psaume LXXXIX, 51-52," *RB* 3 (1976) 380-89.

Tsevat, Matitiahu, *A Study of the Language of the Biblical Psalms* (Philadelphia: Society of Biblical Literature, 1955).

Tucker, Gene M., "Prophetic Superscriptions and the Growth of a Canon," *Canon and Authority*, ed. G. O. Coats and B. O. Long (Philadelphia: Fortress Press, 1977), pp. 56-70.

Torczyner, H. (Tur-Sinai), "A Psalm by the Sons of Heman," *JBL* 68 (1949) 247-49.

Tur-Sinai, N. H., "The Literary Character of the Book of Psalms," *OTS* 8 (1950) 263-81.

Ulrichsen, Jarl H., "JHWH MĀLĀK̂: Einige sprachliche Beobachtungen," *VT* 27 (1977) 361-74.

Voste, J.-M., "Sur les titres des Psaumes dans la Pešittā surtout d'après la recension orientale," *Biblica* 25 (1944) 210-35.

Wanke, Gunther, "Die Zionstheologie der Korachiten," *BZAW* 97 (1966).

Watts, John D. W., "An Old Hymn Preserved in the Book of Amos," *JNES* 15 (1956) 33-39.

__________, "Yahweh Mālak Psalms," *TZ* 21 (1965) 341-48.

Weiser, Artur, *The Psalms.* Old Testament Library (Philadelphia: Westminster, 1962).

Weissmann, A. S., "Ps. 68, 7," *ZAW* 12 (1892) 152.

Westermann, Claus, "Zur Sammlung des Psalters," *Theologia Viatorum* 8 (1961/2) 278-84.

Willis, John T., "Psalm 1—An Entity," *ZAW* 9 (1979) 381-401.

Yeivin, Israel, "The Division into Sections in the Book of Psalms," *Textus* 7 (1969) 76-102.

Indexes

INDEX OF TEXTS CITED

A. Non-Biblical

B. Apocrypha

C. Biblical

INDEX OF SUBJECTS AND AUTHORS